the perfect

the perfect 10

The Blessings of Following God's Commandments in a Postmodern World

Michael G. Moriarty

ZondervanPublishingHouse
Grand Rapids, Michigan

A Division of HarperCollins*Publishers*

The Perfect 10
Copyright © 1999 by Michael G. Moriarty

Requests for information should be addressed to:

⚏ZondervanPublishingHouse
Grand Rapids, Michigan 49530

Library of Congress Cataloging-in-Publication Data

Moriarty, Michael G.
    The perfect 10 : the blessings of following God's commandments in a post-modern world / Michael G. Moriarty.
       p.   cm.
    Includes bibliographical references
    ISBN 0-310-22764-X (pbk.)
    1. Ten Commandments. 2. United States—Moral conditions. I. Title.
    II. Title: The perfect ten.
    BV4655.M57   1999
    241.5'2—dc21   99-19135
                                                 CIP

Interior design by Melissa M. Elenbaas

Printed in the United States of America

99 00 01 02 03 04 05 /❖ DC/ 10 9 8 7 6 5 4 3 2 1

To my lovely wife, who makes my life rich.
I love you, Karen.

And to my precious princesses, Sophia Grace
and Tirzah Rose, who have filled our lives with
many new challenges and incredible joy.

May God grant our family the wisdom, power,
and grace to live out his Ten Commandments
in a rapidly changing postmodern world.

CONTENTS

ACKNOWLEDGMENTS

There is an old proverb that says, "It takes a village to write a book." I owe a deep debt of gratitude to certain people who have shaped my thinking, challenged my ideas, and encouraged me in my research and writing.

I am very grateful to Dr. Walter Kaiser, whose stimulating doctoral seminar on Old Testament ethics revived my love for God's moral law and inspired me to preach and write on the Ten Commandments. Dr. Kaiser has also reminded me several times that it's okay to preach a topical sermon as long as I repent afterwards. Thanks for the encouragement to stay expository.

I am also grateful to M. Blaine Smith for reading portions of the manuscript, giving constructive advice, and getting my creative juices flowing. His wisdom and gentle correction helped to excavate the originality buried deep within my soul.

I am most grateful to my wife, Karen, whose creative analysis and clear thinking have made this a better book. She would dream and agonize with me over chapter introductions, word choices, prose, stories, exegesis—you name it. Her influence transformed the laborious writing process into a labor of love.

Special thanks go to my secretary, Linda McFadden, for typing the entire manuscript and putting up with a legion of revisions. Her patient perseverance kept this project going smoothly.

I am indebted as well to Zondervan's Associate Publisher Lyn Cryderman, who believed in this book from the beginning. His encouragement is much appreciated.

The phrase "practice what you preach" sometimes follows the conscientious minister like a dark cloud. No one can follow the Ten

Commandments with absolute perfection. No one except Jesus, of course. But my parents, Ed and Simmone Moriarty, make it easy to obey the Fifth Commandment ("Honor your father and your mother"). With love and kindness, they have always been of immense support to me. They watched over me in childhood, put up with me in my teens, were concerned about me in college, but never did anything that caused me to question their love. My sweet mom will always be a protective "mother bear." I have followed her example; I am now a protective "father bear."

I am very thankful for the blessing of my wife, Karen. Life with her is a marvelous journey mapped out by a gracious God. She complements and sharpens me. She's my chief exhorter and my most trusted critic. She brings balance and refreshment to a deeply satisfying, yet sometimes emotionally draining, profession. My children, Sophia and Tirzah, have turned their daddy's heart to mush and teach me every day about the preciousness of family life. It is intoxicating, yet sobering. Confining, yet freeing. Demanding, yet rewarding. It is amazing how two such different little girls were created by the same parents. I hope and pray that the truth espoused in this book will guide their lives.

And finally, I am especially thankful to God for giving me a life worth living, a faith worth believing, and a Savior worth knowing.

INTRODUCTION

In the year 63 B.C., the great Roman general Pompey entered Jerusalem with a vengeance. He approached the holy temple and thousands of Jews fell to the ground before him and pleaded with him not to violate the sacred "Inner Sanctum," the Holy of Holies. This piqued Pompey's interest. He had heard rumors that the inner regions of the temple contained great riches and hidden secrets. Some even alleged that the Jews kept their God hidden because they really worshiped the head of a donkey.

As Pompey tore away the veil of separation and marched into the Holy of Holies, a look of amazement flashed across his face. The dark inner chamber was empty. There was no representation or graven image of the Jewish God. Shocked with disbelief, the angry general marveled that he could carry the Jews back to Rome, but he could not lay his hands on their God.

What was conspicuously absent from the pitch-black, windowless Inner Sanctum was Israel's ark. After the exile, a remnant of Jews returned to Judah and rebuilt the temple. Jewish historical sources along with the testimony of Scripture affirms that the ark was not present in the Holy of Holies in the second temple. Its disappearance is a mystery. The search for the ark continues to be a fascinating historical pursuit.

The sacred ark that once stood at the center of the temple and manifested the power and glory of God is lost. But it's what was inside the ark that is important. The character and presence of God were represented most vividly by the tablets of the Law contained inside the ark. The Ten Commandments reflect God's holiness and establish his covenant love. King Solomon reminded God's people that inside the

ark was the "covenant of the Lord" that God had made with their
fathers when he brought them out of Egypt (1 Kings 8:21). This special convenant was God's binding "promise" to liberate and bless those
who committed themselves to him. Before the altar of the Lord, in
front of the whole assembly of Israel, Solomon spread his hands
toward heaven and said:

> "O Lord, God of Israel, there is no God like you in heaven above
> or on earth below—you who keep your covenant of love with
> your servants who continue wholeheartedly in your way."
> (1 Kings 8:23 NIV)

Behind the manifestation of God's power and glory channeled
through the ark was his love. Because what was inside the ark was God's
covenant of love—the Ten Commandments. These tablets of love
reveal God's character and will. They are ten standards to live by; ten
absolutes; the Ten Words to direct us; ten ways to nurture a lasting,
loving relationship with our God. They are still "The Perfect Ten."

The gradual shift from modernism to postmodernism has left Western culture without a moral compass. The church can whine about
moral decline, about the paganizing of America and the fact that we
are no longer one nation under God, but the painful truth is the
church has not sufficiently taught her own people. The steady growth
of biblical illiteracy and the neglect of God's moral law have left the
church with a shaky foundation for living as Christians in a postmodern culture. Without a return to our biblical roots and a renewed
emphasis on God's law, the church will coast like a ship at sea without
a rudder. Until our moorings are recovered, God's people will lack the
spiritual insight and moral authority to resist the aggressive incursion
of cultural decadence. Biblical illiteracy will continue to soar and our
impact on the culture will be minimal. This ought to be a powerful
motivation to renew our understanding of and appreciation for the
bountiful treasure of the Ten Commandments.

In ancient Israel the "Ten Words" were direct evidence of God's
relationship with his people and communicated that his ways were
higher than the ways of the surrounding nations. They stood as his
revealed will for moral conduct and the way life should be lived. Today

they continue to speak to us about what life is all about, bringing instruction, guidance, protection, and blessing to all faithful believers (Ps. 94:12). They are ten steps to liberty.

Christians are prone to blame others for America's cultural erosion. We often point fingers at liberal politicians, secular humanists, New Age gurus, and media elites. But the tragic fact remains: we, too, have contributed to our culture's moral decline by removing the Ten Commandments from our instruction.

The Ten Commandments reveal to us what God wants to be known and that he wants to keep his people free. He is the loving God of relationships who desires that we know him and make him known. To accomplish his purposes we must be healthy. With God's "Ten Liberating Treasures" dwelling richly in our hearts, truth will revive us, love and holiness will be our guiding lights, and the soul of the church will shine brightly in a postmodern world.

GOD'S LAW IN A
POSTMODERN SOCIETY

Several years ago Cable TV mogul Ted Turner proclaimed himself "news king" and declared the Ten Commandments obsolete. Turner, creator of the Cable News Network, told members of the Newspaper Association of America in Atlanta that the biblical Ten Commandments do not relate to current global problems, such as overpopulation[1] and the arms race. "We're living with outmoded rules," Turner said. "The rules we're living under is the Ten Commandments, and I bet nobody here even pays much attention to 'em, because they are too old. When Moses went up on the mountain, there were no nuclear weapons, there was no poverty. Today, the commandments wouldn't go over. Nobody around likes to be commanded. Commandments are out."[2]

Despite his aberrant statement that the Ten Commandments are obsolete, Turner makes an interesting point. People in our fragmented modern era don't generally respond well to commands. Americans tend to value "independence" and "self-reliance" above all else. These qualities are expected to win the rewards of success in a competitive society. Transcendent moral values may be revered in some sense intellectually, but a rampant "individualism" overshadows the prospect of adhering to absolute moral principles.

According to George Gallup, Americans revere the Bible but, overall, do not read it. This has spawned a nation of biblical illiterates. Most Americans cannot recall the Ten Commandments, and even fewer can tell you where to find them in the Bible.[3]

James Patterson and Peter Kim, in their book *The Day America Told the Truth*, have this to say about the tumultuous change that has taken place in America:

> It's the wild, wild West all over again in America, but it's wilder and woollier this time. *You* are the law in this country. Who says so? *You* do, pardner.
>
> In the 1950s and even in the early 1960s, there was something much closer to a moral consensus in America. It was mirrored in a parade of moralizing family TV programs: *Ozzie and Harriet, Father Knows Best, Donna Reed, Leave It to Beaver,* and even *Bonanza.*
>
> There is absolutely no moral consensus at all in the 1990s.
>
> Everyone is making up their own personal moral codes—their own Ten Commandments.
>
> Here are ten extraordinary commandments for the 1990s. These are real commandments, the rules that many people actually live by. (The percentage of people who live by each commandment is included.)
>
> 1. I don't see the point in observing the Sabbath (77%).
> 2. I will steal from those who won't really miss it (74%).
> 3. I will lie when it suits me, so long as it doesn't cause any real damage (64%).
> 4. I will drink and drive if I feel that I can handle it. I know my limit (56%).
> 5. I will cheat on my spouse—after all, given the chance, he or she will do the same (53%).
> 6. I will procrastinate at work and do absolutely nothing about one full day in every five. It's standard operating procedure (50%).
> 7. I will use recreational drugs (41%).
> 8. I will cheat on my taxes—to a point (30%).
> 9. I will put my lover at risk of disease. I sleep around a bit, but who doesn't (31%)?
> 10. Technically, I may have committed date rape, but I know that she wanted it (20% have been date-raped).[4]

The quintessential American pursuit is "finding oneself." Individuals passionately seek lifestyle enclaves to find the self-expression missing from the rest of their lives.[5] The individual self is enthroned as its own source of moral guidance. Patterson and Kim tell us that only one in ten Americans believes in all of the Ten Commandments. "Forty percent of us believe in five or fewer Commandments. We have established ourselves as the authority on morality. We now choose which Commandments to believe and which ones not to believe. Clearly, the God of the 1990s in America is a distant and pale reflection of the God of our forefathers."[6]

In the absence of any objectifiable criteria of right and wrong, the self and its feelings become the supreme moral guide. The objective moral goodness inherent in the Judeo-Christian tradition of obeying God's truth or the Enlightenment quest of following nature's laws is forsaken for the subjective goodness of expressing the full range of human desires. In other words, getting what you want and enjoying it is the desired goal. Utility replaces duty; self-expression unseats authority.[7] What is the driving force behind this intellectual shift—this cultural mood swing?

POSTMODERN TIMES

Several years ago, *Dear Abby* commented on religious disagreements. She printed a letter from one of her critics. "Your answer to the woman who complained that her relatives were always arguing with her about religion was ridiculous. You advised her to simply declare the subject off-limits. Are you suggesting that people talk about only trivial, meaningless subjects so as to avoid a potential controversy? . . . It is arrogant to tell people there are subjects they may not mention in your presence. You could have suggested she learn enough about her relatives' cult to show them the errors contained in its teachings."

Abby replied, "In my view, the height of arrogance is to attempt to show people the 'errors' in the religion of their choice."[8]

Abby's response is unabashedly in line with the popular postmodern mindset so pervasive in our culture. First, she asserts that challenging another's religious truth claims is the "height of arrogance" (e.g., tolerance is the only absolute). Second, personal choice alone validates one's religious commitment (e.g., truth is whatever you believe in your heart).

This pervasive paradigm change demonstrates the rapid mood shift from a modern outlook to a postmodern one. Historically, the modern period can be dated from the end of the eighteenth century in the philosophy of the Enlightenment and its attempt to account for all of reality within the confines of natural reason. The thought and action of the nineteenth and twentieth centuries were governed by the idea of the liberation of humanity. The progress of the sciences, technologies, the arts, and political freedoms held out promises to emancipate the whole of humanity from ignorance, poverty, backwardness, and oppression. Not only would it produce fulfilled individuals but, thanks to modern education in particular, it would also produce "enlightened" citizens, masters of their own destiny.

"Modern" is not a synonym for "contemporary." Modernism refers to a particular time period and the particular ideology associated with it. Modern thought places a strong emphasis on objective rationality and certainty. Human beings determine what happens in history. Advances in science and technology make progress inevitable.

There is a growing dissatisfaction with the modern way of viewing things. The term "postmodern" implies a new vision away from the progress myth that has been the cultural driving force of the West for nearly two centuries. Postmodern thought rejects the modern emphasis on rationality and is highly skeptical of any ideology that espouses certainty. Postmodernism entails a rejection of the optimism of inevitable progress and the emphasis on rational discovery through the scientific method, which provided the intellectual foundation for the modern attempt to create a better world.[9] The Enlightenment belief in unified, universally valid explanations and the bold movement toward a veritable utopia of progress and prosperity has, for the most part, been abandoned.

The emerging postmodern worldview has no fixed moral or spiritual framework. The primary assumption is that truth is not rational or objective, but individually constructed within the context of any given community. While there are many different meanings within postmodernism itself, the golden rule is that all views are equally valid, and respect for differences is a sign of maturity. Absolute claims are "intolerant" and must be dismissed. Tolerance is the new vanguard absolute.

In the past, intolerance meant bigotry or prejudice—that is, displaying an irrational attitude of hostility toward an individual, a group, or a race, or holding an adverse opinion without just grounds or sufficient knowledge. The classic view of intolerance should offend us. But in postmodern usage, intolerance has come to mean simply disagreeing with anyone else's beliefs.[10]

Our culture is postmodern in the sense that people are disillusioned with the modern philosophical bankruptcy and the emptiness of the Enlightenment's ideals. Modern forces, such as urbanization, capitalism, and technology, continue to shape our culture. But modernity's rationalism and ideas of remaking the world are now being viewed as ethnocentric myths spawned by our European cultural conditioning. Postmodernism and New Age consciousness share an overlapping philosophical foundation. This has led to a fresh outbreak of paganism and a fascination with the occult and New Age spirituality. Whoever or whatever one desires to worship or believe in is what is most important. The sacredness of individual choice is the highest good. Objective truth is cast out; morality is a matter of desire; tolerance is the chief virtue. Individuals must act so as to produce the greatest satisfaction of their wants and desires or to express the fullest range of their impulses. Truth becomes "feeling good." Truth isn't discovered; it's personally created. "Truth is ever-changing not only in insignificant matters of taste or fashion, but in crucial matters of spirituality, morality and reality itself."[11]

Our culture's penetrating postmodern shift as it relates to our everyday lives is not necessarily the death of truth in all cases, but a budding skepticism toward the "arrogance of certainty." The emerging postmodern consciousness is hostile toward any worldview that gives us the final word about what truth is.

Although postmodernity has undergone a long incubation period, the gradual decline of modernity has given birth to postmodernity, which is now the primary intellectual molder of Western culture. Art, music, education, fashion, literature, politics, law, theology, philosophy, architecture, and the entertainment industry have all been affected.

Stanley Grenz demonstrates this cultural shift in a comparison between the original *Star Trek* series and the new series, *Star Trek: The Next Generation*. The crew of the old *Enterprise* included persons of various nationalities working together for the common benefit of humankind. The modern enlightenment message was clear: we are all human and must join forces in order to complete our mandate, the quest for certain objective knowledge of the entire universe of which space looms as "the final frontier."[12]

The eccentric Mr. Spock was one of the old *Star Trek* heroes. Being part human and part Vulcan (the only crew member from another planet), his partial alien status actually served as the transcendent human ideal. Spock was the ideal Enlightenment man, completely rational, always holding his emotions in check. His dispassionate rationality repeatedly provided the calculative answers necessary to solve the problems encountered by the crew of the *Enterprise*.[13] The viewer is left with the impression that our problems can ultimately be solved by the application of logic, reason, and rational expertise.

In *The Next Generation*, Spock is replaced by Data, an android. Grenz says, "In a sense, Data is a more fully realized version of the rational thinker than Spock, capable of superhuman intellectual feats. Nevertheless, despite his seemingly perfect intellect, he is not the transcendent human ideal that Spock embodies, because he is a machine. Unlike Spock, he desires not only to understand what it means to be human but in fact to become human. He believes he is somehow incomplete because he lacks such things as a sense of humor, emotion, and the ability to dream (and, indeed, he feels that he has become more complete when he later discovers that his maker programmed a capacity to dream into his circuitry)."[14]

Data is not the primary problem solver on the *Enterprise*. Everyone has answers. One of the distinctive characters is the intuitive Counselor Troi, a woman gifted with the ability to perceive the hidden feelings of others.

The new voyages of the *Enterprise* lead its diverse crew into a postmodern universe. In this new world, time is no longer simply linear, reason is not enshrined, appearance is not necessarily reality, and the rational is not always to be trusted.[15]

Postmodernism is the quest to move beyond modernism and represents a rejection of the foundational assumptions upon which the Enlightenment project was built.

This is the situation we find ourselves in today. Truth is a very slippery concept—it is whatever you sincerely believe. From ancient times until almost the present day, the mindset was different. The Ten Commandments enjoyed unchallenged prestige. The Ten Commandments set a standard that a reasonably determined individual ought to strive to meet. The apostle Paul argues in Romans 2 that there are moral obligations written on the hearts of all human beings and that the human conscience bears witness to those truths. The principles of the Ten Commandments have existed for centuries in hundreds of cultures throughout the world as the moral standards for a just society.[16] But in a postmodern age, truth and morality are culturally conditioned and relative to a community or people group.

Every society needs a moral core to survive. Without agreed-upon objective standards of morality, the social fabric will unravel. The Roman Empire is a prime example. Its loss of moral authority and its bankrupt spiritual dynamic left so many disillusioned that it was ripe for transformation by the principled, heart-changing religion of Christianity. The "whatever makes you happy" type of philosophy will appear to be liberating for a season but, as the experience of ancient Rome showed, a culture cannot long endure when there are no higher standards for human behavior than the appetites and impulses of self-centered individuals steeped in self-expression and individualism.

Our culture is in crisis and people want answers. We have an obligation to reflect the love of God and to care for those around us. We have a calling to be the light of the world and the salt of the earth. The opportunity to present the truth and provide answers is upon us. But in order to be taken seriously we must live out our faith with integrity and authenticity in every area of life. That means getting back to the basic truths that have been shamefully ignored and neglected. We face perhaps the greatest challenge—and the greatest opportunity—since the signing of the Declaration of Independence. To meet the challenge and seize the opportunity, we must first remember that God's transcendent goal is spiritual. We will not make a positive impact if our spiritual lives are barren and our integrity suspect. God's law needs to be brought out of hibernation. The Ten Commandments are absolute treasures rooted in God's covenant love. They are the truths that bring freedom. They must be taught, proclaimed, and lived.

We may debate about just how "Christian" the culture has ever been, but whatever the appraisal of the past, there is less and less doubt that the inherited influence of a Judeo-Christian perspective has largely vanished. In a culture adrift from its biblical roots, is it any wonder that we see a growing array of bizarre religious groups, many of which reek of primitive superstition? Should we be surprised by the proliferation of psychopaths and their serial rapes, murders, and other crimes, all committed without conscience? As respect for our cultural heritage has dwindled, Christianity has been banished from the culture at large—systematically dismissed from public schools, intellectual institutions, and the media. Christian symbols are barred from many public places, and the posting of the Ten Commandments in civil courts and state schools is commonly excluded.

For over four years, Judge Roy Moore of Alabama has been hounded by liberal-interest groups for displaying a little plaque of the Ten Commandments on his courtroom wall. The American Civil Liberties Union (ACLU) and the Alabama Free Thought Association spearheaded the attack by suing Judge Moore to force him to remove the plaque from his courtroom, claiming it violates the First Amendment. Moore is deeply concerned at how the First Amendment has been twisted. What was meant to protect our freedom to acknowledge God has been turned to prevent public officials from acknowledging God. Separation of church and state was never meant to excommunicate God from government. Publicly acknowledging God's moral law is grafted into our cultural heritage and has never been a violation of the First Amendment of the United States Constitution.

Even though Judge Moore still has the Ten Commandments on his courtroom wall, it is possible that this case will be taken all the way to the U.S. Supreme Court. Ironically, the Ten Commandments are permanently engraved in two places at the U.S. Supreme Court. Our cultural dispersion is lamentable, given the fact that the Ten Commandments are barred from many public sectors, but pornography, abortion, and other vices are legal. When a society does away with God's law, it opens the doors to believe and practice just about anything.

The church needs to revive God's moral law and regain a clear understanding of the absolute truth recorded in Exodus 20:1–17 and Deuteronomy 5:6–22. The Ten Commandments reflect the character and nature of God and are therefore obligatory for every believer today. Jesus did not abolish the law, but expressed the law's true intent and meaning (Matt. 5:17–18). The law had been perverted by religious legalists who turned it into a crushing system of works-righteousness. Jesus' teaching represents a definitive fulfillment of the law; it involves the coming of the old into the destiny to which it pointed. Christians are not under the condemnation of the law, but are under its moral guidelines as a rule of life and an objective standard of holiness. The Ten Commandments (the heart of the law) serve as a guide to righteousness and become for us "vital truths" and a joyous source of God's will.

However, in a lawless age, mankind's rebellion is radical and in open view. In spite of the fact that God's invisible qualities—his eternal power and divine nature—have been clearly seen (Rom. 1:20), and that his general law is written on every heart (2:15), these truths have been discarded because of human greed and sinfulness. Moreover, the law revealed by the nature of things is often obscured by cultural prejudices.[17] Mass apostasy is not far behind wherever divine restraints are removed and people are given over to their lusts and corruption (1:24, 26, 28). Whether a society is Christian-based or not, it is always true that righteousness exalts a nation, but sin is a disgrace to any people (Prov. 14:34).

Life without standards erodes into anarchy. Life without standards is easy, at least for a while, but quickly degenerates into selfishness and rebellion. A child who grows up without any standards and does not have a parent or guardian who exhorts him or her to keep standards never experiences committed, covenant love. That child will drift into rebellion, have little respect for authority, and will pace through life with an empty heart.

The child who is given standards is taught respect for self and for other people. Life is given dignity and order. Moreover, if the child knows that the standards are rooted in "parental love," security and freedom are experienced consistently.

The law reflects God's holiness and is grounded in his covenant love. If he were to dispense with his law, he would become an amoral, loveless God rather than a holy, loving God. Grace is God's honest, loving response to the fact that men and women can never meet the standard of holiness the law demands of them on their own. But God's children need law and grace. A balanced relationship between the two is crucial. God's love is carefully expressed in his ten absolute standards that have become known through the centuries as the Ten Commandments. His grace is demonstrated in his giving the law to the people he loves as well as by his encouragement, guidance, and empowerment to keep it. Living according to God's eternal standards frees us to love God and other people. God's law helps us to see life from the divine perspective. Living out the Ten Commandments properly refines us into people of character and grace founded on God's covenant love. This will empower us to be salt and light in a culture that has abandoned God's law.

GOD'S LAW AS A GUIDE TO HOLINESS

Without a moral framework, society crumbles into warring factions and isolated corrupt individuals. The result is a replay of the violence, immorality, and anarchy described in the book of Judges, which at once diagnoses the moral collapse of ancient Israel and definitively defines the postmodernist ethical outlook:[18] "Every man did what was right in his own eyes" (Judg. 21:25 RSV). While postmodern thought does have certain strengths (e.g., its challenge of certain Enlightenment assumptions), believers that uncritically embrace postmodernism ultimately sell out to the dominant culture and become culturally irrelevant. We must understand the contours of the emerging postmodern worldview. As it sets in with a vengeance, unguarded believers often become spiritually disabled by its tenets and fail to develop a rigorous Christian worldview. They become culturally indifferent. For them,

God's love becomes subjective, and his moral law is either ignored or terribly misunderstood.

The law expresses not only God's love but his will for the life and behavior of men and women. The law is not a monolithic unity. There are important distinctions between what theologians have called the civil, ceremonial, and moral laws.[19] The civil law legislated the social responsibility the Israelites were called to have with their neighbors; the ceremonial law legislated Israel's worship life; and the moral law is found principally in the Ten Commandments, which reflect God's covenant love and holiness, identifying his timeless standards of right and wrong. The book of Hebrews shows how all of the types and shadows of the Old Testament ceremonies are fulfilled in Christ. They all pointed to him. Therefore, the ceremonial laws pass away with the coming of Christ whom they were designed to foreshadow (Heb. 9–10).

Some evangelicals would argue that the entire law has been abrogated and has been replaced with another law, the law of Christ.[20] Paul's explanation of the new covenant in 2 Corinthians 3:7–17 is often used to pit law against gospel: "For what was glorious has no glory now in comparison with the surpassing glory. And if what was fading away came with glory, how much greater is the glory of that which lasts!" (vv. 10–11 NIV).

Paul, however, was always careful not to leave the impression that the law was bad (Rom. 7:7), or contrary to God's promises (Gal. 3:21). In fact, he declares the law holy, righteous, and good (Rom. 7:12). The written code (or "letter"), as mentioned in 2 Corinthians 3:6, pronounced a sentence of spiritual death (Rom. 7:9–11), but the Spirit brings eternal life (Rom. 7:6). The law was designed not to kill but to lead believers to Christ (Gal. 3:24). For the believer, it comes to guide in the paths of righteousness and to preserve liberty (Ps. 119:44–45). "The law of the Lord is perfect, restoring the soul" (Ps. 19:7). The greatness of the glory of the old covenant is described in such a way that the glory of the new covenant appears *radiant* in contrast. The contrast is not between that which had no glory and that which was glorious. Both covenants involve a distinctive ministry accompanied by glory, but the glory of the new covenant is destined to be permanent and must be adorned with a far greater glory (Heb. 13:20). The new covenant ministry, based on the finished work of Christ, engraves the law of God on the hearts of men, written by the Spirit (2 Cor. 3:3). The glory of the old enhances the glory of the new. Yet Paul reminds us, "Do we then nullify the Law through faith? May it never be! On the contrary, we establish the Law" (Rom. 3:31).

The moral law carries permanent validity because it stems from the character and nature of God. God's moral standards are objective and do not change. Jesus taught us to distinguish between the weightier and lighter matters of the law and referred to greater and lesser commandments (Matt. 23:23).[21] Most Christian scholars agree that the civil and legal legislation has now been put aside for us as New Testament believers. The basic principles that undergird these ancient practices have carried over into the New Testament, but most of the national civic regulations have been abrogated. Likewise, in different places and at different times the Bible declared the end of the ceremonial laws but never an end of the righteous standard of God's moral law (Heb. 7:11–20; 8:8–13; 9:1–4). The law which the apostle Paul calls holy, righteous, good, and spiritual (Rom. 7:12, 14) is an aid to the gospel and our living out the life of faith.[22] For Paul, righteousness does not come through law, but by faith in Jesus Christ. But the gospel upholds the law in the sense that it is thoroughly in accord with it. Rightly understood, the law supports and confirms the doctrine of faith (Rom. 3:27–31).

"Just as Israel's ceremonial laws prefigured Christ as the great prophet and priest, so her civil laws prefigured Christ as the great King."[23] The Christian, however, is not to go back to the shadows of the promise in the ceremonial laws when we have the fulfillment of that promise in Christ. Likewise, the Christian must not attempt to restore the ancient civil law system or return to the Jewish theocracy which served to preserve and give cohesion to the chosen nation when we have the fulfillment of Christ's kingdom in his spiritual reign through the preaching of the Gospel.[24]

The New Testament expressly forbids any return to the shadows of the civil or ceremonial laws of the Old Testament. However, the New Testament not only repeats the moral laws of the Old Testament many times over but also gives them fuller meaning and explanation.

Although the law cannot give us life—only Christ can impart salvation—the moral law becomes a rule of life for believers, reminding us of God's love for us and our call to emulate the character of God by living righteously.

THE THREEFOLD USE OF THE LAW

Traditionally, biblical scholars have found at least three uses for the law of God. First, the law serves as a guide to society in promoting righteousness in the civil sphere. Second, the law convicts sinners and leads them to Christ (Gal. 3:24). Like a mirror that shows us our blemishes and imperfections, the law shows everyone that they are imperfect sinners in need of a perfect Savior (Heb. 7:19–28). Third, the law teaches and exhorts believers to do God's will. Christians do not look to the law as a way of justification, nor are they under its condemnation, but see the law as the standard of God's guidance for the promotion of righteous living. Far too many believers have not only neglected the Old Testament but have discarded the third use of the law. Dr. Walter Kaiser warns: "There is a positive base for morality and ethical action in the Old Testament, and we will abandon it at the peril of our own ability to walk and live as our God has directed us to go."[25]

As postmodernism has progressively become a fixture on the western intellectual landscape, a growing number of Christians have to some extent bought into postmodernity's new way of viewing reality. While human theological systems have either ignored or repudiated the third use of the law, postmoderns seek to do away with all absolute truth. The result, God's law is exceedingly unpopular. Some declare it obsolete; others say it's too intolerant. Sad but true, lawlessness reigns in many homes, schools, and churches and in the dominant culture.

The postmodern era has in effect replaced truth with tolerance, knowledge with interpretation. The historic Christian view that there is a unifying center of reality that has appeared in Jesus Christ, who is the eternal Word and who perfectly expressed and fulfilled God's law, is viewed as a bygone theory respected only by religious exclusivists. The culture relentlessly continues to put pressure on the church to be more tolerant, to conform to its postmodern outlook that truth is in the eyes of the beholder. Who will the church listen to?

LIVING THE TRUTH

The postmodernist mindset is gaining a foothold within evangelical churches. Can this have something to do with the fact that 53 percent of evangelical Christians actually believe there are no absolutes (as compared to 66 percent of Americans as a whole)?[26] The downplaying of doctrine and objective thinking has given way to "heart-tugging" messages designed to make people feel good. The postmodernist "therapeutic culture" has nurtured the affections of evangelicalism to the extent that psychological well-being, not truth, is the controlling value.[27] As the foundations erode, an insidious religious syncretism looms on the horizon. That is a frightening prospect. George Barna observes:

> As the elements of Eastern religions become more prolific, the most appealing aspects of Christianity (which will be the lifestyle, rather than the central spiritual tenets) will be wed to the exotic and fascinating attributes of Eastern faiths. The result will be a people who honestly believe that they have improved Christianity, and who would even consider themselves to be Christian, despite their creative restructuring of faith.[28]

Without question, postmodernist ideas now permeate the entire culture. For Christianity to compete and present a viable alternative to postmodernism, a resurgence of men and women must arise who exhibit warm hearts and lucid Christian minds leading the way with creative efforts to reach out to the rapidly changing postmodern world. The world needs to see Christians who are biblically and historically literate and who live out their moral convictions in virtuous, authentic, and healing relationships.

The fact that our primary responsibilities are spiritual ("our citizenship is in heaven," wrote Paul in Philippians 3:20) and our worldly civic responsibilities are secondary does not mean that social and political issues are unimportant. "One need only look at the horrors unleashed by atheist totalitarian states—Hitler's Germany, Stalin's Soviet Union, Mao's China, Pol Pot's Cambodia, Mengistu's Ethiopia, to name a few—to see the importance of Judeo-Christian values undergirding the political system."[29] Even in our own nation we are witnessing a serious moral erosion: families are breaking down, crime is in full swing, drugs continue to be an epidemic, over 1.5 million abortions are performed annually, and the political system is high on envy and short on justice.

Christians can play an important role by acting as the polity's conscience, calling it to account for transgressions of God's law.[30] We don't pursue power; we seek a society where government promotes justice and civility in all spheres of the social order. But our convictions must rest on the infallible truth of God's Word. The Ten Commandments are a significant part of God's Word. They must be excavated. They are ten steps to personal freedom, ten disciplines that can lead to cultural renewal through faithful believers. The moral regeneration and repair of a frayed social fabric that this country needs can be realized if more believers apply the treasure of God's commandments and take his law seriously. Solomon put it this way: "Keep the commandments and keep your life; despising them means death" (Prov. 19:16 LB).[31]

Let's begin by looking at the First Commandment. Obedience to this command is crucial for our spiritual lives and is vitally connected to the redemptive influence we will have on society as a whole.

SMALL GROUP DISCUSSION QUESTIONS

1. Read Exodus 20:1–17 and Deuteronomy 5:6–22. Why did God give the Ten Commandments to his ancient people? Discuss the many ways God's moral law applies to us today.

2. What is the difference between modernism and postmodernism? The emerging postmodern worldview has no fixed moral or spiritual framework. How has this affected the culture at large? Discuss some of the ways the church is being impacted.

3. What are the differences between the moral, civil, and ceremonial laws under the old covenant? Why does the moral law take precedence over the civil and ceremonial laws? What is the third use of moral law? How does it apply to believers?

4. Why are the Ten Commandments important to the church and to society? What happens to a society that has no agreed-upon, eternal, fixed moral reference point? Discuss the ramifications of Proverbs 14:34 in reference to moral decline in our culture.

LOVING GOD IN AN
AGE OF IDOLATRY

"I am the Lord your God."

Exodus 20:2

The late Elvis Presley, a teenage rebel from Memphis, Tennessee, with his dark good looks, hipster clothes, daring sideburns, and distinctive singing style, captured the teenage American heart. Elvis could sing everything from gospel and blues to country and pop with the same raw energy and potent sexuality that thrilled rhythm-and-blues audiences and kept people buying records.[1] Over time, his bump-and-grind routine, coupled with his magnetic appeal, elevated him to divine status in the eyes of his many fans.

Millions of people visit Graceland, his Memphis mansion, each year. And Elvis memorabilia is a multi-million-dollar industry. Some fans of Elvis actually worship the "King of Rock and Roll" as a god. It is reported that pockets of semi-organized "Elvis worship" have taken hold in New York, Colorado, and Indiana, where worshipers raise their hands, spell and then chant Presley's name, working themselves into a fervor and praying to the deceased star.

Many followers believe Elvis watches over them. If someone reports seeing Presley, the high priests at the Church of the Risen Elvis in Denver hold Elvis worship services. In an altar surrounded by candles stands an enshrined look-alike doll of Elvis.[2]

By engaging in celebrity worship, people seem to find the fulfillment they lack and are satisfied to admire it, envy it, and identify with it in their imagination. If fame eludes them, they can become a fan, basking in the reflected glory of a star by venerating the star's life, his style and ideas, and even the star's vices. They follow their star like cultists mesmerized by the godlike aura of a guru. Being a close follower helps to bridge the gap between the oversized expectations encouraged by our society and the comparative few awarded public notoriety by this same society. Becoming attached to a celebrity whose stardom has reached its zenith can compensate for a fan's lack of popularity by offering "psychic hitchhiking."[3] Here we see idolatry in two forms: the glorification of the celebrity and the craving for self-worship.

Idolatry covers the globe like a dark cloud. Celebrity idolatry is so widespread in the West that it appears to be contagious. But the ultimate "idol mill" is the human heart. The Bible connects the lustful appetites of human greed, lust, and coveting with idolatry (Eph. 5:5; Col. 3:5). "An idol is something within creation that is inflated to function as a substitute for God."[4] An idol can be anything from physical objects such as a house, car, or money to an image, a pleasure, or a hobby. Idolatry begins with the counterfeiting of God and the erection of a substitute.

King David prayed that the nations abandon their idols when he cried out, "Put them in fear, O Lord; let the nations know that they are but men" (Ps. 9:20 RSV). In Psalm 9 David lashed out at the nations plagued by self-deception. They ignored God's majesty and erected counterfeit idols in his place. The potency of self-deception moved them to scoff at God and exalt themselves. The idolization process gave them an inflated picture of their authority, status, and power.[5]

The idolizing process is at work not only in the contemporary world but also in churches around the globe. God is presented as the enterprise deity who lends almighty support to political crusades, the celestial therapist whose main objective is to make people feel better about themselves, the tame God who won't talk or ruffle our comfortable feathers, or the divine chameleon who conforms to individual spiritual experiences. These gods are always supportive, compassionate, congenial, and very stimulating.

The idolatrous imagination is shamefully creative among evangelical Christians. We who should be "guardians of the faith are falling victim to the world's first and worst sin against faith."[6] While trying to reach out to the culture, many Christians have fallen in. Naïveté about idolatry has not only opened the Christian heart to the diverse "idol mill," but it has spawned an even greater corrupting influence: false views of God! The biblical God of glory is being reduced to more "manageable proportions." The God of Scripture is being trivialized.[7]

The divine decree is that idols misrepresent his nature and character. God is interested in good government and moral values and public policy, but he is not wrapped in red, white, and blue. God never claimed to be an American, yet he is very concerned about the spiritual lives of Americans.

It is important to God that his people experience psychological health and emotional stability, but his greater concern is that we recognize our inadequacy and our need to rest in his sufficiency.

God is personal, close, and available to us, but that does not make him a "divine pussycat," fearful of stepping on any spiritual toes. The holy God of the Bible calls his people to repentance and obedience and cannot be tamed by the creative wisdom of man.

Finally, God wants us to experience the reality of his person and grace. But it is not his chief priority to inject us daily with emotional highs or shivers in our spiritual livers. God calls us to make war against idolatry and to be people of truth.

Tragically, as the culture presses in on the church, many Christians are re-fashioning God to make him more acceptable. The politically correct dragon breathes tolerant, friendly fire. Burned by these flames, Christians are remaking God into a more "flexible" deity. Unguarded confidence in this divine reconstruction has led many to the assumption that God is comfortable with "whatever view I arrive at" regarding his nature and will. "One must ask, 'Who is being served in all of this—God or the god of my understanding?'"[8]

As postmodernity mushrooms in our culture, many Christians continue to get hammered by its alluring, human-centered appeal. Truth begins not with God but with an evaluation of human desires. Concerns often begin with a cause, and then God is re-fashioned accordingly to champion the project. The message that is then grafted into our fragile minds becomes this: Who God really is should not be our primary concern; "what matters is finding an image of God that will be useful."[9]

COMMANDMENTS FOR KEEPING FREE

In Exodus 20:2, God announces himself as the great liberator. He introduces himself as the Lord, as Yahweh, who led Israel out of Egypt, the house of slavery. He is pictured as a holy God—wholly other, different than anything else in creation, awesome in greatness, and utterly supreme in love. In the prologue to the Ten Commandments, God reminds his people that he alone is the God of salvation and that no other so-called god could save or deliver them from the bondage of slavery. Following this great declaration, God reveals in the Decalogue (i.e., the Ten Words or Commandments—*deca* means ten, and *logue* means words) how liberated people should live.

Rightly understood, God's commandments are not narrow restrictions meant to stifle our joy. They are liberating prescriptions that nurture a loving union with our God, a recipe for wisdom and direction in life. They are ten treasures, ten laws of true liberation.

It is fundamental we understand that in the prologue God declares himself to be the Savior, the Liberator. We are told in the first three verses not to look for deliverance in anyone or anything (no other god); only the Lord liberates. The Ten Commandments reflect God's righteous character and announce how his people should conduct their lives.

Unfortunately, God's people have always been prone to idolatry even after liberation. Even as Moses was on Mount Sinai receiving the Ten Commandments, God's people turned from him. They lost patience, then reconceived God according to the felt need of the moment. In their idolatry, "they re-fashioned God to fit their expectations and to service their desires. They reduced God to a more manageable deity; they exchanged the saving God for a trivial god."[10]

The pagan nations surrounding Israel worshiped many different kinds of deities. Roaming gods of love, sex, war, the sky, and agriculture ruled over pagan peoples. But religious devotion was merely a slice of pagan life. While pagan worshipers viewed their deities as more powerful than humans, they sought to use their gods to acquire what they wanted, to satisfy their innermost desires. In paganism, gods exist to make people happy, to bring them personal gratification.

But the sovereign God of the Bible is unlike these resurging views of pagan deities. In the Decalogue, it is revealed in part that God makes all of life a matter of glorifying and enjoying him, not glorifying and enjoying ourselves.[11] He is the personal, transcendent revealer of truth who:

A. Repudiates atheism—"I am the Lord your God" (Ex. 20:2).
B. Renounces deism—"Who brought you out of the land of Egypt, out of the house of slavery" (v. 2).
C. Condemns polytheism—"You shall have no other gods before me" (v. 3).

But the First Commandment was given primarily to guard against "spiritual idolatry." *You shall have no other gods before me* means that nothing is to be placed before God—no person, hobby, philosophy, or purpose. The depth of this prohibition is evident when we take note that this commandment was given to God's people. We are all prone to idolatry and need God's wisdom and grace to stay clean.

God gives us a choice to view him correctly and to follow him according to his Word. Right choosing also means refusing to accept popular views contrary to God's nature and truth. The First Commandment sets the stage for the nine that follow. If we adhere to commandment number one, then the other nine will be joyfully obeyed. If we repeatedly violate the First Commandment, then life will be an uphill climb of ups and downs, obedience and disobedience. The progress and direction of our life must be determined by the First Commandment.

SAY NO TO ATHEISM

Atheism is the active belief that no God exists beyond the universe. Atheism includes many variations (e.g., traditional atheism, mythological atheism, dialectical atheism, etc.). Used broadly, however, atheism holds that no God exists in or beyond the world or universe.[12]

For more than one hundred years—at least since the publication of Darwin's *On the Origin of Species* in 1859—scientists and skeptics in general have excommunicated God from the universe. Replacing the Creator of all things with "natural selection" has been the celebrated theory in American education, but has recently been called into question by a growing number of well-respected scientists. Not only has paleontology failed to produce the fossil "missing links" which Darwin anticipated, but hypothetical reconstructions of major evolutionary developments—such as that of linking birds to reptiles—are beginning to look more like fantasies than serious conjectures.[13]

Most important of all, the discoveries of molecular biologists, far from strengthening Darwin's claims, are throwing more and more doubt on traditional Darwinian evolution. They say that biochemicals are now known to be so enormously complex that "quite explicit instructions" were necessary for their assembly and that other means than "natural selection" were required for life's development.

British scientist Sir Fred Hoyle said that many scientists still cling to Darwinism because of its grip on the educational system and out of fear that any retreat would "open the floodgates of irrationalism. Once a whole society becomes committed to a particular set of concepts, educational continuity makes it exceedingly hard to change the pattern." Hoyle stated, "You either have to believe the concepts or you will be branded a heretic."[14]

Hoyle, an astronomer and mathematician, concludes in no uncertain terms:

> The scientific world has been bamboozled into believing that evolution has been proved. Nothing could be further from the truth. . . . Every competent space mathematician would assure you that such a Darwinian idea had no chance of working. . . . Every computer expert will in fact assure you that throwing random mistakes into a computer is no way to improve it.[15]

As the evidence continues to stack up against evolution, atheism loses more credibility. Some have taken their eyes off Darwin and have once again turned their attention toward the heavens—not to seek after God, the true liberator, but for a cosmic ET in outer space. They are hoping for a higher life form out there that will give our existence meaning, but won't hassle us with morals.

The late Carl Sagan, for example, proclaimed the following in the opening line of his multi-million-selling *Cosmos*: "The Cosmos is all that is or ever was or ever will be."[16] Yet, in spite of his admission that there are "no compelling cases of extraterrestrial visitation,"[17] he still searched through the cosmos hoping to discover evidence. However, nothing is said or done about the enormous amount of evidence for God's existence. The God of the cosmos is abandoned for a cosmic séance.[18] God's testimony does not count.

In the atheistic worldview, values are not discovered by human beings and established by God; they have no need to be discovered because they are established by human beings. In short, when humanity dethrones God, men and women usually enthrone themselves as sovereign.

Herbert Schlossberg, in his book *Idols for Destruction*, astutely observed: "Western society, in turning away from the Christian faith, has turned to other things. This process is commonly called *secularization*, but that conveys only the negative aspect. The word connotes the 'turning away from the worship of God while ignoring the fact that something is being turned *to* in its place.'"[19]

Whenever the one and only true God is absent in an individual's life, you can be sure that some other god will rush in to take his place. Atheists have their gods, whether they are nature, materialism, self-placating moralism, or their own personal egos.

Atheism is repudiated by the First Commandment because it exchanges the infallible God of Creation for the fallible whims of man. It dismisses the sovereign promises of God and banks on the empty promises of man.

Under the head of atheism may be ranked "all presumption, despair, distrust and carnal security."[20]

Although believers repudiate the tenets of atheism, an insidious "practical atheism" is shriveling the hearts and clouding the minds of many who would call themselves Christians. In their heads they may believe in God's existence while their hearts are empty of affection for him. God's direction is sought only in emergency situations. He is rarely thanked or praised, but is often petitioned to divulge material blessings. The pursuit of happiness is supreme, while the pursuit of holiness is barely an afterthought.

Atheism and practical atheism have the same end result: God is dethroned and the self is deified. The difference is that atheists are consistent with their beliefs and practices, but the practical atheist wallows in hypocrisy. He claims to be a follower of Christ, but is a law unto himself, thereby usurping God's prerogative, vilifying God, and using his name. Hence spring selfishness, presumption, and idolatry.

Considering the fact that the First Commandment entails that we love God with all of our heart, soul, and might (Deut. 5:6–7; 6:4–5), practical atheism is a violation of this commandment since God is excluded from the everyday lives of people he loves.

SAY NO TO DEISM

Deism is the belief that God made the world "but never interrupts it with supernatural events. God does not interfere with his creation. Rather, he has designed it to run by immutable natural laws. He has also provided in nature all that his creatures need to live by."[21]

Our third president, Thomas Jefferson, was a staunch deist. A child of the eighteenth-century European Enlightenment, Jefferson helped create the nation with the Declaration of Independence and, for fifty years thereafter, was one of the most influential thinkers the United States possessed.

His religious thought was steeped in the ideas of English deist Baron Herbert of Cherbury and Unitarian clergyman and chemist Joseph Priestley. From these favorite deist writers Jefferson drew authority for his preference for a religion based on the liberal religious Enlightenment view of reason rather than biblical revelation, and his belief in natural law rather than miracles. God does not supernaturally intervene but governs human affairs even as he governs the world of nature by physical laws.[22]

Deism is opposed to the First Commandment because it treats God as a transcendental potentate banished from worldly affairs. God is not an impersonal, heavenly mechanic, but a loving Father who is concerned enough to intervene in a world in which his children need his timely help.

Deism is renounced in the prologue because it denies God's miraculous intervention. A being who could bring the world into existence out of nothing could certainly perform lesser miracles if he chooses.[23] A God who created water could surely part the Red Sea.

God is the almighty, all-good Creator who does not abandon his people, but exercises mercy and grace by miraculously coming to their aid in deliverance: "I am the Lord your God, who brought you out of the land of Egypt, out of the house of slavery" (Ex. 20:2).

Christians, however, must be careful not to surrender to "functional deism." Insisting that God does not have an individual will for our decisions can discourage an intimate, personal relationship with him. This perspective is influenced by Enlightenment rationalism, which viewed God as a transcendent potentate leaving humans to make all of their own choices based on reason. That is not to say that reasonable decision-making is unimportant. Christians should strive to make prudent choices while holding on to the conviction that God can and does offer special guidance.

In an effort to avoid the extremes of backwoods Bible thumpers and mystic televangelists, many believers have stiff-armed God from influencing their personal decisions. We are told to look for God's moral will in the Bible, but personal decision-making is in our court. God has a moral will but not a personal will for his people.[24] Some even warn that if we look for God's guidance in our personal lives (e.g., whether or not I should move or change jobs, etc.), then we open ourselves up to the ravages of mysticism.

The Bible, however, does teach that we should "understand what the will of the Lord is" (Eph. 5:17). The injunction here, in context, clearly goes beyond moral commands and provides a principle for confronting all situations of life—the nonmoral as well as the moral.[25] God guides us in many ways, through the Bible, by special acts of intervention in our lives, as well as by general providential ordering of the world.[26] Our union with God—his presence "with us" and his Word dwelling richly "in us"—is the most important part of guidance. But to say that God only has a moral will but no specific will for his people has some dangers. Dallas Willard shares this concern as he says, generally speaking, "It seems to me that one of the most damaging things we can do to the spiritual prospects of anyone is to suggest or teach that God will not deal with them specifically, personally, intelligibly, and consciously or that they cannot *count* on him to do so as he sees fit. Once we have conveyed this idea to them, it makes no sense to attempt to lead them into an honestly personal relationship with God."[27]

Furthermore, while we may face decisions where there appear to be two or more equal alternatives, that does not mean that God sees them all as equally matched. The sovereign God, infinite in knowing, who sees the minutest intricacies of all human events in precise detail, is certainly able to see the best alternative for the individual seeking guidance. His recognition that one alternative over another would help "tilt the balance of history" at least slightly toward the accomplishment of his purposes would be reason enough for him to guide us specifically.[28] The fact that God can and does guide specifically, however, does not mean that he intends to keep believers constantly under his dictation. "Too much intrusion on a seed that has been planted, or on the life of a plant or a child, makes normal, healthy growth impossible."[29]

Thus, E. Stanley Jones helpfully observes:

> I believe in miracle, but not too much miracle, for too much miracle would weaken us, make us dependant on miracle instead of our obedience to natural law. Just enough miracle to let us know he is there, but not too much, lest we depend on it when we should depend on our own initiative and on his orderly processes for our development.[30]

A redemptive community should not consist of groveling robots or truckling, cringing sycophants, but of mature people who live together in community and communion with the living God. God's perfect will may allow, for a particular person, a number of different alternatives.[31] Although God doesn't exist to solve all of our petty whims, he can and does guide personally and specifically. This is often through his Word and shared activity "because it calls forth to full development that in us which is most in his image and constitutive of our individuality: our understanding, our values, and our will."[32]

Christians need a balanced perspective when it comes to decision-making and the will of God. Certainly God has a moral will for us, but that doesn't negate his personal will in various situations. But just because God can guide us specifically in every situation does not mean he has to or always intends to. Personal guidance is not synonymous with divine dictation. But then again, let's not limit God by surrendering to "functional deism." It is hard to imagine the first-century Christians operating under the philosophical rationalism that objects to God's guidance in personal decisions. There is plenty of evidence in the Scriptures showing that God guides personally and specifically when he wants to (Eph. 5:15–17; Acts 16:6–10; James 4:15, respectively).

SAY NO TO POLYTHEISM

Polytheism says that there are two or more personal gods that have distinct spheres of influence in the universe. "These gods are not creators of the universe but are its shapers and transformers."[33] According to most polytheists, these gods had a beginning but have no end. The gods of ancient Greece, ancient Rome, and modern-day Mormonism are examples of polytheistic gods.

One of the largest and fastest-growing polytheistic religions in the United States and possibly the world today is Mormonism. The founder of the Mormon religion was Joseph Smith, Jr. (1805–1844). Mormonism is the common name given to the Church of Jesus Christ of Latter-Day Saints (LDS), officially founded on April 16, 1830. At the start of the twentieth century, the Church of Jesus Christ of Latter-Day Saints had 250,000 members. By 1950 it had climbed to the 1 million mark, had doubled to 2 million by 1964, and had more than doubled again to 5 million members by 1982. Today the Mormons have more than thirty thousand missionaries in eighty-three countries.[34]*

Mormon sacred scriptures say explicitly that there are many gods; for example, the three persons of the Trinity are regarded as three gods.[35] Mormons believe that God used to be a man but was able to learn how to be a god, and all Mormon men are striving to become gods just like their heavenly Father did. The Mormon church calls this doctrine eternal progression. Lorenzo Snow, former president and prophet of the Mormon church, first coined the famous Mormon phrase "As man now is, God once was; as God now is, man may be."[36] Although Mormons believe that many gods exist, they worship only one—God the Father. At least one Mormon scholar has admitted with qualifications that their doctrine could be labeled "henotheistic"—a

---

*Some religions, such as Hinduism, have polytheistic and pantheistic aspects.

brand of polytheism in which there are many gods, but only one who should be worshipped.[37]

The growing polytheistic phenomenon is elaborated further by David L. Miller, associate professor of religion at Syracuse University, in his 1974 book entitled *The New Polytheism: Rebirth of the Gods and God-desses*. In this book Miller states with approval that polytheism is alive and thriving in contemporary culture. He argues that the death of God has given rise to the birth of the gods.[38] According to Miller, polytheism is western society's answer for hope, harmony, and liberation.[39]

Polytheism is condemned by the First Commandment: "You shall have no other gods before me" (Ex. 20:3). Polytheist David Miller likens Judeo-Christian monotheism to oppressive imperialism.[40] But this is the case only when people fail to understand that the exclusive confession required in the First Commandment is designed to bring about liberation. Human beings were created to be in a personal relationship with God. Union with the true and living God *sets people free*. Forsaking him for false finite gods made in the image of man keeps people in slavery. The one who faithfully serves God will live under his blessing, but the one who serves polytheistic idols will always languish in bondage.[41] Despite their promise of blessing, to cling to idols results in spiritual degeneration. Those who trust in fragile gods of human construction will become like them—spiritually impotent (Ps. 115:3–8). False gods cannot save. Only the great lawgiver can deliver the oppressed and keep people free! Ethical monotheism is the only antidote to the moral decay of our culture, the only hope for a generation consumed by the worship of false gods, sensory indulgence, relativism, utopian political doctrines, and the flight from personal responsibility.

Everybody worships something or someone. People chart the course of their lives based on what they believe really matters. We worship what we supremely value or admire most. We are incurably religious. Whatever our hearts embrace and long for in time of need becomes our god.

During the time of the judges, Israel forsook the Lord and worshiped the Baals and followed other gods (Judg. 2:11–13). Baal was the god of rain, thunder, and fertility. But idolatry comes in many forms. It is not reduced to names or elements. Man's strength can be his god (Hab. 1:1). You can put your "confidence in gold" (Job 31:24); money can be called mammon (Matt. 6:24); and covetousness is explicitly called idolatry in the Bible (Col. 3:5). We can also make our stomach god (Phil. 3:19).[42]

The First Commandment treasure is an absolute truth that brings freedom. It denounces spiritual idolatry and promotes liberty! It is a gift of grace from a loving God who jealously strives to keep his children free.

A body that takes in the proper food, nourishment, and exercise experiences good health. The junk-food junkie who lives to be a couch potato gradually deteriorates. Similarly, individuals who place their confidence in the one true God and feast on his truth maintain their freedom and keep their spiritual filters clean. Those who are seduced by foreign gods become enslaved to the idols of the age and are led astray.

God painfully declares that his people are destroyed for lack of knowledge (Hosea 4:6). It is a sad commentary that bears witness to the fact that many of God's children can't even name the First Commandment, let alone explain what it means. Biblical illiteracy is rampant in the Christian church, and idolatry continues to flourish. Many Christians are no better at recognizing and resisting idols than contemporary secular people are. This is a major reason for our postmodern cultural captivity. There will be no spiritual revival or cultural transformation without a discerning eye to the detection and destruction of idols. It takes a sincere love and commitment to God and a growing knowledge of his Word for idolatry to be uprooted. Entering into that covenant love and commitment means there is no room for any other gods.

THE SUMMATION OF THE LAW: LOVING GOD

The First Commandment calls us to a covenant relationship with God. In atheism, human beings are all alone in this gargantuan universe. Life is an incredible accident as the result of an impersonal evolutionary process.

Deism espouses a god who is distant and doesn't care. He is not interested in initiating a relationship with little people.

Polytheism promotes gods of all shapes and sizes who manipulate people and can be manipulated by them. The mystical gods of polytheism are interested in power and control, not a relationship.

The God of the Bible is a personal being of love who cares how we live our lives. The Ten Commandments are absolute declarations of love telling us what real life and real relationships are all about. The First Commandment thunders a warning against those who are tempted to develop a relationship with something or someone other than the one true God.

In the Sermon on the Mount, Jesus articulates the essence of the Ten Commandment principles. Righteousness is not a matter of external performance, but of a pure heart (Matt. 5:20). Murder and adultery are matters of the heart (vv. 21–28). The religious leaders buried God's revelation under a load of human tradition, elevating external performance as the way to please God. Jesus challenged the Pharisees' interpretations ("You have heard that the ancients were told") with his declarations ("But I say to you"). Jesus was not abolishing the law or teaching contrary to it. The Pharisees were the ones setting aside God's law. Jesus came to fulfill the law by expressing its true intent and meaning (Matt. 5:17–18). Jesus goes to the very heart of life and proclaims the priority of the one true God, the sacredness of the marriage covenant, and the importance of having a heart free of deadly emotions. He was not the new Moses or the new lawgiver, but the fulfiller of the law.

Fulfillment was not about doing away with the law, but restoring it to its original purpose of guiding and penetrating the interior life. The moral law has always expressed the divine intent: "For thou dost not delight in sacrifice, otherwise I would give it; Thou art not pleased with burnt offering. The sacrifices of God are a broken spirit; a broken and a contrite heart, O God, thou wilt not despise" (Ps. 51:16–17). It is better to obey from the heart than simply go through the motions of a ritualistic sacrifice (1 Sam. 15:22).

Jesus brought the law to completion by entering history as God's promised Messiah. His life and teaching represent a definitive step forward; his life involves the coming of the old into the destiny to which it ultimately pointed.

Tragically, the religious leaders who opposed Jesus did not understand the law because they didn't understand God's love. Genuine love for God had, over time, degenerated into external rules and ways of impressing others. Jesus stressed that what God wants is not a good performance, but warm hearts in relationship with him. That requires internal change.

Jesus summarized the Ten Commandments in two great commands: "Love the Lord your God with all your heart" and "love your neighbor as yourself" (compare Deuteronomy 6:5 and Leviticus 19:18 with Matthew 22:37–40). He brilliantly unites theology and ethics. Loving God impacts our moral values and the way we treat others. The First Commandment shines like a sparkling jewel when seen in this light. Everything we think, say, or do is connected to our relationship with God. The insightful A. W. Tozer said: "What comes into our minds when we think about God is the most important thing about us."[43]

The First Commandment directs the course of our lives. A loving relationship with the God of truth profoundly affects our relationships with other people. Fellowship with false gods or surrendering to the idols of the age has disastrous consequences.

The Canaanites, for example, worshiped a variety of gods. One of their chief deities was the mother goddess of fertility, passion, and war known as Asherah.[44] Violence and cult prostitution were associated with Asherah. The Canaanites sacrificed newborn babies by burning them alive as part of their religious rites. They performed a ceremonial ritual of tying together the legs of a woman in labor and leaving her until she died.

A god conceived in the darkness of a fallen heart will quite naturally bear no real likeness to the true God. False gods generate spiritual and moral erosion. That is why God wants us in a relationship with no other god but him.

The effects of idolatry in the twentieth century are spellbinding. We see the destructive aftermath of idolatry in a tyrant like Adolph Hitler, the decadent lives of so many rock stars, the selfish ambitions of entertainers, the hypocrisy of showy spiritual leaders, and the prideful hearts of everyday people whose thinking has become futile, who worship "vain gods" made in their own likeness (Rom. 1:21–23).

As we approach the new millennium, the effects of idolatry in a postmodern age are both blatant and subtle. The gruesome killings taking place in our society are not performed by primitive Canaanites on pagan altars. They're committed by seemingly normal people. In New Jersey, Amy Grossberg and her boyfriend checked in to a hotel room, gave birth, and killed their baby. Another teen, the "Prom Mom," gave birth in a restroom, dumped the baby in the trash, and returned to the dance.

Postmodernism's rejection of universal truths has led to a decline in our society's moral recognition of the universal dignity of human life. These teenagers' actions are the desperate outcome of postmodern self-centeredness carried to its chilling conclusion.

The early modernist mindset is conveyed in René Descartes's famous dictum, "I think, therefore I am." In contrast, the postmodern mood is, "I feel, therefore I am." It's a quest for oneness with the divine spirit that leaves room for the mystical and carries a deep skepticism toward Christian certainty in absolute biblical truth.

However, such a subjective quest only leads one into an empty, esoteric spirituality where thoughts about God are entertained that are totally unworthy of him. That is the essence of idolatry. It is a one-way ticket to deception, self-righteousness, and shame (Isa. 42:16–17).

Obedience to the First Commandment protects our hearts from spiritual oppression and sets us on a steady course to follow the other nine. The second tablet in the Ten Commandments protects the dignity of human beings and keeps us from mistreating others. But this requires a close relationship with the one and the only true God. A person who loves God will grow in his or her desire to honor and please him, which is why Jesus summed up the entire law in one great command, "Love God."

C. S. Lewis once said, "Our problem in life is not that we love things too much but that we don't love God enough."[45] Perhaps the reason why so many Christians have a love affair with worldly things is because they do not have one with God. Lewis candidly said, "Every Christian would agree that a man's spiritual health is exactly proportional to his love for God."[46] Our personal agendas and self-indulgence suffocate our love for God. Meager love is our greatest enemy. Could this be why the church has given the great commandment to love God so little attention?

Three times Jesus asked Peter life's most important question: "Do you love me?" (John 21:15–17). He moves Peter to probe to the depth of his being to search out his deepest passion. Passion, when cut off from its living source in the one true God, degenerates into destructive, addictive, exploitative, narcissistic choices. But when rooted securely in God, passion opens us up to receiving the fullness of God's life (John 10:10). The First Commandment regulates all our values, ambitions, and desires, bringing them into union with God's truth. Passion opens our souls, challenges us to take calculated risks, and sets us free to live out our life in God.

Biblical love is not heartless obedience, but passionate following. Jesus warned that obedience that flows from an unchanged, passionless heart is not genuine love, but a legalistic adherence to a human system. It's like the little boy who, reluctantly sitting down after being told to do so three times, said to his dad: "I'm sitting down on the outside, but I'm standing up on the inside." A private in the military may obey his sergeant but despise him. His obedience is not motivated by genuine love. But a man and a woman who love each other deeply, from the heart, will flourish in their relationship (Song 8:6–7). God is not pleased by legalistic rituals or heartless obedience (Amos 5:21–23). He delights in those who love him with all their heart, soul, strength, and mind.

The goal of the Christian life is transformation.[47] Discipleship is life which springs from God's loving grace as we passionately abide in him (John 15:5). Our response to the First Commandment is to nurture a loving, faithful relationship with our God. Loving God gives us a greater capacity to love others. St. Augustine made the famous statement: "If you but love God you may do as you incline."[48] If we truly love God and strive to keep his commandments, we will be inclined to please God and do the right thing. As Paul says, "The very spring of our actions is the love of God" (2 Corinthians 5:14 PHILLIPS). Our spiritual lives will become fountains of grace and truth, making a powerful impact on the world.

The Ten Commandments are God's "covenant of love" (1 Kings 8:23 NIV). A God who loves is a God who cares about how we conduct our lives. Every day we make decisions of the heart. When we choose to love God and build an authentic relationship with him, we refuse excess and idolatry. Jesus emphasized that God's purpose and intention all along was to have a covenant relationship with his people, not an external legalism. To have "no other gods" before the true and living God demands intimate fellowship with him. Obedience to the First Commandment keeps us free.

SMALL GROUP DISCUSSION QUESTIONS

1. How does the author define idolatry? Discuss some of the ways idolatry is at work not only in the world but also in the church. What idols are you currently struggling to overcome?

2. Rightly understood, the Ten Commandments are not narrow restrictions meant to stifle our joy but absolute truths to keep us free. How do they keep believers free? See Exodus 20:2 and Psalm 115. What do these Scriptures teach us?

3. Why are atheism, deism, and polytheism forbidden by the First Commandment? What are the implications of practical atheism and functional deism for Christians? Can a Christian fall into polytheism or a form of it? Why or why not?

4. Read Deuteronomy 6:4–9 and Matthew 22:37–40. Why does God's law and Christ's summarization of the law and the prophets exalt loving God as supreme? What prevents believers from loving God as they should? How can we grow in our love relationship with the one and only true God?

MAKING AN IMPACT
ON AN IDOLATROUS CULTURE

"You shall have no other gods before Me."

Exodus 20:3

Today's pervasive individualism has changed the public ethos, the public standards, ideals, and beliefs, breaking up the subtle ties that bind people together. No longer is our society guided by virtue or tradition. Individual passions breed freely, unrestrained by the idolatrous pursuit of pleasure. Cut loose from a transcendent basis of authority, morality has collapsed into individual choice. The stability of our culture is being threatened like never before. How do we find ourselves in this predicament?

Between the close of the seventeenth and the eighteenth centuries, the intellectual history of Europe and America underwent such momentous development that the entire era has been named after it. This is the age of Enlightenment. While the philosophies of the Enlightenment varied from nation to nation, Enlightenment writers believed that human autonomy and unbounded confidence in human reason would displace church authority and religious tradition. The emphasis during the so-called Age of Reason "was often placed on empirical observation, apart from divine revelation. As nature was their church, so reason was their bible."[1]

Two central aspirations of the Enlightenment were: (1) reason would replace authority, and (2) the "individual" would be freed from the chains of tradition. The twin movements of rationalism (of René Descartes) and empiricism (of Francis Bacon) depicted the "self" as a discoverer of truth. The duty of reason was to mentally uncover and document truths already out there in the world.[2] As the critical mind studies the monuments of past culture and the natural world, it will eventually discover those prescriptions of reason that are absolute, universal, and unchanging.[3] Progress will result when the individual translates those universal truths into terms that "the mass of humankind" can find intelligible and that correspond to reality.

The advent of Romanticism in the late eighteenth century appears as a transitional movement, a stage on the way from the sacramental world of the late Middle Ages to the self-filled, intuitive world of modernity. "First expounded by such figures as the English poet William Wordsworth, the German theologian Friedrich Schleiermacher, and the American essayist Ralph Waldo Emerson, this romantic orthodoxy still governs as the central ideology of modernity in the West."[4]

The Romantics reacted fiercely against the rational categorizations of the Enlightenment which, they believed, had so distorted the nature of the spiritual dimension that it frustrated human passion and interest in spirituality. The theologians of the Romantic period* sought to justify the place of religion in human life while maintaining the cardinal principle of autonomy by celebrating the "inspired self." For Emerson and other romantics, the truth discovered within the self was a mirror image of the truth hidden within nature.[5]

Ironically, the Romantics had the same premises and goals of the Enlightenment project. They were merely challenging the means that the Enlightenment chose to pursue its ends. Romanticism repudiated Enlightenment rationalism and empiricism but embraced the major assumption that the "inner self" could discover universal moral and spiritual truths. Emerson told the students of the Harvard Divinity School in the summer of 1838 that the true source of revelation is not a transcendent God who spoke definitively in the life of an ancient race and a first-century carpenter. No, revelation, he said, has its source in the inspired self filled with the "sentiment of virtue."[6]

---

*Some historians speak of the "Romantic period" between 1780 and 1830 where these principles and ideas came into growing prominence.

While the Romantic aspirations of utopian progress have cooled, the understanding of the Romantic self is still in vogue. Today's postmodernist is in many ways a child of yesterday's Romanticist. Both stand insightfully alone in nature, defying demands upon the self and searching for that which will bring fulfillment.[7] Unlike the Romantic self, the postmodern self no longer looks for "universal truths" or "absolute principles." Instead, driven by the ideals of consumption, self-improvement, and self-fulfillment, it seeks, by whatever means will work, a personal vision of success. With no authoritative guidelines, psychological gratification replaces morality, and individual choice unseats authority. In a postmodern culture of individualism, there is nothing to direct the self except its desires.

It is easy to see how postmodern individualism violates the First Commandment. God's law is abandoned for the inner regions of the self. God is dethroned and the individual is enthroned in his place. Sociologist Robert Bellah interviewed a woman, Sheila Larson, who described the prevailing spirit: "I believe in God. I'm not a religious fanatic. I can't remember the last time I went to church. My faith has carried me a long way. It's 'Sheilaism.' Just my own little voice."[8]

The idolatry is intensified by various contemporary New Age religious philosophies that often teach that human beings are God. Oscar-winning actress Shirley MacLaine declared in her best-selling autobiography *Out on a Limb*, "The tragedy of the human race was that we had forgotten we were all Divine."[9]

The abysmal results of modern and postmodern individualism are clear. Modernity's quest for progress, the attempt to build a utopian society that would end human conflict once and for all, in turn has been a crucial ingredient in modern totalitarianism and its horrific practices. In the name of inevitable progress, both communist and fascist totalitarian regimes thrashed their opposition and killed millions of innocent human beings who stood in their way. Some of the greatest intolerance and oppression, as well as a new kind of authoritarianism, can also be seen in postmodern settings, such as is found in political correctness, where only one answer is permitted.

The relentless attack upon tradition by modernists and postmodernists has encouraged an extravagant individualism that has strengthened our culture's lack of moral conviction. Even an agnostic professor emeritus of political science at the University of Massachusetts, Amherst, stresses that freeing individuals from the constraints of inherited beliefs rooted in the Judeo-Christian tradition "has led to the spread and toleration of all kinds of harmful behavior and has weakened one of the most important traditional institutions of society—the family."[10] Moreover, individualism has ignored the fact that all rational searching or enquiry is "embodied in tradition"; it has remained blind to the fact that "to be outside all traditions is to be a stranger to enquiry; it is 'to be in a state of intellectual and moral destitution.'"[11]

The brilliant French statesman Alexis de Tocqueville celebrated our nation's character traits by writing that Christianity's moral authority assures the transmission of a stabilizing set of moral values from generation to generation. But he also saw the danger of individualism, describing with alarm the prospect of every person "thrown back on himself alone," and the danger that individuals may imprison themselves in the solitude of their own hearts.[12]

The abdication of "tradition" and the denial of "absolute values" for the sake of modern rationalism and/or a postmodern spirit of openness threaten our ability to make a distinction between good and evil. Abandoning God and his law, resulting in the consequent loss of all objective standards of right and wrong, opens the door to barbarism.

Unfortunately, the poisonous attraction of individualism has injected its venom into the veins of evangelical Christianity. For some, *spirituality* is reduced to personal fulfillment. Church attendance becomes whenever it's convenient, and biblical commands, fellowship, and accountability are all open for interpretation.

In *American individualism* people form the habit of thinking of themselves in isolation and imagine that their entire destiny is in their hands. They forget their ancestors and isolate themselves from their contemporaries.[13]

In *evangelical individualism* people think of their personal relationship with God in isolation ("Just me and Jesus") and forge their destiny apart from any church authority. While holding relatively low opinions of history, tradition, and the church, they turn to the experiences of self and isolate themselves from their brothers and sisters in the faith.[14] True spirituality is perverted as it becomes a quest for inner stimulation rather than growth in biblical knowledge and the application of truth in community. Healthy Christians do not live in isolation!

Unlike pantheism, which robs human beings of their distinctive character as persons created in God's image for a relationship with him, Christianity recognizes the dignity of individuals. However, the Scriptures indicate that we were made for community. No Christian can thrive without the spiritual nutrients of fellowship and encouragement. There should be a depth of *togetherness* present in local bodies where believers devote "themselves to the apostles' teaching and to fellowship, to the breaking of bread and to prayer" (Acts 2:42). In a world committed to self-seeking and the thirst for individual rights, the church must work hard to create a genuine community based on self-sacrifice and mutual commitment. Committed love must mark the local expression of the body of Christ.

The moving story of a young mentally challenged runner at the national finals of the Special Olympics is instructive. The event was the difficult 440-yard dash. The eager mentally retarded boy led the field all the way from the starting gun into the home stretch. Suddenly, he collapsed with muscle spasms and cramps. As the second- and third-place runners drew alongside, they could have pulled ahead for the gold and silver. Instead they stopped and picked up the fallen competitor. With his arms around their shoulders, they finished the last ten yards and broke the tape *together*. The crowd cheered. Everyone won. No one lost. All were impacted by a tender, profound demonstration of self-sacrifice and mutual commitment.

To make an impact on a postmodern culture, we must live out the truth together in community, not as isolated religious consumers who feel no more sense of commitment to the church than does a consumer to a shopping mall, but as believers committed to the church who build up and encourage "one another." An idolatrous culture is positively influenced by well-salted saints living in passionate obedience to God and committed to functioning in community.

THE QUEST FOR CULTURAL RENEWAL

Spiritual hunger is swelling the heart of American culture. After decades of Enlightenment rationalism and the advance of secularism, there is a spiritual thirst sweeping across the land.

Hunger for personal spirituality, however, does not mean an interest in Christianity or traditional morality. The New Age movement is one sign of this increasing desire to experience the supernatural. New Age ideas include beliefs in channeling, crystals, horoscopes, paranormal psychology, UFOs, reincarnation, and Eastern occultic practices. New Age advocates do not preach a coherent set of doctrines but provide services to aid people in their search for self-fulfillment and enlightenment. Yet the crisis in the character of our culture remains. The values that restrain inner vices and develop inner virtues are withering on the vine. Postmodernity's cultural grip, scorning our moral heritage and strangling the notion of any controlling values for society, is weakening the very pillars upon which our civilization rests.

The term "culture" describes the knowledge, beliefs, customs, and habits of a particular society or people group.[15] Historically, many Christians have seen themselves engaged in a convulsive struggle to change a world that has gone drastically awry. The Christian is not called to be a spiritual recluse or to dwell in milk-toast neutrality, but is to be an agent of God's transforming power. As individual Christians themselves are transformed by God's grace, they go about the business of changing their culture by making disciples throughout the social structure. Progressively, the knowledge, beliefs, and habits of that culture begin to change as believers bring biblical principles to bear on their spheres of influence.

Throughout biblical history, one of the great shortcomings of God's people has been syncretism. The ungodly practice of fusing principles from alien faiths into the Christian message is still a problem. Eastern ideas enter many churches packaged in attractive spiritual clothing. New Age ideas are the most prevalent. They seem to be floating around everywhere—in business, psychology, religion, and entertainment, to name a few. The New Age is a conflicting mixture of Eastern and self-help ideas with no internal consistency. Christians knowingly and unknowingly eagerly glean certain tenets from the New Age package. Our culture's consumer mentality empowers this cafeteria-style approach to spirituality. It is imperative that Christian leaders help their parishioners to discriminate between competing ideas and identify them for what they are. We are supposed to influence our culture. This is difficult when prevailing pagan ideas have found a home in our churches.

The bottom-line question is this: Is our faith germane to our current life situation, and is it impacting the lives of people around us? Martin Luther astutely remarked that "if you are not applying the Gospel of Christ to the specific problems of your age, then you are not communicating the Gospel at all. Merely talking about the problems won't suffice."[16] Believers who retreat from society often find themselves rootless and insecure. The church has the responsibility to be salt and light, challenging conventional public and private immoralities and standing as a sentinel of decency, civility, and justice. To neglect or ignore this responsibility is to become, as Millard Fuller suggests, parrots who have learned to chirp "I love Jesus, I love Jesus" without having an inward and outward reality that keeps us moving for the kingdom.[17]

Dr. Martin Marty of the University of Chicago described contemporary evangelical Christianity in the *Wall Street Journal* several years ago in this way: "If you're part of the evangelical subculture, it's your whole life ... you go to church, you buy religious books, you watch the television programs. But if you're not part of the subculture, you never know it exists."[18] Those words—"you never know it exists"—continue to send chills up my spine. Christianity is deemed to be so inward focused that it's declared essentially irrelevant.[19] Christians who retreat from society to snuggle into their nests of private devotion withdraw from the world they were called to illumine with the truth of God; they make Christianity "look like another form of psychological self-help rather than a coherent structure of truth."[20] The Christian movement is called to be "outward bound."

God's truth is a precious treasure. We must guard it diligently. The attempt to blend alien faiths with the Gospel is idolatry. Syncretism breeds error and can lead an entire nation away from the living God (1 Kings 12:28). Idolatry is so insidious that it must be guarded against regularly.[21] Believers must return to the first principles, to the First Commandment, and arise again to the challenge faced by first-century Christians when the Christian movement was first making its way in the Roman Empire. We are called to deliver redemptive answers and actions and to persuade people that our primary aim as human beings is to honor the one true God. When God is not honored and his truth is ignored, the culture erodes into an amoral assemblage of competing, self-centered interests destructive of the general welfare of society. The choice before us is between honoring God and applying his law in order to encourage cultural renewal or to accept the hedonistic consequences of postmodernism.

It is our Christian and civic responsibility to overcome cultural decadence and disintegration by bringing Christian presuppositions to bear on a broad range of subjects usually neglected by the church, such as philosophy, political theory, economics, literary criticism, technology, and music, just to name a few. Tragically, while Christians have been absent from culture, many of the banal elements of culture have not been absent from the church, so that Christians are all too often "of the world, but not in the world."[22] Christians who never question their culture are usually molded by public opinion rather than biblical principles. This is the danger believers face as the new millennium approaches. Christians must think clearly about truth, move toward cultural interaction, "and seek ways to combine efforts with other concerned believers who desire to see a Christian worldview at work in our communities."[23]

Separation of church and state does not mean the separation of religion from public life. Pluralism does not mean all views are equally valid. It simply means that all views deserve to be fairly heard. In this era of postmodernism, where reality is fluid and truth depends on the beholder, principles of renewal and a solid moral foundation are desperately needed. English scholar John Stott has stressed that "the principles of the Bible work whether or not one acknowledges their source."[24] To recapture a unified moral ethic based on a Judeo-Christian value system, where the moral authority of God's Word once formed the foundation for societal life and law, is desirable. But we must keep in mind that while it is important to call men and women to repentance by the proclamation of God's law, we cannot force the Ten Commandments on a godless society. Just as we should not dictate the personal behavior of individual Christians beyond Scripture, we should not dictate public morality *in the name of God* beyond that which is written into the human heart by creation.[25]

Cultural renewal through our social, political, and economic institutions is important, but it cannot eclipse the more important reason for our existence on this earth—spiritual renewal. Christ did not call us primarily to save America, but to save Americans.[26] Changing the culture is the glorious result of reaching one person at a time. Cultures are changed only when people are changed. If we lose sight of personal spiritual transformation, we will end up on a battlefield fighting the culture rather than on a mission field winning the people.

Rabbi Harold Kushner, best-selling author of *When Bad Things Happen to Good People*, admits that Christianity is "God's chosen instrument for redeeming the world from paganism."[27] In our current cultural climate, a postmodern-pagan interface has the bewildering potential to unleash an amoral anarchy impossible to restrain by the resources of its own thought. Without a "transcendent standard for ethical evaluation all moral protest or prescription must philosophically obliterate itself."[28] Kushner is right; Christianity is redemptive. And, I would add, our culture's only hope for survival. This postmodern age can only be "illumined" by the character and hope transmitted by God-fearing believers who radically confront idolatry, live in obedience to God's Word, and apply the life-giving message to all areas of human society.

In his lectures on "Christianity and Culture," T. S. Eliot admonishes us to take up the challenge of conceiving anew a Christian society. By a Christian society, he did not mean one that was composed solely of Christians, but one in which human life is ordered to ends that are morally just and honoring to the true God. "It would be a society in which the natural end of man—virtue and well-being in community—is acknowledged for all, and the supernatural end—beatitude—for those who have the eyes to see it." Only God can give ultimate meaning to our lives and a clear direction to our society. "The First Commandment is the theological basis for a just and human society."[29]

Robert Wilkin, in his essay entitled "No Other Gods," tells a story he heard years ago in Germany when Walter Ulbricht, the German Communist leader, was head of the German Democratic Republic. It was said that Ulbricht once had a conversation with Karl Barth about the new society that was being built in East Germany. Ulbricht boasted to Barth that the Communists would be teaching the Ten Commandments in the schools and that the precepts of the Decalogue would provide the moral foundation for the new society. Barth listened politely and then said, "I have only one question, Herr Minister. Will you also be teaching the First Commandment?"[30]

SMALL GROUP DISCUSSION QUESTIONS

1. How have the different forms of individualism influenced our ideas and shaped American culture? What effect does this have on our society's understanding and allegiance to the Ten Commandments?

2. What is religious syncretism? Why does God condemn it in the Old and New Testaments?

3. Why can't we afford to be indifferent about our culture? What difference would it make if the overwhelming majority of believers took God's law seriously and applied the First Commandment to all areas of life?

PROTECTING GOD'S NATURE

"You shall not make for yourself an idol, or any
likeness of what is in heaven above or on the earth
beneath or in the water under the earth."

Exodus 20:4

Back in my Bible college days I struck up a friendship with a man from the Far East. Before his conversion to Christianity, the worship of man-made wooden images and human-like deities was a way of life. As a little boy, the question came to his mind one day, "Why do I worship gods of wood and stone? They can't talk, and they don't seem interested in me."

He went to his father and asked why he was taught to pay homage to muted gods who appeared lifeless and oblivious to the world. "Why should we worship objects that we create?" my friend had asked.

Good questions for an inquisitive boy. To his disappointment, his father could not provide any satisfactory answers. Not long after, my friend walked away from his idols and looked toward the heavens for help, answers, a sign—he just wanted to know the truth. As he did for Cornelius in the New Testament (Acts 10:25–31), God sent this young seeker a Christian missionary. Gradually, the knowledge of the Sovereign God who loved humanity came alive to him through the Scriptures. He found out quickly enough that when you serve the one and only true God, there is no place for idols.

Idols, however, are not just gods of wood and stone on pagan altars. As we saw in the last chapter, idols come in many forms, attaching themselves to the human heart. Idolatry begins with counterfeiting God, making him remote and his commandments irrelevant or unrealistically prohibitive.[1] Even though idols in and of themselves are non-existent, (e.g., false gods), they germinate in the imagination of the human heart and come between us and God.

As we take up this Second Commandment, it is important that we understand that it "was not meant to stifle artistic talent but only to avoid improper substitutes that, like the idols of Canaan, would steal hearts away from the true worship of God."[2] It is also important to recognize that the First and Second Commandments are different. The First Commandment forbids the worship of other gods. The Second Commandment forbids the making of other gods for worship. The First Commandment was given to guard against spiritual idolatry. The Second Commandment was given *to protect the basic nature of God as a spiritual being.*

God is a living Spirit—infinite, immense, eternal, invisible, and incorruptible. To make any corporeal representations of him is unworthy of his being and a disgrace to his nature.[3]

Idol production is always a futile endeavor. God is misrepresented and the mind of the manufacturer is contaminated. The essence of paganism is to construct representations of God by creating carnal, corruptible images of him (e.g., beasts, serpents, half-humans, etc.). The Israelites surrendered to this pagan notion when they represented God by a golden calf and suffered immeasurably for their idolatry (Ex. 32:31).

In the following two sections I explore and examine the effects of two technological giants: television and cyberspace. Both have the power to shape cultural trends, attitudes, and values. Both have the electrifying potential to change our concept of reality.

TELEVISION: THE POSTMODERN CULTURE SHAPER

In the half century since its commercial unveiling, television has become the undisputed master of communications media, revolutionizing the way postwar generations have viewed the world.

On the whole I believe that technology is a friend. It makes life more efficient, much cleaner, and exceedingly more comfortable. Yet there is a dark side to this friend. Its gifts have a high cost. Cultural critic Neil Postman warns that the "uncontrolled growth of technology destroys the vital sources of our humanity. It creates a culture without a moral foundation. It undermines certain mental processes and social relations that make human life worth living. Technology, in sum, is both friend and enemy."[4]

As we examine the effects of television, keep in mind that an idol is not exclusively a wooden god carved for pagan worship. An idol can be anything that captures the human heart and is inflated to function as a substitute for God. The Second Commandment was given to protect God's nature as a spiritual being and has everything to do with our spiritual well-being. In understanding and obeying it we find our freedom and our great worth as divine image bearers. Those who worship worthless idols will themselves become worthless (2 Kings 17:15).

Marshall McLuhan's famous aphorism ("The medium is the message") may be controversial among Ivory Tower scholars. In practicality, however, where feelings often define truth, McLuhan is unquestionably on target. Television presents a stimulus but makes no demands on response. The passive viewer is often blinded to the influence of compelling images, desensitized by fiery imagery, and duped by television's tightly packaged, quick-moving, oftentimes illusionary news and entertainment programming that is more designed to "impress" and galvanize the imagination than articulate a coherent worldview.

Neil Postman, a professor of communications, analyzes the impact of television in our society in his book *Amusing Ourselves to Death*. He traces the effects on our society's cultural development in our transition from a print culture to an age of television information.

In the eighteenth and nineteenth centuries, our society was typographic. A typographic culture is dominated by print. Writing freezes speech and in doing so gives birth to the grammarian, the logician, the rhetorician, the historian, the scientist—all those who must hold language before them so that they can see what it means, where it errs, and where it is leading.[5] Postman explains that every scholar from Erasmus in the sixteenth century to Elizabeth Eisenstein in the twentieth confirms that reading produces habits of mind that encourage the process of rationality. By developing the ability to reason effectively through reading, one can uncover lies, confusions, and overgeneralizations and detect abuses of logic and common sense.[6]

Postman convincingly argues that America's all-consuming love affair with television has led to a steady decline in reading and a passion for amusement over truth. The sovereignty of television has obscured the pursuit of truth and ignites the fascination of visual imagery and entertainment. Truth is no longer determined by careful analysis, examination, and evaluation, but is perceived by impressions of sincerity, feelings of authenticity, attractiveness, or charisma. As a culture moves from orality and writing to printing, to televising, its ideas of truth move with it. Every discipline is affected—law, politics, philosophy, journalism, advertising, the news, and religion.

Television arranges our communication environment for us in ways that no other medium has the power to do. This new medium creates moods and conditions us to exalt visually entertaining material and visually attractive people, regardless of the truth or value content. The decline of the Age of Typography and the ascendancy of the Age of Television has powerfully influenced the way people determine what is important, relevant, or true.

For example, it is highly unlikely that anyone like our twenty-seventh President, the multi-chinned, three-hundred-pound William Howard Taft, could be nominated as a presidential candidate in today's world. As Postman argues: "The shape of a man's body is largely irrelevant to the shape of his ideas when he is addressing a public in writing or on the radio or, for that matter, in smoke signals. But it is quite relevant on television. The grossness of a three-hundred-pound image, even a talking one, would easily overwhelm any logical or spiritual subtleties conveyed by speech. For on television, discourse is conducted largely through visual imagery, which is to say that television gives us conversation in images, not words."[7]

Furthermore, in an image-based culture, people are less prone to communicate openly with each other and more prone to entertain, manipulate, and charm each other. They do not exchange ideas, they exchange images. They do not dialogue with clearly reasoned analyses; they argue with good looks, sex appeal, flashy smiles, and celebrity power.

Television favors moods of conciliation featuring attractive prime-time faces and is at its best when substance of any kind is muted. Knowing that, Postman levels this indictment:

I think it is both fair and obvious to say that on television, God is a vague and subordinate character. Though His Name is invoked repeatedly, the concreteness and persistence of the image of the preacher carries the clear message that it is he, not He, who must be worshipped. I do not mean to imply that the preacher wishes it to be so; only that the power of a close-up televised face, in color, makes idolatry a continual hazard. Television, after all, is a form of graven imagery far more alluring than a golden calf.[8]

The blazing images of television can often obscure the eternal while glorifying a made-up human image. Both the television and those who appear on it are idols in many homes. Images are that powerful. Because image rather than word is the dominant form of communication in our culture, the chances of people being duped, manipulated, or swept into some type of sophisticated "graven imagery" is much greater.

Television, with its rapidly moving images, erodes the ability to concentrate. It discourages analytical thinking by reducing complex ideas to images that communicate immediately and intuitively.[9]

"Words, on the other hand, communicate through abstraction and analysis. Words communicate in linear, logical form; something communicated in words can thus be judged to be true or false."[10] Words are carriers of meaning. The idea of a universal sovereign deity cannot be expressed in images but only in words.

Gene Edward Veith, in his book *Reading Between the Lines*, explains why: "The heart of our religion is a relationship with God—and relationships thrive on communication. We can't know people intimately by merely being in their presence. It takes conversation to share thoughts and personalities. Christians are meant to have an ongoing conversation with God. We address Him in the language of prayer and He addresses us in the language of Scripture."[11]

A culture that is rooted more in images than in words "will find it increasingly difficult to sustain any broad commitment to *any* truth since truth is an abstraction requiring language."[12] Images stimulate the senses and numb the consciousness, making idol production more subtle. This serves a postmodern culture well since there is no real commitment to truth. Because of this, television plays a significant role in shaping behavioral lifestyle. The pulsating images of television dance in the mind like Fourth of July fireworks in an open sky. Those images tamper with our imagination, influence us in a certain direction, and even beckon us to be something or someone that we are not. How can we guard against the negative effects this powerful medium can have on our mental faculties and sensibilities?

First, it is important that we understand the potential intellectual hazards of high-tech electronic imagery and a fast-paced media culture.

Neuroscience research has shown for years that growing brains are physically shaped by experience. This is particularly the case with children. The way children use their brains causes physical changes in them. Neuroscientists understand that experience—"what children do every day, the ways in which they think and respond to the world, what they learn, and the stimuli to which they decide to pay attention—shapes their brains."[13] Not only does it change the ways in which the brain is used (functional change), but it also causes physical alterations (structural change) in neural wiring systems.[14]

Dr. Kenneth A. Klivington of the Salk Institute in San Diego, California, says that "*Structure and function are inseparable. We know that environments shape brains; all sorts of experiments have demonstrated that it happens. There are some studies currently being done that show profound differences in the structure of the brain depending on what is taken in by the senses.*"[15] In other words, if you change what a child does with his or her brain, you are physically going to change that brain. Therefore, it is wise to encourage children to make choices from a selected variety of available challenges, both environmental and intellectual. In an age when we need "enriched" minds to grapple with increasingly complex problems, we should not encourage, or even condone, large doses of passive observing or absorbing for growing brains. Such learning passivity profoundly contributes to lagging academic and mental skills.[16]

Moreover, we stand a better chance for cultural survival (and renewal) with mental equipment flexibly engineered and properly developed for the challenges of an ever-changing world. Thus, human brains and the culture they generate are intertwined. As the culture acts to modify our brains, they, in turn, act to modify the culture.[17] The insidious "downward spiral" is frightening. The more promiscuity and sensuality we watch, the more promiscuous and sensual our culture becomes. The more violence we take in, the more angry and violent our culture becomes. A culture is fashioned by human brains shaped by the information and images they absorb. At any age we take an active role in shaping our own brains according to what we choose to notice and respond to.[18]

A culture that yearns for entertainment reveals its deep spiritual anorexia. There is a longing for something beyond. There is that sense of cosmic emptiness apart from God. In a godless postmodern culture, people are seduced by entertainment and the visual arts and are driven to consume it in greater doses. The taste for "higher things" is often blunted by the electronic media. Truth-starved hearts struggle to fill the void, but satisfaction is never reached.

In Christ that emptiness is conquered as the longings of the human heart are met and the struggles of the intellect are answered. Jesus is Lord over the arts and of all creation. He is the master artist who holds all things together and has played the ultimate role in the greatest drama of all—the drama of redemption. The Word of God commands us to reflect on excellence, training ourselves to love higher things that challenge our mind and build our character. That means seeking out whatever is true, noble, right, pure, admirable, and to "think about such things" (Phil. 4:8 NIV). Our worldview must be defined by these truths and our sensibilities shaped by them. Otherwise, the salient characteristics of the media will overwhelm our perceptual faculties and our ability to respond to that stimulus in an upright manner.

We can also protect our vulnerable mental wiring by learning *what not to watch* and *how to watch*. We are hopelessly naïve, for example, to think that we are immune to the effects of sexually explicit imagery and innuendo. Not only are our beliefs, convictions, and attitudes threatened, but we become desensitized in the process. Like the frog boiled to death by degrees, many Christians are being misled and desensitized to sexual sin.[19] Many parents feel under siege from a culture that seduces their children with a nonstop flow of crude sensuality devoid of genuine love or commitment. The fact that more than 2 million kids tune in to *The Jerry Springer Show* every day is alarming. Topics include a woman who is pregnant by her half brother while married to his stepbrother. Add a mother who lives with her 13-year-old's ex-boyfriend. The *Springer Show*'s hedonistic mixture of sex, humor, and violence is particularly lethal. There's no integrity and no remorse. Kids are especially vulnerable since they lack the maturity to put such imagery into some type of moral framework.[20]

We must also learn how to watch. Postman asserts, "No medium is excessively dangerous if its users understand what its dangers are."[21] We need to be careful observers, evaluating the ideas, discourse, and the vast spectrum of biases woven into the tapestry of television. Biblical discernment is essential for cogent decision-making. Moreover, parents must train themselves and their children to cultivate inner immunity to "mediated" imagery and immoral content.

Banishing the "menacing medium" from the home is the path some have chosen. For certain people that may be a prudent decision. When the television becomes a "plug-in drug" it is time to nuke the idol! There are, however, other ways to approach the concerns raised by the tube, as previously mentioned (learning what and how to watch). Author and professor David Augsburger points out: "Separate a young man from all contact with evil; and when he is suddenly faced with opportunity, he has little power to refuse it. It is not the sterile safety of perfectly pure surroundings that we need, but inner resistance. Inner immunity to evil."[22]

Whatever decision is made, we must be discerning about this potentially addictive medium. Television's rapid growth of immoral content and its mesmerizing ability to detach us from reality, to fixate us in fantasies, will consume us if we become spiritually or intellectually complacent. We must hold fast to the truth and remember that television does not traffic in truth.

TV screenwriter Lloyd Billingsley observed in the movie *Network*:

"There is something to be said for the counsel of Howard Beale," the mad prophet–anchorman who was another central character in the Academy Award–winning movie. "If you want truth," he screams to his audience, "don't come to us. We'll tell you anything but the truth. Go to God. Go to your gurus. Go to yourselves. But don't come to us."[23]

Truth is not found on talk shows, sitcoms, or soap operas. It is found in God's law. Idols subvert truth and bring people into bondage. God's truth sets people free (John 8:31–32).

VIRTUAL GODS: SPIRITUAL CONNECTIONS IN CYBERSPACE

The term "cyberspace" was coined by William Gibson in his book *Neuromancer* to describe a shared virtual universe operation within the sum total of all the world's computer networks. Gibson describes cyberspace as a place of "unthinkable complexity," with "lines of light ranged in the non-space of the mind, clusters and constellations of data. Like city lights, receding."[24] Considering the present power of cyberspace—the immediate access to knowledge in bit-streams of data that can lure one all over the world—Gibson's idealized vision appears within reach.

The World Wide Web (WWW) is the most sophisticated and powerful gateway of the Internet (worldwide digital network). In a matter of seconds one can go from New York to Rome, then Moscow, then to a small city in Colombia. This is often referred to as "surfing the Net."

Cyberspace is an electronic genie with unique promises. It claims to be an instrument that can entertain, educate, and expand the boundaries of knowledge and experience. "Yet, the very instrument that can invade the mind enough to bring a cornucopia of sensate delights could also enter the hidden recesses of the mind and its most private thoughts. As well, it could have the power to corrupt, deceive, control, police, and perhaps even enslave someday. It is not an instrument to be taken lightly."[25]

Virtual reality is the most titillating, complex doorway of cyberspace.[26] Cyber-punks and cyber-pundits are prophesying that one day a full immersion into a computer-generated alternate reality will be accessible. People will be able to escape the constraints of bodily existence and enter a world where reality is alterable and freedom is unlimited.[27]

The popular virtual reality movie *Total Recall*, starring Arnold Schwarzenegger, dramatizes the seamless synthetic illusions that can bend and shape perceived reality. In this futuristic blockbuster, the science of virtual reality has reached the point of incredible sophistication where a powerful computer chip—a biochip—is able to reach the visual and auditory neurological centers directly, producing a level of virtual reality that equals and, in some instances, surpasses reality. This is observed when Schwarzenegger has the biochip implanted in his brain by a high-tech corporation promising to give him the ultimate virtual vacation. The seamless illusion is touted to be as tangible as reality itself because the consciousness is altered, causing the brain not to know the difference. The mind-bending story lives up to its basic virtual theme. The viewer is left unsure of whether the high-tech adventure was a virtual-reality experience or something that actually happened in reality.

This is an idealized vision of where cyberspace is boldly headed. Virtual reality is projected to be a $4.5 billion industry by the year 2000. Could our journey into cyberspace, with all of its images and seductions, subvert our commitment to God and enhance the philosophy of postmodernism? Can becoming too cyberspace-minded be dehumanizing? Will flirting with virtual reality, with all of its simulations and stimulations, put one at spiritual risk?

Before answering these questions directly, I turn to the insightful comments of social analyst Neil Postman, who is concerned about our society's obsession with what he calls the "god of technology." This life-altering invention is a god, according to Postman, "in the sense that people believe technology works, that they rely on it, that it makes promises, that they are bereft when denied access to it, that they are delighted when they are in its presence, that for most people it works in mysterious ways, that they condemn people who speak against it, that they stand in awe of it, and that, in the born-again mode, they will alter their lifestyles, their schedules, their habits, and their relationships to accommodate it."[28]

The god of technology casts a wide and usually imperceptible influence on our society like the powerful spells of the mystic sorcerers of medieval lore. Social critic Langdon Winner wonders why it "is that we so willingly sleepwalk through the process of reconstituting the conditions of human existence."[29] He notes, "In the twentieth century it is usually taken for granted that the only reliable sources for improving the human condition stem from new machines, techniques and chemicals."[30] As technology grows in sophistication and power, the powerful spells become more convincing and overpowering. How can we evade the influence of the virtual gods seeking to connect us with techno-idols of another kind?

First, our commitment to growing in the grace and knowledge of Jesus Christ and his Word must be stronger than ever. The residue left behind or the sensibilities that are created and reinforced by cyberspace interactions do have a pervasive effect on society. The desire for more immediate information generates a superficial surfing mentality. One runs the danger of becoming imprisoned in cyberspace. Any addiction stifles the human spirit and damages relationships. Cyber-addiction is no exception and, perhaps, is more psychologically potent. The answer, however, is not to become reactionary Luddites* who want to destroy new technologies simply because they alter our forms of life. After all, the good news of the Gospel can be spread over the Internet. Souls can be saved in cyberspace. As we enter the third millennium this may be an important medium to keep truth in full circulation. Author Douglas Groothuis correctly informs us that "Cyberspace technologies excel in communicating information faster than previously possible and in linking information between computers. In areas where speed is paramount and personal contact is irrelevant or marginal, we can embrace and endorse these technologies—so long as our involvement does not adversely affect our souls in our offline lives."[31]

But we must not overlook the fact that technologies are *not* neutral. Machines are created by humans who bear the image of God and have a sin nature. In a postmodern society we can expect that cyberspace will be inundated with techno-pagans and "reality hackers." Online Christians will only be able to detect and withstand the high-tech relativism and cyber-charged hedonism if they are "tuned in" to the living God and his unchanging Word. Moreover, Christians slowly getting hooked on cyberspace gadgetry must be made aware that "endless experimentation with identities in cyberspace is not the way of edification or sanctification. It

*In the early nineteenth century, a group of workmen in England destroyed laborsaving machinery as a protest against technological change.

may well be the way of madness. We are already fragmented enough as individuals and as a culture. Cyberspace may only make this worse."[32]

Second, cyberspace can deceive us into mistaking connectivity with community.[33] Information can be distributed widely and quickly via cyberspace, but the transformational touch of personal presence is lost.

Theologian David Wells laments, "Our computers are starting to talk to us while our neighbors are becoming more distant and anonymous."[34] The heart of Christianity is its "incarnational nature." God the Son became man that he might redeem men and women and allow us to experience him personally. The apostle John wrote, "What was from the beginning, what we have heard, what we have seen with our eyes, what we beheld and our hands handled, concerning the Word of Life" (1 John 1:1). The kind of community required to make an impact on a postmodern culture requires the grace that comes through the human touch, the human voice, the human gaze.[35]

Jesus demonstrated that transformational ministry cannot take place from a distance. Biblical discipleship, fellowship, and worship must be incarnational. Cyberspace may connect us with people across the Atlantic, but if we are "disconnected" from our spouses, children, churches, and neighbors, we are doing everyone a disservice.

Douglas Groothuis says:

> Genuine community shines through the human presence of truth expressed personally. Cyberspace can only mimic or mirror these experiences (however convincingly); it cannot create them. It can, however, beguile us into mistaking connectivity for community, data for wisdom, efficiency for excellence, and virtual democracy for an informed and active citizenry. It can even beguile us into worshipping the works that our hands have made. If cyberspace is kept closely fastened to the real world, and if we refuse its temptations to replace the literal with the virtual, it can in some ways enhance the natural bonds of humans in society. If not, it may instead eclipse much of what is good and true in genuine community.[36]

Finally, the mind-machine interface of virtual reality is a computer chip away. At present, the cumbersome body gear and head-mounted display used to immerse the user into a creative three-dimensional world can be distracting. But bioengineering is progressing so fast that these obstacles will soon be overcome. This progression inspires a deeper quest for knowledge, power, heightened abilities, and god-like powers. In the midst of modern-day builders of a new Tower of Babel, God's Word still holds: "And now nothing will be restrained from them, which they have imagined to do" (Gen. 11:16 KJV).

The infamous gateway where human minds combined with computer wizardry form this god-like alliance is the imagination. "Virtual reality intersects human vulnerability where desires and longings meet the imagination."[37] Here, the ultimate technological quantum leap will emerge through untapped potentials unleashed deep within the consciousness. Cyber-technology's much anticipated virtual world where man can express his creative power unhindered by the confining forces of the material universe evolves to a kind of virtual immortality.

We must be aware that the idealized utopian hope of cyberspace is Eastern in worldview. Not only is cyberspace the perfect medium to illustrate the postmodern view that there is no normative self, but also, by its very unitive structure, it leans towards a functional pantheism. The new Tower of Babel, bringing global unity to the world electronically, is the cosmic dream.

Idols always pretend to do what only God can do. The seductiveness of what could become a high-tech idol for the Christian is that it promises to get things done, to be more efficient, to exude power, to make positive changes—but by using means that may conflict with God's means.[38] Tal Brooke is on target in saying: "As man creates his universe with no other gods in it but himself, his creation will ultimately grow dark. The human creator who himself is long estranged from his Creator, the Living God, will now try to play God as he creates alternative realities. Virtual realities can never be more than either a poor mirror of the actual reality that God created, thus borrowing from whatever is already in existence, or they will simply be mutations and perversions of these previously created things."[39]

Fleeing reality invites deception. It is a rejection of God's creation which he pronounced good (Gen. 1). It is an abandonment of the one who created reality and "richly supplies us with all things to enjoy" (1 Tim. 6:17). Our minds will be victimized, adulterated, cheapened, or deceived through the fascinations of cyberspace if we substitute electronic circuitry for the natural and beautiful world of landscapes, mountains, clouds, oceans, animals, and human beings.[40] Virtual communities in cyberspace cannot teach us "what a walk through a pine forest is like. Sensation has no substitute."[41] God's wonderful world of realities gives testimony to the fact that "the heavens declare the glory of God" (Ps. 19:1). The verdict of God is that cyberspace "can't touch" or doesn't compare to the magnificently created *real world* of the five senses where human beings connect in divinely intended personal relationship.

The qualitative transformation brought about by new technology competes as a psychological counterfeit of the immanence of God. The quasi-exponential development of technoscience summons our attention and, all too often, our emotional and psychological surrender. Idols are not only on pagan altars but dwell in the recesses of the human imagination. The apostle John's closing warning to first-century Christians is relevant today: "Children, guard yourselves from idols" (1 John 5:21).

IDOL CONSEQUENCES

Idolatry has consequences. This is stated quite forcefully in the Decalogue: "You shall not worship them or serve them; for I, the Lord your God, am a jealous God, visiting the iniquity of the fathers on the children, on the third and the fourth generations of those who hate Me, but showing lovingkindness to thousands, to those who love Me and keep My commandments" (Ex. 20:5–6). If God is not honored, the idolatrous, sinful, and even addictive behavior of the parents will be transferred to their children and subsequent generations. This is not a divine threat but a description of the way things are in human existence. Our actions have consequences and those consequences don't die when we do. The transference is not a mystical one, nor is this a reference to transgenerational demons. This means, essentially, that God has so delicately constructed human beings and so carefully ordered the offspring that children emulate parents' patterns of behavior, whether good or bad. This parental influence is incredibly powerful. Vices of the parents are often adopted by their children. When God is not honored, the negative behavioral patterns are often passed on to the children. We are told that a whole generation was lost because of the spiritual neglect of their parents (Judg. 2:10–11). We see in the Old Testament historical books that idolatry and rebellion were passed on from one generation to another until the nation was ultimately sent into exile (v. 15). King Solomon's idolatry brought God's judgment and caused the nation of Israel to divide (1 Kings 11:11). His idolatrous heart was passed on to his son, Rehoboam, who led Israel into deeper idolatry and male cult prostitution (14:22–24). Israel had reached their darkest hour as their spiritual heritage crumbled from within. Chaotic conditions prevailed in the wake of idolatry.

There is an abundance of research that demonstrates that when parents are dominated by idols of some sort (excessive drinking, drugs, promiscuity, etc.), the negative behavioral patterns are often passed on to the children. This impacts the home, the community, and the society at large. When it comes to divorce, for example, research data show that children often follow in their parents' footsteps. The more divorces and remarriages a child lives through, the more likely that child is to divorce as an adult. Lawrence A. Kurdek followed newlywed couples for five years and discovered that one of the best predictors that a marriage will fail was a history of divorce on the part of one or both spouses, especially if the wife brought children from a previous marriage into the new union.[42] Thus over time divorce begets more divorce.

Maggie Gallagher, in her book *The Abolition of Marriage*, is candid about the divorce cycle:

> In the next generation, daughters affected by the cycle of divorce—divorce begets divorce begets illegitimacy, which begets more of both—are more likely to both divorce and become unwed mothers. Daughters raised in single-parent households launch into sex earlier—because they are less supervised, they often crave male attention, and they have observed their own mothers' romantic lives. A mother with an active postmarital sex life may be less interested in or effective at postponing her teenage daughter's premarital sex life.[43]

God respects an individual's freedom to either serve or reject him. For those who love their idols, whether they take the form of drugs, power, sex, or something else—as the idolaters wish—God lets them pursue their vices. If God's law continues to be ignored, the idols go on to mold and shape the children of future generations.

Children who repeat the sins of their fathers evidence it in personally hating God, in that they forsake him for idols. The good news is that the sinful generational chain can be broken by anyone who abandons their idols and chooses to love and obey the living God; "but showing lovingkindness to thousands, to those who love Me and keep My commandments." The prophet Ezekiel made it plain that the children would not bear the iniquity of their parents if they lived righteously (Ezek. 18:20). God makes it plain that his infinite mercy, his faithfulness, his lovingkindness extend the entire length of a person's life as long as that person loves and honors God.

Idolatry has consequences. But when idols are abandoned and God is given ultimate priority, a pattern of life is established that will benefit generations to come.

WORSHIPING THE RIGHT GOD THE RIGHT WAY

One of the great longings of the human heart is to worship; yet, within that hungry nature there are toilsome tugs in many directions that ultimately defile the essence of worship. Whether one bows down at a pagan altar, invokes prayers to a false god, or becomes enamored by the psychological molding power of new technologies—all are idolatrous substitutes that clearly contradict the essence of worship.

The Second Commandment was given to guard against idol production and to protect the nature of God as a spiritual being. God is spirit. He is a spiritual essence, infinitely above corporeal matter, and is not honored by any form of imaginative worship that is not consistent with his spiritual nature.

We worship the God of the Bible because he is the true and living God, the God who is worthy of our worship based upon his spiritual nature and his unique attributes. He is the only spiritual, infinite, holy, eternal, self-existing, Sovereign Creator who alone fits the definition of a God worthy of worship. He holds and exhibits all the defining qualities of God.

Therefore, the right exercise of worship is grounded on the spirituality of God and his divine attributes. He is the only one who is qualified (worthy) to be worshiped. We do not honor God if we do not honor him as he is.[44]

Our English word *worship* simply means "worth-ship." We worship that which we deem worthy. "Worthy art Thou, our Lord and our God, to receive glory and honor and power; for Thou didst create all things, and because of Thy will they existed and were created" (Rev. 4:11). Neither man, nor beast, nor machines, nor idols of any kind are worthy of worship. Only the one eternal God is worthy. What a person worships is a good indication of what is really important to him.

The famed Archbishop of Canterbury William Temple defined worship in these terms:

> Both for perplexity and for dulled conscience the remedy is the same: sincere and spiritual worship. For worship is the submission of all our nature to God. It is the quickening of conscience by His holiness; the nourishment of mind with His truth; the purifying of imagination by His beauty; the opening of the heart to His love; the surrender of will to His purpose—and all of this gathered up in adoration, the most selfless emotion of which our nature is capable and therefore the chief remedy for that self-centeredness which is our original sin and the source of all actual sin. Yes—worship in spirit and truth is the way to the solution of perplexity and to the liberation from sin.[45]

Ben Patterson astutely says, "We who worship the true, living God would be better if not completely different if we worshipped Him better. For to worship Him as we ought is to become what we ought."[46] Worshiping the right God must be done the right way. We are the beneficiaries when we worship the right God the right way. Right worship leads to enrichment and enablement, the kind of spiritual strength that empowers our lives and sharpens our witness. But it must be as Jesus prescribed: in spirit and truth.

> God is spirit, and those who worship Him must worship in spirit and truth (John 4:24).

Jesus instructed us that right worship must be God-centered. Worship in spirit involves our entire being: our intellects, our senses, and our feelings. Worship in truth must be on the basis of God's revelation concerning his nature as a spiritual being. In the fullness of his revelation, we worship him out of the fullness of the supernatural life we enjoy ("in spirit") and "on the basis of God's incarnate Self-Expression, Christ Jesus himself, through whom God's person and will are finally and ultimately disclosed ('in truth'); and these two characteristics form one matrix, indivisible."[47]

The application of truth to every area of life must be a priority. We should have a deep knowledge of the true God and an unquenchable desire to worship him. John Piper ties things together with this picture: "The fuel of worship is the truth of God, the furnace of worship is the spirit of man, and the heat of worship is the vital affections of reverence, contrition, trust, gratitude and joy."[48]

Although God has made us to live in a material world, he calls us to worship him as he truly is, as a spiritual being who transcends the material world. To worship a false god or the true God in an incorrect manner will lead to presumptions, superstitions, and idolatry (Isa. 44:9, 16–17).

The idol maker bows down to an extension of himself—whether the objects are fashioned from wood or words, images or ideas. His idol-making is a thinly veiled glorification of his subjective longings, but he refuses to face the truth about his egocentric pursuit. The grand delusion of idolatry is that we can find rapture in ourselves—and therefore gain both inspiration in and command over our god. Since the creation reflects God's majesty, worshiping the creature allows us to counterfeit right worship without bowing before the majesty of God.

The Second Commandment demands that we represent God correctly. God is a spirit of infinite majesty; therefore we must come before him with humility and knowledge, worshiping him in spirit and truth.

"For the people of God there is no other way because there is no other God. There is one God, there is no god but God, and there is no rest for any who rely on any god but God."[49]

SMALL GROUP DISCUSSION QUESTIONS

1. What is the difference between the First and Second Commandments? Why do you think it was necessary for God to give two commandments against idolatry?

2. What are some of the positive and negative elements of technology? How is television a powerful culture-shaping device? In what ways has it shaped your ideas and opinions?

3. What are the ups and downs of computers and cyberspace? What are some of the dangers of virtual reality? How can we guard against cyber-addiction? What are some steps we can take to make sure that the technological giants (television and cyberspace) do not become idols in our lives?

4. How does Exodus 20:5–6 relate to our culture today? To your situation? What is the context of this passage? How can the sinful generational chain be broken?

5. What does it mean to worship God? How does worshiping in spirit and truth relate to the Second Commandment? What effect does idolatry have on true worship?

PROTECTING GOD'S REPUTATION

"You shall not misuse the name of the Lord your God."

Exodus 20:7 NIV

Elmer Gantry was an unusually appealing man. He stood six-foot-one, was broad, big-handed, and had a large face. He was as handsome as a young Burt Lancaster, with a swirl of thick black hair worn rather long. His dark eyes were venturesome. His smile was friendly and he spoke with an arousing baritone voice. He could make "Good morning" seem as profound as Einstein's theory of relativity, welcoming as a brass band, and uplifting as a cathedral organ. He was born to be a Broadway star but he became a professional preacher. He was a greedy womanizer, a villain, and was vastly hypocritical. He brought to the pulpit the methods of commercial salesmanship. Gantry was a flamboyant man who had a passion for publicity that equaled the most carnal Hollywood icon. Yet his formidable appearance and enchanting speech hid his pretension.

The popular Sinclair Lewis novel *Elmer Gantry* is today recognized as a landmark in American literature. His portrait of a golden-tongued preacher who rises to power within his church—a saver of souls who lives a life of hypocrisy, sensuality, and ruthless self-indulgence—is also a portrayal of real-life religious figures steeped in greed and vulgarity.[1] This novel scandalized readers when it was first published, causing Lewis to be "invited" to a jail cell in New Hampshire and to his own lynching in Virginia.[2]

Critics of *Elmer Gantry* repudiated the story, claiming its author was a drunk with an axe to grind. Even a close friend of Lewis was later to charge that the last thirty thousand words of the novel were written in a state of drunkenness. One may well question the accuracy of that charge, but the fact remains that he had barely delivered the manuscript to his publisher when he was taken off to a rest home to be "dried out."[3]

Whether Lewis was a drunk or not is not the issue. He angered many religious folk in the early 1900s by bringing to light, through a fictional character, the shenanigans and deceitful scheming of pompous preachers out for themselves. The truth hurts, but it should not be hidden. People have been *using* God's name for centuries. The Third Commandment is often shamefully ignored, but it still stands to rebuke the disobedient: "You shall not misuse the name of the Lord your God" (Ex. 20:7 NIV). God places great value in his name. When it is used in vain or abused by a glory hound, everyone suffers.

God is the life-giver who delights in having his name used properly. He delights in being known for who he really is. When we properly understand and observe the value of his name, then protecting our Lord's reputation becomes central in our lives.

God's Name Is to Be Hallowed

God takes pleasure in being known for who he really is. His name is not a mere designation, but a description of *character* and *purpose*. He is the faithful God of the covenant who keeps his promises to his people. He is the missionary God who delights in having his name lifted up among the nations; "For this very purpose I raised you up, to demonstrate My power in you, and that My name might be proclaimed throughout the whole earth" (Rom. 9:17).

Over and over the Scripture says that God does things "for his name's sake." God's commitment to the salvation and growth of his people is grounded not in his people but in himself. "His passion to save and to purify feeds itself not from the shallow soil of our value but from the infinite depth of his own."[4] God takes pleasure in liberating human beings, but liberation will not be experienced if his name is not hallowed. Surrendering to the God whose name is to be praised brings redemption and deliverance from false gods.

"And what one nation on the earth is like Thy people Israel, whom God went to redeem for Himself as a people and to make a name for Himself, and to do a great thing for Thee and awesome things for Thy land, before Thy people whom Thou hast redeemed for Thyself from Egypt, *from* nations and their gods?" (2 Sam. 7:23)

God's name was so sacred to the Jews that it was pronounced only once a year by the high priest when giving the blessing on Yom Kippur, the Day of Atonement (Lev. 23:27). The Lord (Yahweh—YHWH) was the majestic, faithful, promise-keeping name of God that would not be misused. It is interesting that the Third Commandment does not simply say, "You shall not misuse my name." God speaks of himself here not in the first person but in the third person. The reason is striking and apparent. It is to focus attention on the proper name—Yahweh (the Lord). His name is intentionally mentioned. It is not merely, "You shall not misuse my name," but, "You shall not misuse the name of Yahweh, your God."[5] His name is not to be confused with or viewed on an equal par with Baal, Asherah, or the false gods of Egypt. Yahweh is the true and living God and he alone is Lord.

A person's name not only brings to mind the kind of person he is, but included in that name is his "whole being."[6] When Solomon's *fame* was known to all the surrounding nations, his *name* was attributed to his unsurpassed wisdom (1 Kings 4:31, 34). Here "name" refers not to what he was called but to what he actually was. Attacking his name or treating it lightly meant not taking seriously the wisdom of Solomon.[7] David's name was also highly esteemed because of his wisdom (1 Sam. 18:30). But Shimei attacked David's name. Instead of honoring him as the Lord's anointed king, he cursed David, threw stones at him, and called him worthless (2 Sam. 16:5–7). The word "cursing" here contains the idea of declaring someone a trifling, despicable nonentity. David's reputation was being slandered and his status was being changed from heavyweight to lightweight.[8]

The name of the Lord is befitting his level of majesty. He is a heavyweight. He made a name for himself as Creator. He did the same as Redeemer, choosing Israel to live by his life-giving truth and to make a reputation for him. Yahweh is the God of relationships. That is why he made himself known by the name YHWH (meaning "I am who I am"—Exodus 3:14). In other words, "I exist as Savior and Liberator,

I make real what I say, I do what I have promised."[9] In the New Testament, the church is also described as chosen by God to make a name for him in the world (1 Peter 2:9). To misuse or attack his name is to dishonor his authority, spurn his perfect character, and declare him a worthless nonentity.

Honoring God's name means living for him and according to his law. Proclaiming his name with integrity enhances his reputation.[10] In order to make a worldwide reputation for himself, "God has graciously licensed the use of His name to anyone who will use it according to His written instructions. It needs to be understood, however, that God's name has not been released into the public domain. God retains legal control over His name and threatens serious penalties against the unauthorized misuse of this supremely valuable property."[11] The abuse or misuse of his name not only hurts God's reputation in the world but also has consequences for the abuser. God's purposes are stifled by those who portray him incorrectly or use his name for their own fame. Their fate is ultimately in his hands. Nevertheless, God's plan is not defeated, only temporarily frustrated. His reputation is tarnished in the process by self-aggrandizing individuals out to bask in their own glory.

How, then, is God's name, his reputation, violated?

By Using God

Throughout history God's name has been damaged by ministers and preachers using techniques of commercial expansion to make money and a name for themselves. Markets once flourished in cathedral towns, and the Medieval church shared the profits. Johann Tetzel, a Dominican friar, sold indulgences to collect money for the construction of a massive new basilica. It was a splendid bargain for the buyer. The purchase of an indulgence would buy a confessing believer God's forgiveness or could be applied to a soul in purgatory. Tetzel's drastic proverb was: "As soon as the money in the coffer rings, the soul from purgatory's fire springs."[12] At the time, a fervent university theology professor by the name of Martin Luther denounced this as religious blackmail. The door of the Protestant Reformation had cracked open.

In the late 1980s, the collapse of Jim Bakker's PTL ministry brought many things to public attention, including a new gospel of materialism that made the contemporary world its friend. Bakker wanted to be Billy Graham, Johnny Carson, and Walt Disney rolled into one. Bakker told people that they did not have to prove their Christianity by making the world an enemy. Author Laurence Moore in his book *Selling God* observes: "The world belonged to them if they would just take it. Like his wife, they could paint their faces, collect shoes and love the sounds of country-western music. Only by enjoying in Christian form the full range of pleasures offered by commercial culture could they signal their control over modern technology. Bakker's world was a sort of reckless Pentecostal antinomianism."[13]

Bakker repented of his ostentatious sins while serving a lengthy prison term. In his humiliation, loneliness, and loss of dignity, inmate 07407–058 began to realize that his former life and ministry was a sham. This is documented in his book *I Was Wrong.*[14] He writes:

> As the true impact of Jesus' words regarding money impacted my heart and mind, I became physically nauseated. I was wrong. I was wrong! Wrong in my lifestyle, certainly, but even more fundamentally, wrong in my understanding of the Bible's true message. Not only was I wrong, but I was teaching the opposite of what Jesus had said.[15]

While the God of the Bible is quick to extend mercy and grace to the repentant, human beings react in a variety of ways. Blatant moral failure hurts the cause of Christ in the world. Oftentimes it reinforces people's distrust for ministers, which may have been softened by good examples but hardens again, perhaps permanently, because of hypocrisy. Using God's name to satisfy human greed and cravings for power inevitably taints his reputation before a watching world.

A corporate example of how God's name was terribly misused is exemplified by the institutional church of Germany in the first half of the twentieth century. The German church discredited God's name by *using* Holy Scripture and reformulating biblical terminology to support National Socialism and to justify allegiance to Hitler's elitist ideology. The people were captured by the spirit of the age and saw their role as helping blot out the shame of the past and bringing about a prosperous future. The church at the time was spiritually weak and was swept away by the cultural tide of German utopianism. The influence of theological liberalism had taken its toll. The historic Christian faith was, for the most part, abandoned for a sterile brand of religious Protestantism. A foundationless church was shaped by the popular themes of German culture. The preparation for Nazi deception was well under way before Hitler came to power. Swept away by the cultural tide, the church was unable to challenge the assumptions of German nationalism.

Adoration for Hitler gushed forth from the pulpits of Germany. The evil swastika, with the cross of Christ sometimes neatly planted in the center, adorned many churches. One pastor enthusiastically proclaimed, "In the pitch-black night of church history, Hitler became, as it were, the wonderful transparency for our time, the window of our age, through which light fell on the history of Christianity. Through him we were able to see a Savior in the history of the Germans."[16]

In his *Nicomachean Ethics* Aristotle wrote, "Men start revolutionary changes for reasons connected with their private lives."[17] Tragically, God's name is often invoked to justify the self-serving ideas of men. In cases like the gross hucksterism of greedy preachers, the Holocaust, and others, such as the Crusades, slavery, and South Africa's apartheid, the exploitation of God's name brings enormous discredit to the cause of Christ in history and tarnishes God's grand reputation.

In the last twenty years, God's name has been pathetically used to justify American patriotism, "militarism, opposition to child care for working mothers, and even such debatable issues as the retention of the Panama Canal."[18] During the 1992 National election, one organization sent out a brochure announcing the "Christian" position on many issues. Many were surprised to discover that God was in favor of limiting congressional terms and lowering taxes.[19] This is likened to using God as a mascot to peddle mere human convictions. Using God's name as a blank check to push our own agenda is tantamount to religious exploitation and, in some cases, flat-out spiritual child abuse. God's name must be protected, not used!

We must always be cognizant of the fact that we are God's representatives on the earth. God is included in the charges the world makes against confessing Christians who live scandalous lives. The first and most important prayer that can be prayed is, "Hallowed be Thy name." Beginning with this great prayer and ending with, "In Jesus' name," means that the glory of God's name is the goal and the ground of everything we pray.[20] To pray this way means we must live this way. God's reputation is guarded when we do what we say, when we walk in integrity. Paul summed it up well in his letter to Timothy where he told the Christians to live in obedience to God's Word so that the name of God and the teaching may not be defamed (1 Tim. 6:1).

FALSE DOCTRINE AND ERROR

It is no secret that mainline churches have been dying for years. Not only have they declined sharply in membership in recent decades, but even "friends and insiders have acknowledged that the mainline churches have lost their impact, their zeal, even their meaning."[21] The mainline churches are today commonly called the old-line churches and sometimes, perhaps unfairly, the sideline churches. Yet the sad facts are that many churches have alienated their orthodox members and lost their strongest adherents. When God's absolute truth is replaced by false doctrine, the Third Commandment is violated and God's name is degraded. God's people, however, are called to proclaim with confidence:

> "Give thanks to the Lord, call on his name;
>   make known among the nations what he has done,
>   and proclaim that his name is exalted." (Isa. 12:4 NIV)

The issue of biblical Christianity versus cultural Christianity is immediately relevant to our context today. The intense struggle in the church between evangelicals and theological liberals is also over the authority of Scripture versus the authority of alien, non-biblical ideologies, between the church's faithfulness to the lordship of Christ and the glory of his name versus an accommodation and reconstruction of Christianity to the spirit of the age. When Scripture is twisted to conform to the spirit of the times, God is mocked and the Third Commandment is desecrated.

Rudolph Bultmann, one of the influential critical scholars to arise out of Germany, was the most discussed continental theologian of the 1960s.

He was a New Testament scholar at the University of Marburg for thirty years (1921–51). His theological aim was to make biblical Christian faith understandable to the modern mindset. Bultmann felt strongly that no modern individual living with all the benefits of science and technology could accept miraculous Christianity, a grand assumption to say the least. The evolving scientific world could not accept the New Testament record as it stood with its healings, demons, exorcisms, and bodily resurrections. So Bultmann set out to recover the core of the Gospel, hidden within the "mythology" of the New Testament, by a process of demythologization. He did not aspire to rid the New Testament of its mythical elements—the legends, myths, and inventions of early Christians—but rather to understand these elements correctly, in accordance with their underlying purpose of pointing one to the Christ of faith. According to Bultmann, myth was problematic not only because it was unacceptable to the modern mind but because it distorts the message, inhibiting personal encounter with the Christ of experience.

For Bultmann, the mission of the church was to recover the actual words that Jesus had spoken. The process of demythologization was like peeling back the layers of an onion to get to the heart. Bultmann's anti-supernatural approach, however, was destined from the start to produce an aberrant portrait of the biblical Jesus. In the end, he concluded that all we know for sure about Jesus of Nazareth was that he lived and died.

Interestingly enough, the famous humanitarian Albert Schweitzer wrote a book entitled *Quest of the Historical Jesus* (1906) that became one of the causes that led to the collapse of liberal theology in Germany. Schweitzer showed that the so-called "quest of the historical Jesus" was not only a subjective approach to historical knowledge about Jesus, but it was also based on a naive view of the objectivity of human judgment. Some critics observed that the German theological professors made Jesus look and sound just like a German professor of theology. Far from rediscovering Jesus, German theologians were projecting their own ideas, values, and hopes onto Jesus, making him a child of their own minds. "A Kantian made Jesus sound just like a Kantian. A liberal made Jesus sound just like a liberal. And a rationalist made Jesus sound just like a rationalist. It was all rather like Hans Christian Andersen's story of the emperor's new clothes. Once someone had the courage to expose the delusion, everyone rushed in to join the fun."[22]

The damage, however, had already been done. The Bible took a beating in Germany and has yet to regain its proper place of authority there. Furthermore, Bultmann's theories saturated the universities of the continent and much of Great Britain. From those venerated shrines of learning, his theories sailed the Atlantic to the prestigious divinity schools of the northeastern United States. Some of the most promising students of the vast spectrum of Protestant denominations began to venture out to theological liberal institutions like Harvard Divinity, Union Theological in New York, or to the continental bastions of learning in Europe. There they were dazzled by the erudition of the Bultmannian protégés. An impressionable young student sitting in a seminar at Union Theological Seminary or at Germany's Tübingen School met a different face of Christianity. Instead of a well-meaning, semi-degreed, passionate home pastor, he met smug, confident, multi-degreed, cosmopolitan liberals who intimidated him from the very beginning. Due to institutional peer pressure, psychological turmoil, or simply as a matter of intellectual pride, the Bible was traded in for mind-poking human theories. The fresh-faced kids who showed up in seminary class were indoctrinated with faith-sapping biblical criticism and routed back to pastor churches. Some, who showed promise, went on to become influential faculty members at other major seminaries.

J. Gresham Machen, the brilliant professor of New Testament, pounded the liberal gospel in the 1920s in his book *Christianity and Liberalism*. The entire book was uncompromising and clear, stating that despite the use of traditional phraseology, modern liberalism not only is a different religion from Christianity but belongs in a totally different class of religions.[23] Liberals in no uncertain terms butchered the basic fundamentals of the gospel and replaced them with a watered-down version of the original. H. Richard Niebuhr summarized the core of liberal theology in a single sentence: "A God without wrath brought men without sin into a kingdom without judgment through the ministrations of a Christ with a cross."[24]

There is a price to pay when Ivory Tower theologians are unwilling to allow for some divine mystery and concede that God is not totally comprehensible to the finite human mind. By insisting on bringing him within the compass of twentieth-century mundane knowledge, liberals courted modernity by embracing it. Embrace turned to erosion. The faith of hundreds of thousands was either lost or marred because many mainline churches too eagerly sacrificed the wisdom of their traditions rooted in the historic Scriptures in favor of surrendering to cultural demands. The cultural civility which capitulated to the idolatries within the permissive culture was soon indistinguishable from polite paganism.

As in Germany, where the general erosion of traditional belief and dissatisfaction with the established church sparked a return to pagan nature religions, likewise, in liberal North American churches we find clergy and laity yearning for new spiritual nectar to satisfy a very old thirst. One dismal example of this was the "ReImagining 1993" conference in Minneapolis where 2000 women and 85 men, including leading staff members of certain liberal Presbyterian and Methodist denominations, gathered to experience cutting-edge theology. Unfortunately, the new theology *cut out* the heart of the Gospel and *carved up* a false god.

The conference featured the goddess "Sophia, Creator God," a workshop on belly dancing, a ridiculing of the Atonement of Christ ("I don't think we need folks hanging on crosses and blood dripping and weird stuff. . . . We just need to listen to the god within"), and rites from other religions such as the American Indian tobacco ritual.[25]

Bishop Earl G. Hunt, of the United Methodist Church, commented, "When the church seems to be losing its struggle with powers and principalities, weird things begin to happen."[26] Some were surprised that a "golden calf" was not displayed for ecumenical worship. This return to pagan forms of thought and behavior is the opposite of biblical faith and is an explicit reinvention of the fertility-worship of Baal and Ashtoresh, against which the faith of Israel defined itself through the centuries of history with the Lord God.[27]

Most recently, sociologists Benton Johnson, Dean Hoge, and Donald Luidens have found that the majority of mainline church members are "lay liberals who have no clear understanding of what Christianity is or why they are Christian. They vaguely know that it has something to do with belief in God and respect for Jesus and the Golden Rule."[28] The churches, according to this study (among many), somehow "lost the will or the ability to teach the Christian faith and what it requires."[29] According to theological liberals, Jesus is "God-light"— an insightful moral teacher who founded an earthly kingdom built on the fatherhood of God and the brotherhood of love. According to the Bible, Jesus is "God," who entered the space/time world as God incarnate, the Savior of humankind (John 1:1, 14; 3:16; 8:24, 58; Col. 1:15–18; Titus 2:13). The memorable words of C. S. Lewis in his book *Mere Christianity* still stand to rebuke those who would reduce Jesus to a great moralist or a great human teacher.

> That is one thing we must not say. A man who was merely a man and said the sort of things Jesus said would not be a great moral teacher. He would either be a lunatic—on a level with the man who says he is a poached egg—or else he would be the devil of hell. You can shut him up for a fool, you can spit at him and kill him as a demon; or you can fall at his feet and call him Lord and God. But let us not come with any patronizing nonsense about his being a great human teacher. He has not left that open to us. He did not intend to.[30]

False doctrine disrespects God's competence in providing his people with divine truth and generates massive division. Liberals who advocate "Rodney King" type theology ("Can't we all just get along") ignore the scriptural principle of unity in the truth. Changing God's revealed truth to appeal to the cultural mood and to tamper with God's nature by making Jesus less than who he claimed to be is condemned by Holy Scripture (Gal. 1:6–8; 2 Cor. 11:3–4, 13–15). It is also condemned by the historic confessions and creeds (e.g., Councils of Nicea, A.D. 325, and Chalcedon, A.D.451) which uphold the foundational Christian teaching that Jesus is true God and true man. It should be no surprise then why the Bible commands believers to separate themselves from false teachers (Rom. 16:17; 2 John 9–11) and to stand together in unity against those who deviate from essential Christian truth.

The liberal theology still germinating in mainline churches treats the Third Commandment as chaff. God is reshaped into a finite, benevolent servant who has no plan of redemption and no sure word to guide his people. Holy Scripture is aborted in favor of eccentric interpretations of reformulated biblical teachings. The end result is a careless misuse of God's name and an innocuous blending with shifting cultural surroundings where energies will continue to be dissipated in irrelevancies and leadership will continue to limp along the sidelines of churches in desperate need of renewal.

The trajectory of the Gospel of God moving from the biblical Jesus to the subjective weak-kneed Jesus of theological liberalism subverts the foundation of Christendom. When the very basis of the Gospel is undermined, the door of hospitality opens to pagan spirituality and contentless mysticism, and God's name is misused.

OTHER WAYS THE THIRD COMMANDMENT IS VIOLATED

The first thought that comes to most people when they hear "You shall not take the name of the Lord your God in vain" is swearing or using vulgar language. The demise of civility in everyday language is a tragic reality of postmodern culture. In a postmodern age where language is more a producer of subjectivity than a meaningful product of autonomous subjects, it has become increasingly irreverent and vulgar to man and God precisely because there has been a depreciation of both man and God.

Paul Galloway, writing for the *Chicago Tribune* in the fall of 1992, described a "striking linguistic comparison between William Shakespeare's *Julius Caesar* and Chicago playwright David Mamet's *Glengary Glen Ross*, noting that while both treat human greed and ambition, they are exactly 232 obscenities apart. Shakespeare managed to muddle his way through without a single blankety-blank, while Mamet managed his Herculean 232 blankety-blanks with an astonishing 152 variations of his favorite vulgarity."[31]

God's name is misused when it's used as a filler for absent syntax ("O God"), is profaned when irreverently used as a divine exclamation point ("Jesus" and "Christ"), and is debased when used as a curse word (damning something or someone). Using the name of the Lord as a curse word is an attack on his power and majesty (Rev. 13:5–9). By treating that which is holy as common, we engage in a violation of the Third Commandment.

Believers can also misuse God's name by saying over and over again, "Praise the Lord, hallelujah, praise God" as a Christian equivalent of "That's great!" I have an old friend who lets the catchphrase "praise God" roll off his tongue whenever he hears anything remotely positive. Excessive repetition has embarrassed him more than once. On one occasion when informing him of my sister's brain surgery he promptly spouted "praise God." Within a few moments, he realized his blunder and quickly apologized. Yet this kind of repetition not only dishonors God but can damage the testimony of a pious believer despite good intentions. God's name should not be used in an idle manner.

There are things to verbally praise the Lord for. However, casual use of God's name by merely repeating words over and over again wears away our sensitivity to the honor we owe it.

Another way people misuse God's name is by breaking an oath or a promise. Swearing an oath by God's name and breaking it was a flagrant misuse of God's name in biblical times. David wrote that God honors one "who keeps his oath even when it hurts" (Ps. 15:4 NIV). In the ancient world, when entering into a covenant with another party, the covenant was sealed with an oath (Gen. 26:31). In Israel an oath was used in legislating important matters of business and commerce. However, it was not permissible to swear by anyone other than the true and living God. Moses' writings repeatedly emphasize this: "And you shall not swear falsely by My name, so as to profane the name of your God; I am the Lord" (Lev. 19:12).

By New Testament times the biblical teaching regarding oaths had come under enormous abuse. In Matthew 5:33–37 Jesus is not prohibiting oaths but is refuting both Jewish casuistry and superficial swearing.[32] The swearing of oaths had degenerated to a clever system. In order to escape the binding biblical requirement of an oath, people swore "by heaven," "by earth," by the life of a king (as Abner did in 1 Samuel 17:55). By avoiding mentioning God, people did not have to be very careful about telling the whole truth since they were cleverly swearing only by human authorities. Jesus brought his word of correction against this deceptive use of oaths: "But I say to you, make no oath at all, either by heaven, for it is the throne of God, or by the earth, for it is the footstool of His feet, or by Jerusalem, for it is the city of the great King. Nor shall you make an oath by your head, for you cannot make one hair white or black. But let your statement be, 'Yes, yes' or 'No, no'; and anything beyond these is of evil" (Matt. 5:34–37).

Jesus is not rejecting *all* oath-taking. He is merely rejecting every kind of swearing that uses an oath for deceiving someone.

People today are as flippant about oath-taking as they were in the first century. Oaths are continually mingled with everyday speech: "I swear on my mother's grave"—"I swear to God"—"on the Bible"—"as God is my witness" and on and on. All of this generates a moral schizophrenia: "I'm really not lying, but I'm also not telling the truth."[33] Adults end up acting like children who play the game "I had my fingers crossed!" Using God's name in such an empty, insincere manner is a grievous breaking of the Third Commandment.

Finally, to give credence to theories like macro-evolution that reject a supreme designer and attempt to excommunicate the name of God from the culture at large (from the schools, the intellectual establishment, and oftentimes the media) is a violation of the Third Commandment. When the master of the universe, the Creator of heaven and earth, the artist of Creation is ignored, when God's name is deleted, erased from his creation in a diversity of ways, and the credit is given to an unproven, mathematically impossible, evolutionary hypothesis, the Third Commandment is broken.

Edith Schaeffer correctly observes: "To give God's praise to *chance* and to declare that everything we know in the world and that the universe came by accident is to sign 'chance' to all of God's creation. It is an insult to his name as much as it would be an insult to Bach's music, or Michelangelo's statues to sign 'chance' where the name of the composer or artist should be."[34]

While we live in a culture that regularly ignores God and misuses his name, we must make every effort to revere his name. His name must be exalted by us in the marketplace, at work, during activities and recreational events, in the classroom, and in the home. We revere and protect God's name because salvation has come to us by calling upon the name of the Lord; "Whoever will call upon the name of the Lord will be saved" (Rom. 10:13). In the Old Testament, God's people were referred to as "My people who are called by My name" (2 Chron. 7:14) in contrast with those who tried to make a name for themselves at the Tower of Babel (Gen. 11:4).[35] God's name is defamed by self-promoting spiritual hustlers who dishonor the Word of God (Titus 2:5).

For nineteen centuries the church has been telling the world to believe in the Gospel. Yet today, in the late twentieth century, the world is "watching" more closely than ever and asking why the church should be listened to. Jesus proclaimed our biblical responsibility: "Let your light shine before men in such a way that they may see your good works, and glorify your Father who is in heaven" (Matt. 5:16). The word "glorify" (*doxa* in the Greek), when applied to God in the New Testament means "to enhance God's reputation."[36] Certainly, no human being can improve on who God really is. He is sovereign, great, and perfect. But his reputation does not always measure up to reality. There are people who think God is unfair, unkind, and unloving. God's reputation is weak among certain people. When a Christian represents God well by living a godly life and upholding central biblical truth, the reputation of God is enhanced and God has been glorified.

The Third Commandment is concerned about protecting God's reputation and exalting his name. He must be hallowed in our interior so that he shines through to our exterior. Keeping the Third Commandment points people to the Sovereign God who desires a relationship with people. It also leads right into the Fourth Commandment, which points people to the life-giver who makes that relationship possible.

SMALL GROUP DISCUSSION QUESTIONS

1. Why must we take God's name seriously? What qualities are behind his name?

2. What does it mean to "use God"? Discuss the personal and corporate sins of using God (i.e., Jim Bakker and the German National Church). What does this do to God's name?

3. What personal and corporate changes take place in the church when the Bible is reformulated to keep up with the spirit

of the times? What can we do to prevent this from happening in our own lives and in our churches?

4. How is false doctrine or prophecy a violation of the Third Commandment? Why is the liberal mainline teaching about Jesus being a great moralist or simply a good example to follow a violation of divine truth? Read John 1:1, 14; 3:16–18; 8:24, 58; Col. 1:15–18; Titus 2:13. What do these verses tell us about Jesus?

5. Consider the different ways people today misuse God's name. How should we respond to people who consistently dishonor God's name? What can we do to ensure that honoring God's name is a priority in our lives?

POINTING TO THE LORD
OF THE SABBATH

"Remember the Sabbath day by keeping it holy."
Exodus 20:8 NIV

It was a cold, brisk winter morning. Huge snowflakes fell from the sky. The glowing white countryside looked like a Christmas postcard. Church was still on. The minister of a fundamental Scottish congregation had to travel some distance in order to lead the worship service. Since the river that flowed past both his home and the church was completely frozen, he decided to skate to church. Attenders shuffling into the building were surprised to see their pastor on skates—shivering but ready to conduct the service.

The episode stirred a debate as to whether or not the pastor should have skated on the Sabbath. The elders held a lengthy formal meeting to discuss the eye-raising incident. Arguments were launched back and forth surrounding the question of whether the practicality of getting to church or the keeping of the Sabbath should be the prime consideration.

Finally, the all-important, ground-breaking question was asked of the pastor: "Did you enjoy skating up the river?"[1]

Why have so many people over the centuries viewed the Lord's Day and fun activities to be mutually exclusive? Was the Sabbath originally designed to be primarily a day of rest? Before answering that question, the origin of the Sabbath institution must be examined.

THE ORIGIN OF THE SABBATH DAY

The Fourth Commandment to keep the Sabbath holy was a new law for the people of God. The Sabbath was God's gift to Israel as a day of rest (Ex. 20:8) and a day for the joyful celebration of freedom from the bondage of slavery (Deut. 5:15). Each text gives a different reason (or emphasis) for keeping the Sabbath, but as we will see, they are intimately connected and unfold beautifully in God's brilliant plan of redemption.

Genesis 2 informs us that after the six-day Creation scheme, God rested on the seventh day (2:2). God celebrated a divine Sabbath for himself by blessing the seventh day and making it holy, because he rested from his creation work (v. 3). God created the Sabbath rest because he had finished his work, not because he was tired and needed a break. As theologian Karl Barth declared, by resting God takes pleasure in what he has made; God has no regrets, no need to go on to create a still better world or a creature more wonderful than man and woman. In God's day of rest, his free love toward humanity takes form as time shared with them.[2] God also establishes a "genesis rhythm," an arrangement of time that flows in seven-day cycles. At the end of the weekly cycle built into the divinely framed cosmos is the day that God sanctified for himself.

God did not institute his divine Sabbath as a "creation ordinance" (a universally binding institution for all humanity), as some have maintained. There is no command in Genesis 2 for humanity to observe the Sabbath. Everything is centered on God. The first time we come across Sabbath observance in the Old Testament is in Exodus 16. This is a special prelude to the giving of the Fourth Commandment, where God's people were being prepared for the Sabbath law soon to come.

Dutch scholar J. Douma, in reference to Genesis 2, correctly states:

> Strictly speaking, we read no more than that God rested on the seventh day, and also blessed and sanctified this day. The passage does indeed speak about rest—the rest of the Lord—but not about the Sabbath as a prescribed rest for man.[3]

It is not until the Mosaic institution of the Sabbath that we read, "Therefore you are to observe the Sabbath, for it is holy unto you"

(Ex. 31:14). What God prescribed for himself with regard to the seventh day (sanctified the day, making it a special divine-focused day) he now mandates for "his people."

THE PURPOSE OF THE SABBATH

Too many believers have carelessly reduced the Sabbath to a day of inactivity. The Sabbath is often viewed simply as a day to rest the weary mind and body. Even though there are no intricately detailed, uniform guidelines given to individuals to construct their Sabbath day, many have developed Pharisaical rules and regulations that have turned what was meant to be a day of joy into drudgery and have negated the primary purpose of the Sabbath rest. The 1648 Westminster Larger Catechism, although not taking it to this extreme, does state that the central emphasis of the Sabbath is human rest from employment and recreation.

> The Sabbath or Lord's day is to be sanctified by an holy resting all the day, not only from such works as are at all times sinful, but even from such worldly employments and recreations as are on other days lawful; and making it our delight to spend the whole time (except so much of it as is to be taken up in works of necessity and mercy) in the public and private exercises of God's worship: and, to that end, we are to prepare our hearts, and with such foresight, diligence, and moderation, to dispose and seasonably dispatch our worldly business, that we may be the more free and fit for the duties of that day.[4]

The highly esteemed Confession obviously views the Sabbath as a creation ordinance placing its primary emphasis on rest from physical labor and recreation. Worship is stressed but its focus on physical rest leads one away from the central theological significance of the Sabbath. I say this advisedly and carefully, because I hold the Westminster Confession in high regard and rarely disagree with its contents.

The purpose of the Sabbath is not the practical service it provides for us. The primary purpose of the Sabbath institution is surprisingly overlooked. The Sabbath was the "shadow" which pointed to Christ the reality. Its primary significance was in its *sign-bearing* function. The primary use of the commandment was the forward look, pointing to Christ, that anticipated the "spiritual rest" believers would enjoy in him. The old covenant Sabbath bore a greater significance than a continuing regulation of activity on a specially designated day of the week. It foreshadowed the new covenant spiritual rest realized in Jesus Christ.

The New Testament is clear that Jesus came to fulfill the law, to bring it to completion. Jesus portrays the law as having a forward look, anticipating a "fuller" significance to come. The law is from God and cannot be destroyed (Rom. 7:22; 8:7). Jesus' teaching expresses fully and ideally the righteousness anticipated in the old covenant foreshadowing. The law was not complete in itself; it looked forward to the One who would bring it to completion.

As Walter Kaiser says, "The law cannot be properly understood unless it moves toward the grand goal of pointing the believer toward the Messiah, Christ."[5] The law anticipated a fulfilling which in Christ's teaching finally came to perfect realization.[6] Jesus views himself as the fulfiller—the divinely appointed Messiah called to finish the work which the law and prophets had left incomplete. The New Testament in effect completes the story that God began in the Old Testament.

As the one who portrayed the law as having a "forward look," anticipating a fuller significance, Jesus promised rest to anyone who would come unto him (Matt. 11:28). Later he pronounces himself "Lord of the Sabbath" (Matt. 12:8). Jesus claimed authority to exercise his own prerogatives over the Sabbath law. It wasn't the time for Jesus to explain the full meaning of this disclosure. Oftentimes, the people were not ready for new disclosures (John 16:12). But "we are left with the distinct impression that as a result of his coming, the Sabbath will undergo some kind of transformation."[7]

Hebrews chapter 4 provides us with further revelation, giving a definitive answer regarding the primary purpose of the Sabbath. It tells us that God rested on the seventh day because he had finished his work, not because he was tired (4:3). God rested in peace and satisfaction with his creation, but did not become inactive. His day of rest extends as he enjoys redemptive relationships with his people.

The Sabbath rest is significant because it offers to men and women the opportunity to enter his rest but has no effect if it is not received by faith in the one and only true God. The Israelites failed to enter God's rest because of unbelief (Heb. 3:12–19). Hebrews chapter 4 cites Psalm 95:11 concerning that failure, where the Lord declared, "Therefore I swore in My anger, Truly they shall not enter into My rest." The writer to the Hebrews later states that the believers who finally did enter the Promised Land understood that it was still only a shadow of the eternal Sabbath rest: "But as it is, they desire a better country, that is, a heavenly one" (11:16).

Those who rejected God and his promises were refused admission not only to God's earthly rest but his heavenly rest as well. The same is true today—there remains a heavenly rest open to believers, but closed to the disobedient:

> It still remains that some will enter that rest, and those who formerly had the gospel preached to them did not go in, because of their disobedience (4:6 NIV).

The good news hasn't changed. It still must be received by faith (4:2). But its fuller expression is realized in the eternal work and purpose of Jesus Christ—the Lord of the Sabbath. Under the old covenant the Sabbath rest pointed toward the fundamental redemptive truths realized in Christ who established the new and better covenant (8:6–11). God invites us into his eternal Sabbath foreshadowed by the earthly Sabbath.

The foundational text is Hebrews 4:9–10: "There remains therefore a Sabbath rest for the people of God. For the one who has entered His rest has himself also rested from his works, as God did from His." Through a redemptive relationship with Jesus Christ one enters God's spiritual family—his eternal Sabbath rest. The apostle Paul said, "For by grace you have been saved through faith; and that not of yourselves, it is the gift of God; not as a result of works, so that no one may boast" (Eph. 2:8–9). Like the Israelites of old who forfeited his rest "because of unbelief" (Heb. 3:19), many today are barred from entering God's eternal rest because they refuse to receive God's free gift of eternal life and attempt to enter the Promised Land (God's eternal presence) by their own efforts. God calls it disobedience (Heb. 4:6).

In Hebrews 4:8 the author develops a striking parallel between Joshua (the son of Nun) in the Old Testament and Jesus (the Son of God) in the New Testament. The words for "Joshua" and "Jesus" are exactly the same in the Greek—Jesus was named after Joshua. The Old Testament "Jesus" (Joshua) had led his followers into the temporal, earthly Canaan. But there was an eternal heavenly rest to come: "For if Joshua had given them rest, He would not have spoken of another day after that" (v. 8). The New Testament "Jesus" (the Savior) is the author of salvation (2:10) who leads the heirs of the new covenant into their heavenly rest.

Jesus Christ is the eternal Sabbath rest. Those who work to gain God's favor or strive to earn their salvation will not enter. "For the one who has entered His rest has himself also rested from his works" (Heb. 4:10). When we trust in Christ alone we close the doors to works-righteousness and enter God's rest. By our spiritual union with Christ, "we are already living in the seventh day, the eternal Sabbath of God."[8]

Michael Horton correctly asserts that the main point of all God's laws, including the Sabbath decree, is theological. "It teaches us something about God, not something about ourselves. It points the way to enjoying God, not to enjoying ourselves. It is not concerned with making life easier for us, but with teaching us about the age to come that God has prepared."[9]

While the Sabbath did serve the best interests of the people by providing physical rest, it was intended to be a God-centered institution, not a human-centered one. Salvation is granted to those who "rest" from their works and receive the free gift of eternal life through the One whom the Scriptures pointed to—Jesus Christ. The physical rest in Exodus 20:8–11 prefigured the eternal new covenant heavenly rest. In Deuteronomy 5:15 the emphasis on God's redemption of the people of Israel from slavery in Egypt pointed forward to the heavenly rest as the definitive rest. Liberation is the theme. The new covenant Sabbath is unique. It is eternal life in the presence of God.

DOES THE SABBATH HAVE ANY OTHER CONTINUING SIGNIFICANCE?

The command to rest is not a rule that restricts, it is a rule that liberates. Physically, mentally, and spiritually we are freed to function better if we live within God's "design specifications." God has arranged time in such a way that it unfolds in seven-day cycles. Some have tried to improve upon this seven-day pattern only to repent later. During the French Revolution, anti-Christian leaders abolished the seven-day week, but they found that the health of the nation weakened, and they had to reinstate it.[10] Certain communist systems, such as the former Soviet Union, proclaimed the new man theory and inaugurated a ten-day week. The social experiment failed, and the venturesome Marxist thinkers were left standing irrelevantly puttering on the sidelines. God's seven-day rhythm is best for men and women because God created them.[11]

The mind and body need rest. But does that mean that the Christian must cease from all labor because of a Saturday Sabbath command? The New Testament tells a different story.

The theological significance and application of the Fourth Commandment changes in the New Testament. The ancient Jewish practice of a seventh day Saturday Sabbath is superseded by a new day. The New Testament indicates that the Christian day of worship was changed to Sunday, which was called "the Lord's Day" (see John 20:19, 26; Acts 20:7–11; 1 Cor. 16:1–2; Rev. 1:10). Sunday, the first day of the week, was the day Christ rose from the dead (Matt. 28:1; Mark 16:1–2; Luke 24:1; John 20:1). Early in the second century A.D., Ignatius of Antioch noted that "those who followed ancient customs [that is, the Jews] have come to a new hope, no longer celebrating the Sabbath but observing the Lord's Day, the day on which our life sprang up through Christ."[12]

Interestingly enough, worship, not rest, appeared to be the priority in the post-apostolic church. In fact, many Christians worked on the Lord's Day. A day of rest was impossible for many at first—especially for the poor and the slaves.[13] Worship and work went together on the Lord's Day.[14] People either gathered in the early morning or in the late evening on Sunday, while the time between was used for daily labor.

Sunday labor was prevalent until Emperor Constantine instituted Sunday as an official day of rest in A.D. 321. Even then, "Constantine let farmers work on Sunday, because Sunday was often the best day for sowing and planting. In Constantine's opinion, one should not pass up any appropriate opportunity offered by God's propitious providence."[15]

In any event, the early Christians saw the Saturday Sabbath rest pointing forward to its more distinctive Lord's Day significance—worshiping the risen Savior.

The primary purpose of the Fourth Commandment is fulfilled by those who enter God's eternal spiritual rest through Jesus Christ. For the Christian, every day is a Sabbath since one is in union with the Lord of the Sabbath. Furthermore, the Sabbath-keeping practice of cessation of labor belongs to the "ceremonial" part of the law. The writer to the Hebrews clearly shows that the ceremonies and rituals were abrogated by Christ's substitutionary death and resurrection. The "moral" part of God's law is eternally binding on believers in both testaments since it is based on the character of God. The ceremonial and civil laws functioned only as further illustrations of the moral law.[16] The shadows of Christ in the ceremonial and civil laws are set aside when the reality appears. The Sabbath was the "shadow" which looked forward to Christ the reality.

The entire flow of the New Testament confirms this conclusion. God's moral commands are found throughout the New Testament, but the ceremonial and civil laws are not repeated. Every one of the Ten Commandments is stated and reiterated over and over in the New Testament—with the exception of the Fourth Commandment. The command to keep the Sabbath, following Christ's death and resurrection, is nowhere to be found. The Sabbath is unique among the Ten Commandments, pointing the chosen community of God's people forward to Christ.

In Colossians 2:16 the apostle Paul includes the Sabbath observance in the ceremonial part of law and specifies that it must not be laid upon us as obligatory because the One whom it anticipated has now come: "Therefore do not let anyone judge you by what you eat or drink, or with regard to a religious festival, a New Moon celebration or a Sabbath day. These are a shadow of the things that were to come; the reality, however, is found in Christ" (Col. 2:16–17 NIV). By placing the Sabbath day alongside the other rituals and great feasts of the ceremonial law, Paul was demonstrating that the shadows disappear when the real thing has come in Christ.

Although rest is the emphasis of the Fourth Commandment in Exodus 20:8–10, its primary theological significance pointed forward to Christ who is the Sabbath (eternal rest) for his people. That is not to devalue physical rest. Without question, the human body needs rest. Overworked Americans need to rest more. Time flows in seven-day cycles, and a day of rest from normal routines prepares our minds and bodies for the days to come. The New Testament, however, does not pigeonhole believers into resting on a certain day of the week. Finding a suitable day of rest is important, but it does not necessarily have to be Saturday or Sunday. Most pastors would find it next to impossible to rest on Sundays since they are generally filled with ministry demands.

Christians should try to be as consistent as possible in finding sufficient rest every day. That is certainly consistent with our daily New Testament Sabbath rest in Christ. Working yourself ragged six days a week and then falling asleep in church on Sunday hardly upholds the divine prescription to rest. Poor Eutychus, who fell sound asleep as the apostle Paul preached and fell out of a third-story window, learned the hard way (Acts 20:7–12). Work that goes on day after day, week after week, without a genuine pause for rest will not only take its toll on the body but will drain the heart of vitality and joy. Our emotional and spiritual gauges are freed to more loving and effective performance if we live within God's design specifications. We were not only made to work but also to rest.

Simply on pragmatic grounds, European countries have observed some of the benefits of a day of rest. They see the value of closing down public shops and companies one day a week for the general good of society. I was recently in France and learned that "Sunday closing" is a public institution written into legislation. Traveling to the celebrated city of Paris one Sunday evening, my wife and I, upon arrival, walked several blocks before finding a restaurant that was open. [17]

Not one of God's commandments was given primarily for its usefulness, but they all end up serving useful ends.[18] A day of rest has great benefits. Better yet, getting the proper daily rest keeps us fresh and ready to face the everyday challenges God brings our way. But the secularization of society, not to mention the passing away of the civil laws, brings with it an increase in Saturday and Sunday work. It would be difficult, if not impossible, to fully obey the Sabbath commandment with the rigor required by Old Testament law without reinstituting a theocracy.[19] We have no theological justification for applying to the United States passages from the Old Testament that were obviously intended for a time when God worked through a visible kingdom on earth, the nation of Israel. There is no reason to assume God has a similar covenant arrangement with the United States.

Finally, the Lord's Day is a day of distinction and corporate worship. It is a day where God's people gather together to concentrate on God's Word and to refocus ourselves as a community toward the fixed center of reality—Jesus Christ. Those who get into the habit of neglecting Sunday worship in order to sleep in, clean the house, or participate in their morning soccer event are in danger of spiritual erosion. This was the fear of the writer to the Hebrews: "Let us consider how to stimulate one another to love and good deeds, not forsaking our own assembling together, as is the habit of some" (Heb. 10:24–25).

Most people think they are stronger than they really are. Yet statistics show that if you don't go to church for a month, the odds are almost two to one that you won't go for more than a year.[20] Without the spiritual encouragement to persevere that is provided by corporate worship, the ministry of the Word of God, and the fellowship of the people of God, there is a much greater tendency to backslide and erode spiritually.

Sunday should be a true day of joy for the Christian. Worship in the morning and an activity in the afternoon does not dishonor the Lord's Day. Skipping out on worship does. Going to the early service and then charging out to engage in eight hours of afternoon and early evening hedonism does as well. But afternoon activities can be very healthy. The axiom "praying and playing" are two elements woven in and out of all the healthy biblical Jewish and Christian observances.[21] John Calvin led his congregation in worship in the morning and in the afternoon went among the people of Geneva and played skittles, an ancient version of bowling.[22] My favorite activity on Sunday afternoons is a good "nap." There are many ways to relax and recharge the physical batteries. It is a shame when believers develop a legalistic human system of deprivation, turning the Lord's Day into a dull, joyless time. The Lord's Day must be set aside for corporate worship and the enjoyment of his creation. Enjoying God and each other is central.

We must remember, for the Christian every day is a Sabbath. Having entered God's eternal rest, we commit every day to the Lord. On any given day, whatever we do, we do it to the glory of God (1 Cor. 10:31).

THE LORD OF THE SABBATH

The Old Testament points forward to Jesus Christ. The New Testament completes the Old Testament story. The focus of that story is Jesus. He is the divine string that binds the pearls together. He embodies the promise of eternal life that is prefigured in the Sabbath. As Lord of the Sabbath, Jesus opens the doors to eternal life in the presence of God. He is the eternal Sabbath rest.

The world is fascinated with the person of Jesus Christ. No other name is better known. Even in places where Christianity is sparse, large numbers of people know about Jesus. The power of his name and reputation over the last two thousand years has left profound imprints on nations, tribes, and cultures.

The name of Jesus is used for cursing and blessing, for praying and healing. Have you ever heard the name of Buddha, Allah, or Krishna taken in vain? Yet Jesus is largely misunderstood, and his teachings are misinterpreted and misapplied. If people lived as he instructed, love, justice, and civility would fill the world. Imagine how cultures would be transformed if everyone followed the Golden Rule—loved their enemies, prayed for those who persecuted them, clothed the naked, fed the hungry, and worked toward unity, not divorce.

The teachings of Jesus fulfill the real objectives of life—true love, acceptance, kindness, compassion, and purpose—that most people seek through other means. Unfortunately, in a postmodern world those teachings are ignored or deemed irrelevant by those who look to the self as the source of truth and reality. There are now revisionists and postmodern academicians who have even concluded that Jesus was an illiterate first-century peasant. Amazing.

This is in sharp contrast to the biblical portrait, supported by mounds of historical evidence, that Jesus was full of wisdom, and the multitudes were amazed at his teaching (Matt. 7:28–29). He knew the law ("You have heard that it was said") and corrected the abuses and misunderstandings of the law that had arisen in his day ("But I say to you" Matt. 5:21–30). Jesus was beyond brilliant. He was wise. In him there was no guile. He was full of grace and beauty. He was watchful, observant, and always spoke and acted at just the right time. He astonished the crowds by speaking the truth with wisdom and authority.

In a postmodern world there are no controlling rules or standards. The culture idolizes "openness" and "tolerance." Not even God has the right to say what is true.

In such a world, Christians must maintain a biblical worldview in order to stay spiritually healthy and to speak effectively to post-modernity. We must be shaped by God's law, not relativistic theories. Our perspective must be rooted in the eternal, not the temporal. A renewed confidence in the biblical, historical Jesus and a faith that is grounded in where we have come from historically is fundamental to our mission as Christ's disciples.

Jesus is the focus and the message of the historic Old Testament. Written centuries before he was born, the inspired Old Testament Scriptures give impressive evidence for Jesus being who the first-century disciples said he was: God incarnate, the Messiah of the Jews, the only true light for the Gentiles, and the Savior of the world. Virtually all of the central events of Jesus' life found in the Greek New Testament are foretold in the Hebrew Old Testament: the Messiah was to be a descendant of Kind David (Jer. 23:5; Acts 13:22–23), born in Bethlehem (Mic. 5:2; Matt. 2:1–6), attested to by the miracles he performed (Isa. 61:1–2; Luke 4:18–21), rejected in the end as he suffered for the sins of other people (Isa. 53:2–6; Mark 15:1–39), and subjected to the humiliation of being crucified, with his tormentors gambling to decide who would take his clothing (Ps. 22:15–18; John 19:23–24).

Jesus brought the purposes of the law into full realization. In fact, the Ten Commandments mirror the perfect righteousness of Jesus Christ.

He perfectly embodied God's moral law. He perfectly expressed God's "covenant of love." Jesus is the grand display of God's love for us, our Sabbath rest—eternal life in the presence of God (Heb. 4:9–11).

The story of Jesus is the story of reconciliation and love. He is the unifying center to reality, the architect of the drama of redemption. Jesus personifies the promise of God to bring salvation to the world and healing to the human heart. The Lord of the Sabbath stretches forth his saving arms: "Come to Me, all who are weary and heavy-laden, and I will give you rest. Take my yoke upon you, and learn from Me, for I am gentle and humble in heart; and you shall find rest for your souls" (Matt. 11:28–29).

SMALL GROUP DISCUSSION QUESTIONS

1. What was the primary purpose of the old covenant Sabbath? Discuss the Sabbath's *sign-bearing* function. What is the new covenant spiritual rest?

2. The law cannot properly be understood unless it moves toward the goal of pointing the believer to Jesus Christ. With this in mind, what did Jesus mean when he said: "Do not think that I came to abolish the Law or the Prophets; I did not come to abolish but to fulfill. For truly I say to you, until heaven and earth pass away, not the smallest letter or stroke shall pass from the Law until all is accomplished" (Matt. 5:17–18).

3. What did Jesus mean when he pronounced himself "Lord of the Sabbath" (Matt. 12:8)? How does this relate to Hebrews 4:1–10? Read also Psalm 95:11 and Hebrews 3:12–19. What do these verses teach concerning the eternal Sabbath rest?

4. Is it a sin to work on Sunday (e.g., a job, around the yard, at a restaurant, etc.)? Is it a sin to skip out on church once a month to attend your favorite sporting event? What does Hebrews 10:24–25 teach us?

HONORING AUTHORITY IN AN AGE OF DISRESPECT

"Honor your father and your mother."
Exodus 20:12

We live in an age where parents are the heirs of respect or the recipients of disrespect. Some think of their parents as heroes. Basketball star Michael Jordan's father, James Jordan, was murdered in the summer of 1993. Before that happened, Michael said this to columnist Bob Greene:

> My heroes are and were my parents. It wasn't that the rest of the world would necessarily think that they were heroic. But they were the adults I saw constantly, and I admired what I saw. If you're lucky, you grow up in a house where you can learn what kind of person you should be from your parents. And on that count, I was very lucky. It may have been the luckiest thing that ever happened to me.[1]

To Michael Jordan, good parents meant as much to him as his extraordinary basketball skill. For others, however, their parents don't get the same kind of respect. Some people wrestle with angry feelings toward their parents. For some, the word "parents" does not spell love, but abuse, authoritarianism, rejection, or even abandonment.

The Fifth Commandment may appear archaic or naive to those who struggle with bitter feelings toward Mom or Dad. But this command, like the other nine in the Decalogue, is designed to keep God's people free. The absolute standard "to honor your father and your mother" flows out of God's covenant love and extends his concern that we respect those in authority over us. This starts with the most important social institution—the family. We are told to honor our parents primarily because they have given us the most priceless of treasures: the gift of life.

God created the first parents from the dust of the ground and a human rib (Gen. 2:7, 21). They were told to be fruitful and multiply. God's design was for husband and wife to go on and populate the human race. Obedience to his plan honors him. God gave the first parents the gift of life, and they are told from that point on to give this gift to their offspring. In short, when we honor our parents for the priceless gift of life, we honor God.

LOVE IS SUPREME

The starting point and goal of all God's commandments is love.[2] Jesus declared that the Ten Commandments are summarized in two great commands: love toward God and love toward neighbor (Matt. 22:37–40). The first four commandments relate specifically to our vertical love for God. The last six deal with our horizontal love for people. But God is the ultimate foundation in the love of the genuine believer. Everything else is built upon this foundation. So it naturally follows that the more passionate our love for God, the greater our ability to love people.

This truth is powerfully exhibited in the life and ministry of the well-known missionary Hudson Taylor. When he heard others suggesting that he gave his life to the Orient because he loved the Chinese, whom he unquestionably did love, Hudson Taylor countered gently and responded thoughtfully, "No, not because I loved the Chinese, but because I loved God."[3]

Therefore, flowing out of the vertical love imparted by and grounded in the first four commandments, the fifth divine treasure commands that we love and honor our closest of kin—"Honor your father and your mother, that your days may be prolonged in the land which the Lord your God gives you" (Ex. 20:12). This is God's absolute standard which, if adhered to, will bring both domestic and national blessing. Keeping God's covenant of love, his Ten Commandments, inspires us to live in harmony with others. The Fifth Commandment speaks to children, parents, and authorities throughout the social and political structures of society. But God starts with the most foundational social institution—the family.

HONOR TO WHOM HONOR IS DUE

In Hebrew, the word for "honor" comes from a verb that means to be "heavy." The person who must be honored is held to be someone of weight.[4] The office of parenthood deserves to be respected, held in high esteem. The opposite of honor is disrespect, treating the office as if it were light and worthless.

Parents are first to be honored for the bestowal of a gift that only they can give—life. The ultimate violation of the Fifth Commandment is soberly brought to light by nationally known cases of children murdering their parents. One example is the much publicized Eric and Lyle Menendez trials of 1993. The brothers admitted to killing with premeditation both their parents with a shotgun at point-blank range as the parents were eating ice cream and watching television. This is a gross violation of the Fifth Commandment. The greedy duo snuffed out the very source of their own life.

One New Testament reference to the Fifth Commandment exhorts children to obey their parents in the Lord, for it is right (Eph. 6:1). Children are told to get under their parents' authority and to listen respectfully. In contradiction, many in our society say we need to free children from parental authority. The good parent does not depend upon wielding power, but allows the child room to pursue unbridled freedom. Following Dr. Benjamin Spock's essentially psychoanalytic model of parenthood, the child-rearing prophets of the 1970s and 1980s touted a new democracy in the home where children are accepted as equal partners in the affairs of the family.[5] Even worse, the entertainment media have combined this model of the democratic family with the notion of the clumsy, irresponsible, superfluous father. This negative stereotype is given disrespectful punch in comic strip and TV characters such as Dagwood Bumstead, Homer Simpson, and Al Bundy.

The Bible says, "Honor your father and your mother." This is to be a lifelong commitment. Even when childhood obedience ends, the honor continues.[6] If respect and obedience are learned in childhood, it will provide a solid foundation that will remain steadfast throughout life. Respect for authority starts in the family and will produce harmonious relationships in the home and in society. Respectful children are a "national treasure."[7] They grow up to be the kind of people who make human relationships work on any level. They bless society with their righteous example and act as a healing balm to a relationally fragmented culture.

Even the early pagan moralists, both Greek and Roman, taught that parental authority is right and necessary for unity in the family and a just society.[8] Virtually all civilizations have regarded the recognition of parental authority as indispensable to a stable society.[9] Disobedience and disrespect in the home engender a decadent society.

While it has been stated that the last six commandments deal with our relationship to others, the Fifth Commandment surely brings the honoring of our parents into our duty to God. During our childhood they represent God's character and mediate his authority and love. As obedience naturally recedes when transitioning into adulthood, respect ascends to become the dominant way mature children honor their parents and acknowledge the parents' God-given position of authority. The blessings of a more prosperous life and of social stability to the community are the results of a respect for authority and a strong family life (Eph. 6:2–3).[10]

THE RESPONSIBILITY OF PARENTS

The April 6, 1990, issue of the *Wall Street Journal* reported that, on the average, American parents spend less than fifteen minutes a week in serious discussion with their children. For fathers the amount of intimate contact with their children is an average of seventeen seconds per day.[11] The important role parents play in socializing children and character formation is a difficult task, but it is an impossible one if the parents fail to bond with their kids. The result is that children and adolescents are increasingly disrespectful and disobedient to adults and to each other.

The Bible instructs parents to bring their children up in the discipline and instruction of the Lord (Eph. 6:1–4). They are to instill the godly values and principles that are not only supported by Scripture but have also stood the test of time and proven to be regenerating truths for any society. Helping children acquire character benefits both parents and children. It makes life easier for both. Well-behaved children are happier and they grow into a happier, more stable adulthood.[12]

Parents who rear their children to acquire behavior and attitudes that honor God's Word and profit the community are building a heritage of honor. Well socialized children have learned to cooperate and share with others and to respect the directions of legitimate authority figures such as parents and teachers. Poorly socialized children have not.[13] Good character reflects the ability to restrain impulse gratification. A civil society is dependent upon virtuous citizens who have developed the capacity to delay impulse gratification.[14] It follows naturally that well-socialized children generally become well-socialized adults. Poorly socialized children generally do not.[15]

Sheila Weller, in her book *Saint of Circumstance*, reveals the untold story of Alex Kelley, who was convicted of rape in 1996. When Kelley was initially indicted he fled to Europe, spending more than eight years on the run, leading a comfortable lifestyle. Kelley's lawlessness finally caught up to him and he was arrested and brought back to the United States. He was later found guilty of rape.

In her book, Weller uncovers a town that seemed to encourage its coddled youth to act above the law: teens left alone to drink themselves into oblivion, kids jeering at local police as they broke up nightly parties, and students ridiculing teachers in the classroom.[16] It came as no surprise to many that when Alex lived overseas as a fugitive from justice, his parents supported him wholeheartedly.

Failing to correct young adults when they break the law or leading them to believe they are the special few who can live above it is malicious parenting. Encouraging them to run from the law is "child abuse." When families fail at their task of socializing children, a civil society degenerates.

When parents exercise authority with the proper combination of firmness and love, the effect is increased love and respect for the parent.[17] According to psychologist William Damon, respect for the parent who exercises proper authority leads to respect for legitimate social institutions and to respect for law. In his book *The Moral Child*, Damon writes, "The child's respect for parental authority sets the direction for civilized participation in the social order when the child later begins assuming the rights and responsibilities of full citizenship." Damon calls this respect "the single most important legacy that comes out of the child's relations with the parent."[18]

THE IMPORTANCE OF MOTHERS AND FATHERS

Men and women are the kings and queens of God's marvelous creation scheme. God originally designed his earthly royalty to function together in the most sanctified of all relationships: marriage. God reveals his glory through all created things. God's grand goal in marriage is to reveal his love, truth, holiness—his essential characteristics. His ultimate goal is to reveal his glory.[19]

Rebellion against God has circumvented his intention for marriage throughout history. High divorce rates, extramarital affairs, and shattered families were the norm in the first-century Roman world. When Christ established his church, a biblical definition of marriage was established with it: the legal union of one man and one woman for life.[20] For the state, this view of marriage composed the foundation for social and political stability; for the church, it was the core institution for the rearing of successive righteous generations. For at least 1,700 years the church and state agreed on this standard, seeing it as foundational to a prosperous, firmly rooted society. The idea of marriage as a lifelong commitment was etched into Western consciousness (except for extreme cases of violence or perversion) until the galloping ideas of "individualism" took root, giving rise to an increasing appetite for personal satisfaction at the expense of personal responsibilities.[21]

Selfish ideas have consequences. Divorce is up 700 percent in this century, with most of the rise occurring in recent decades.[22] Undeniably, a two-parent family is important for the development and well-being of children. Divorce rattles a child's confidence in the existence of a morally ordered, meaningful world. But from a Christian standpoint, the problem starts with the lack of commitment to God and to each other. With the dissolution of far too many Christian marriages, one wonders what kind of spiritual leadership the father brought to the family. While there are some exceptions, I believe one of the major reasons for divorce in Christian homes is because fathers have not exercised godly leadership in the marriage and family.

The result of these relational blowouts, of which Christians are a part, is that "almost 75 percent of American children living in fatherless households will experience poverty before the age of eleven, compared to only 20 percent of those raised by two parents. Children living in homes where fathers are absent are far more likely to be expelled from or drop out of school, develop emotional or behavioral problems, commit suicide, and fall victim to child abuse or neglect. The males are also far more likely to become violent criminals. As a matter of fact, men who grew up without dads currently represent 70 percent of the prison population serving long-term sentences."[23]

There are, of course, thousands of single moms who are doing an exceptional job of parenting and beating the odds. I do not mean to demean single parents or overlook their diligent efforts. But most social scientists conclude, based on numerous studies, that the moral impoverishment of today's youth bears a strong relationship to fatherlessness.[24]

Former Vice President Dan Quayle was slammed by the liberal cultural elite for criticizing the television show *Murphy Brown* for exalting a single-parent lifestyle and implying that children didn't need their fathers. In a May 1992 campaign speech, Quayle pointed out that the poorest and most disorderly American neighborhoods were places where fathers had disappeared, and boys gleaned models of manhood from gang leaders.

Although Quayle's remarks were greeted with protests and wisecracks from the media establishment, the wisecracking was soon silenced by social scientists who came forward to support Quayle's allegations about fatherless homes. Even President Bill Clinton played a part in drowning the catcalls by later voicing his agreement with Quayle. Research shows that illegitimacy and divorce are "by-products of an ideology of expressive individualism that had seized postwar generations and driven them to put self-realization before their children's needs."[25]

Interestingly, the Christian ethic for a husband to love his wife intimately and sacrificially was light-years beyond the formal domestic ethics of the first century. Rome had a law called *patria potestas*, which literally means "the father's power." The law allowed and encouraged the father to dominate his wife and family. Needless to say, this fertilized the ground of self-serving attitudes and immoral ideas. In the midst of unethical surroundings, the Scriptures called a Christian man to love his wife, to honor her as a fellow heir of the grace of life, and to take special care of his family (Eph. 5:25; 1 Peter 3:7; 1 Tim. 5:8).

God's truth speaks candidly to our contemporary situation. It is time that Christian fathers get their noses out of the rotting ideas of the culture and start to inhale the sweet fragrance of biblical truth. The father's role is absolutely pivotal. Fathers must encourage the development of good habits in their children—habits that will shape character. The Puritans viewed the family as a little church and a little commonwealth. The home was to be a place where spiritual and moral development was nurtured—a smaller culture that impacted the larger culture.

One of the surest routes for bringing morality back to this society is for fathers to rededicate their lives to passing on a moral legacy. The influence of one godly father can be monumental. He can impact in a positive way not only his children but also his grandchildren and great-grandchildren.

Jonathan Edwards, referred to by some as the "Last Puritan," is a good example. He is regarded by many scholars as the most brilliant mind America ever produced. A pastor, writer, and, later, president of Princeton University, he and his wife, Sara, had eleven children. Of his known male descendants,

- more than 300 became pastors, missionaries, or theological professors;
- 120 were professors at various universities;
- 60 were prominent authors;
- 30 were judges;
- 14 served as presidents of universities and colleges;
- 3 served in the U.S. Congress; and
- 1 became vice president of the United States.[26]

Jonathan Edwards left a majestic legacy because he was a godly father who invested in his children. The child who is nurtured in a healthy moral environment will pass on the same enduring virtues to future generations and will be more resistant to the growing array of moral diseases circulating in the larger culture. As it says in the Psalms, "Then our sons in their youth will be like well-nurtured plants" (Psalm 144:12 NIV).

James Dobson and Gary Bauer in their book *Children at Risk* articulate the importance of the father's leadership and his role in the children's emotional development and moral education: "Fathers must be there to tame adolescent boys, to give a young son a sense of what it means to be a man, and to explain why honor and loyalty and fidelity are important. For daughters, a father is a source of love and comfort that can help her avoid surrendering her virtue in a fruitless search for love through premarital sex."[27]

Of course, the mother's role in the family is vital. After all, it was through the special care and prayers of mothers like Jochebed (the mother of Aaron and Moses) and Hannah (the mother of Samuel) that freedom from bondage and national revival for the Hebrew nation began. I have spent considerable time discussing the problem of father-lessness since it is primarily the fathers in America who have abdicated their place of leadership and responsibility in the home. Mom is left to parent solo. What children need to develop sound character is the combination of what mothers and fathers bring to the home. Christian parents socialize their children by teaching biblical truth and modeling godly behavior. Simply put, most lessons in the laboratory of life are better "caught than taught." If there is a discrepancy between the parents' talk and their walk, children will be far more likely to do what the parents do, not what they say. As Ben Franklin once observed, "The best sermon is indeed a good example."[28]

It is clear that a child's benevolent behavior is affected much more by what he observes his models doing than by the words they speak. That is why it is so important for a father to show love and affection for his wife. Boys learn how men should treat women through observing how fathers treat mothers. If fathers treat mothers with contempt and cruelty, then it is likely their sons will also. If fathers treat mothers with dignity and respect, then it's likely their sons will grow up to treat women with dignity and respect.[29]

As I mentioned in chapter 4, both the blessings and the sins of the parents have an impact on successive generations (Ex. 20:5–6). Because this is the reality of human existence, we need God's commandments to guide us. We live in an age of disrespect because parents have not modeled behavior worthy of respect and honor. Christian parents can turn the tables by teaching their children that family life is linked to a larger vision and purpose than itself. The history of the world "is not the record of its great wars but the history of its households. No nation can be lifted higher than its homes."[30] A society will unravel if the demands of human dignity and respect are not written into our conscience from early childhood. Parents committed to building stable, secure families are constructing national treasures. No doubt succeeding generations will thank us for keeping the Fifth Commandment.

SHATTERED FAMILIES: THE GENERATION X EXPERIENCE

Author Douglas Coupland coined the phrase Generation X in his 1991 novel *Generation X: Tales for an Accelerated Culture*. The boundaries of this generation are variously described as "those born between 1961 and 1981," or "1965 to 1976," or "1965 to 1981." This is the generation that has grown up "in an age of social malaise, urban decline, inept government, corrupt government, ineffective school systems, soaring national debt, increasing environmental concern, racial polarization, high divorce rates, and declining values."[31] The shattered families and fractured relationships have left this generation angry, fearful, and insecure.[32] Needless to say, they have little respect for authority. Yet they yearn for intimacy. Close, durable relationships give Xers the opportunity to tell their stories and to share their joys, fears, and vulnerabilities. Absolute truth is not immediately accepted by this group. Rather, truth is established through certain tribal groups to which one belongs and is experienced in community.[33]

According to George Barna, this is the "first generation raised without the assumption that Christ is the starting place for religious expectations."[34] Generation X is the first consolidated postmodern generation.

Many in this generation are not sure what a family is supposed to look like. Between 1950 and 1979 the American divorce rate tripled. By 1986 the United States had the highest divorce rate in the Western world.[35] Many Xers come from highly dysfunctional backgrounds where family feuds are commonplace. Do these familial sins and frustrations mean that Generation X is exempt from the Fifth Commandment?

The command to "honor your father and your mother" is not the divine standard to be obeyed only by those who happen to have "perfect parents." Obviously, no parent is perfect. Everyone has shortcomings. Parents are to be honored for the life-bearing position they occupy, not because they've proven to be supermoms or superdads. God has fashioned a world where parents are the procreators (Gen. 1:28). They have given their children the most precious gift of all—life. Their position should be honored.

This commandment is difficult for children who have been verbally and/or physically abused by their parents. But honoring an abusive parent does not mean ignoring the mistreatment or in any way suggesting that the abuse was justified. Honoring an abusive parent does mean working toward forgiveness. Allowing the past to pollute the present locks one in a cycle of anger and hatred. Evil is not overcome by evil, but with good (Rom. 12:21).

To forgive is just what the word says—to offer a gift before it has been earned or deserved. That is how God treats us. But we cannot offer forgiveness with our own strength. We need God's grace and power to forgive and to heal. But the beauty of forgiveness is its boomerang effect: The gift we send out is what we will get back, and more. We get freedom. Peace of mind. A heart being healed. When the Fifth Commandment is honored under the guidance of God's Spirit, we find liberty and God is glorified.

The emergence of Generation X opens the door of opportunity to the church—the family of God. Believing Xers who have abusive family backgrounds can find hope and healing in God's community. A loving community that reaches out to the needy and hurting and bears one another's burdens fulfills the law of Christ (Gal. 6:2).

Reaching unbelieving Xers with the Gospel requires love and authenticity. As Leighton Ford says: "The story of God's grace must not only be told in words. We must model an evangelism of grace. We must communicate not only with a clear voice, but with the authentic touch of grace. Our evangelism must be hands-on evangelism, in which we roll up our sleeves and dare to touch human lives. Our voice must be clear and our touch must be real."[36] Real people living out the truth in community inspires most people, even postmodern Xers.

One positive aspect of postmodernism is its emphasis on community. The church is being challenged to regain its purpose as a community of hope and love. Jesus did say that people will know us by our love (John 13:35). A community of love is a powerful apologetic for the gospel message. However, Jesus did not say that love will set people free. He said rather, "The truth shall make you free" (John 8:32). While the postmodern Xer is governed by the concept of preferences and has been taught to disparage ultimate truth, God's Word must be proclaimed. Love will draw them in, but truth will keep them free.

Keeping the Fifth Commandment still brings about liberation. The church has a golden opportunity to teach journeying Xers the value of respecting God's authority structures. If we fail to keep this commandment, we add to the cultural anarchy. Obedience to this command keeps us free and establishes a chain of blessing to our future descendants. The outcome is a more secure, stable society.

AUTHORITY IN SOCIETY

The Fifth Commandment extends to other areas of authority in society. Zacharius Ursinus, the principal author of the Heidelberg Catechism* wrote in his seventeenth-century commentary, "The design or end of this commandment is the preservation of civil order, which God has appointed in the mutual duties between inferiors and

*The Heidelberg Catechism is an instruction guide where the main points of Scripture are systematically arranged in the form of questions and answers. It is designed to impart the basic principles of the Christian faith down through the generations.

their superiors. Superiors are all those whom God has placed over others, for the purpose of governing and defending them. Inferiors are those whom God has placed under others, that they may be governed and defended by them."[37] By learning to respect parental authority, one learns to respect the authority of other superiors, such as teachers, ministers, policemen, and state and federal officials— right up to the president.

The average Hebrew household numbered anywhere from 40 to 100 people. Jacob's household consisted of 66 (Gen. 46:26). These families were like small villages made up of several adjacent buildings.[38] Fathers could become tribal heads (Gen. 10:21). Heads of families and elders exercised authority and sat by the city gate to administer justice (Ex. 12:21; Deut. 22:15). David wore many hats being a father, the tribal head, and king of the nation. Clearly, the Fifth Commandment is broader than the narrow Western view influenced by the nuclear family model. This commandment is a call for a well-ordered society. Clear lines of civil and political authority must be established to which we submit; otherwise, anarchy will follow.

The New Testament elaborates on this command to honor those in authority over us: "Submit yourselves for the Lord's sake to every human institution, whether to a king as the one in authority, or to governors as sent by him for the punishment of evildoers and the praise of those who do right" (1 Pet. 2:13–14). God has established such patterns of authority for the orderly functioning of human life, and it both pleases and honors him when we submit ourselves to them.

Here evangelicals must tread carefully and prayerfully. Far too many believers have entered the public square with nonsubmissive attitudes and vengeance in their hearts. Fed up with intrusions into their private world by Supreme Court decisions in the sixties (prayer in public schools) and the seventies (abortion rights), many evangelicals have prepared for political battle.[39] Whether their arguments are right or wrong is not the issue I wish to address. My concern is the spirit and attitudes portrayed. Let's face it, even if we are right, the absence of love and humility is wrong.

Some Christians are still so obsessed with trying to convince everyone that America is a Christian nation that their rhetoric is often interpreted by the public as a new brand of "religious totalitarianism." The emotionally charged term "Christian Nation" leaves people of other faiths and persuasions wondering how far Christians will go in the application of their beliefs. Does this mean Christian domination and the establishment of a "national religion"?

"If by Christian Nation one means either that the republic's roots were primarily—though not exclusively—Christian or that the Christian faith has been the prominent faith in America, few would disagree."[40] However, the U.S. Constitution is not a Christian document. The basic fundamentals of the Christian faith are not included. A nation cannot exclusively be considered a "Christian Nation" if its foundational documents do not clearly set forth the fundamental truths of Christianity. Biblical principles were ingrained in the political sphere during the writing of the Constitution, but the writers, some of them Christians, granted full political protection for followers of different faiths, including atheists and agnostics who practiced no religion at all. James Madison, the author of the First Amendment, argued that a state-sponsored religion undermines the integrity of evangelism and ultimately destroys the vitality of faith it seeks to protect.[41]

No doubt there is a fair share of anti-Christian bias and prejudice in many sectors of American society today. As columnist Patrick J. Buchanan wrote upon release of Martin Scorsese's film *The Last Temptation of Christ*, "We live in an age where the ridicule of blacks is forbidden, where anti-Semitism is punishable by political death, but where Christian-bashing is a popular indoor sport; and films mocking Jesus Christ are considered avant-garde."[42] Evangelicals should certainly be concerned about the turbulent moral erosion and growing volume of anti-Christian bigotry. But should this motivate us to proclaim a special entitlement to dominate this country or to hurl scathing denunciations at our cultural enemies? Jesus commands us to love our enemies and to pray for those who persecute us (Matt. 5:44).

Loving those with whom we disagree is not accomplished by mobilizing for "cultural warfare," but by working side-by-side with our non-Christian neighbors, leading peaceful, responsible lives so that we may win the respect of outsiders (see 1 Thess. 4:11–12). The apostle Peter exhorted believers to "keep your behavior excellent among the Gentiles [unbelievers], so that in the thing in which they slander you as evildoers, they may on account of your good deeds, as they observe them, glorify God in the day of visitation" (1 Pet. 2:12).

This is not an exhortation to become evangelical doormats. We must never cease proclaiming God's law and Christ's gospel. If the state tells us to stop teaching God's truth, we politely inform them that we are under divine obligation to proclaim God's Word (Acts 4:19–20, 29–31). If the president or top government officials command us to worship a human authority, we boldly declare that we worship no other god but the one and only true God (Ex. 20:3; Dan. 3:17–18; 6:10–15, 23). If a law is passed that is immoral and contrary to God's truth, we can openly protest and voice our anger. Yet in our anger we must not be drawn to sin (Eph. 4:26). We're still called to "speak the truth in love" (Eph. 4:15).

Our righteous indignation must never provoke us to proclaim judgment or vengeance. God says, "Vengeance is Mine, I will repay" (Heb. 10:30). He is the infallible judge. Our views can still be expressed purposefully while maintaining Christian humility. Bold love preserves a godly witness. Vengeful power plays destroy our love for those with whom we disagree. If we gain the political clout to remove mountains but do not have love, we are nothing (1 Cor. 13:2).

The Christian Gospel calls us to be responsible and concerned citizens who embody a loving witness before all people. We should be concerned about the shape of our public policies, but our convictions must be expressed prudently. Richard John Neuhaus has wisely advised us "to build a world in which the strong are just, and power is tempered by mercy, in which the weak are nurtured and the marginal embraced, and those at the entrance gates and those at the exit gates of life are protected both by law and love."[43]

God's covenant of love is a decalogue of liberty. There is no liberty without authority and order. The family forms the foundation for well-ordered relationships in the entire social structure. The husband encourages his wife; together they train and influence their children, who go on to impact their friends, community, and culture. The Fifth Commandment is filled with wisdom for every sphere of authority in society. By working for a just society, if we show concern only for our own groups or our own convictions, then we run the risk of worshiping the holiness of our own convictions instead of our holy God.[44] Biblical holiness concerns not only our love for God but our love for others as well. Our ultimate allegiance is to his law. Our ultimate "hope [is] in his unfailing love" (Ps. 147:11 NIV).

SMALL GROUP DISCUSSION QUESTIONS

1. What does it mean to "honor your father and your mother" (Ex. 20:12)? What are some ways we can show honor to our parents? How can those who have had cruel or irresponsible parents show honor? Does the Fifth Commandment apply to them?

2. Discuss the importance of godly parents and their influence upon their children and society? What happens to a society when the majority of the homes fall apart? What is the father's role in the family? The mother's?

3. How can we encourage those who have gone through a divorce or come from a dysfunctional family? Does God's truth speak candidly to our contemporary situation? How can we relate the truth to postmodern Generation Xers, many of whom do not know what a family is supposed to look like?

4. The Fifth Commandment extends to the major authority structures of society (e.g., the government, the church, and the family). What is our Christian responsibility as citizens in regard

to honoring those in authority over us (read Rom. 13:1–7 and 1 Peter 2:13–19)?

LOVING OUR NEIGHBORS
IN AN ANGRY CULTURE

"You shall not murder."

Exodus 20:13

One of the best-known high-profile killers of the late 1980s was serial murderer Ted Bundy. Estimates are that he raped, mutilated, and killed as many as a hundred young women from the West Coast to the East Coast, outwitting for years various police departments who sought his arrest.[1] He was finally convicted in the state of Florida for the dreadful murders of two college coeds in their sorority house bedroom and for the brutal slaying of a twelve-year-old schoolgirl, Kimberly Leach. Bundy was later executed for his crimes.

The grisly crimes of a serial killer bring the dark side of human nature to the surface. Such horrific evil is seen on a broader scale when examining the horrors unleashed by Hitler's Germany, Stalin's Soviet Union, and Mao's China. Inner rage is often cited as one of the compelling reasons given for a killer's mad rampage. But when one carefully probes the underworld of human iniquity, another reason is uncovered: false ideas.

For example, the Cambodian tyrant of the 1970s, Pol Pot, left a legacy of hunger, torture, and death in his country. The "killing fields" of Cambodia, where the deaths of more than 2 million people took place, were orchestrated by Pot and seven other French-speaking, middle-class Cambodian thinkers who had all studied in France in the 1950s. There they were schooled in philosopher Jean-Paul Sartre's doctrine of "necessary violence," which justified violence to overthrow unjust institutions.[2] Pot was an undistinguished student, but won a scholarship to Paris probably because of his family's royal connections. He absorbed the works of eighteenth-century philosopher Jean-Jacques Rousseau and would later disastrously try to impose the ascendant new ideology, communism.

In an attempt to create a perfect society, Cambodian Communists, with Pot at the helm, unleashed a blood bath that has been compared to the Nazi murder of 11 million Jews and others, to Stalin's collectivization in Russia, and to Mao Tse-tung's ill-named Great Leap Forward that may have caused more than 30 million Chinese to starve. Pot's goal was to turn pastoral Cambodia into a modern socialist state in four years. Instead, millions starved, succumbed to illness, or were executed as enemies of the state.

Richard Weaver's familiar phrase comes to mind: "Ideas have consequences."

How does all this relate to the Sixth Commandment? First, God's Ten Commandments are ten absolute truths, rooted in his love. God's law flows out of his covenant love. *Unrighteous anger* is contrary to God's love. *False ideas* are opposed to his truth. Bundy and Pot stand as two lawless models whose evil actions mock God's love and truth. Yes, they are two of the worst offenders, but their lives show how unrighteous anger and faulty ideas can corrupt a heart and ravage a society.

The negative commandments ("You shall not. . .") include positive commands as well. When we consider "You shall not murder," we must also acknowledge God's calling to "love our neighbors." God's law requires it (Lev. 19:18).

Hidden Murder: The Heart of Unlawful Killing

The goal of all instruction is love. Love flows from a pure heart (1 Tim. 1:5). Holiness in Scripture concerns not only our love for God but love for our neighbor as well. Positively, the long reach of the Sixth Commandment requires that we show interest and concern for the spiritual health and physical/emotional well-being of our neighbor. The Heidelberg Catechism asks, "Is it enough then, if we do not kill our neighbor in any of these ways? No; for when God condemns envy, hatred, and anger, he requires us to love our neighbor as ourselves, to show patience, gentleness, mercy, and friendliness toward him, to prevent injury to him as much as we can, and also to do good to our enemies."[3] The Sixth Commandment penetrates down to the root of murder. It unmasks not only wrong actions but forbids sinful attitudes of the heart.

The New Testament not only repeats the moral laws of the Old Testament but also gives them a fuller explanation. In the Sermon on the Mount, Jesus clarified the meaning and application of the commandment. "You have heard that the ancients were told, 'You shall not commit murder,' and Whoever commits murder shall be guilty before the court; and whoever shall say to his brother, 'Raca,' [an Aramaic term meaning "empty-headed, good-for-nothing swine"] shall be guilty before the supreme court" (Matt. 5:21–22). Jesus gets to the heart of the matter by declaring that the Sixth Commandment is violated in *action* because of the heart's hateful *intent*. When vengeance and wrath brew in the heart, sinful actions follow.

Jesus showed in his great Sermon that the law had been perverted. He said, "You have heard that it was said, 'You shall love your neighbor and hate your enemy.' But I say to you, love your enemies and pray for those who persecute you, so that you may be sons of your Father who is in heaven" (vv. 43–45). Nowhere in the Old Testament, however, is it written, "love your neighbor and hate your enemy." Unscrupulous religious leaders misled the people to believe this based on their erroneous interpretations of Scripture. Jesus was repudiating a particular tenet of Jewish tradition, not the law.

Jesus used the law to bring to light the full extent of God's covenant love. The difference between the religious leaders and Jesus "was the difference between laying down the law for a group of prison inmates and living the law of love in a family. In prison the goal is to keep the inmates from hurting one another. In a family the goal is to show love to one another."[4] Jesus probes beneath the surface to the root of the act of murder itself to expose the anger and hatred that incite evil deeds. To restrict the application of the Sixth Commandment to the literal act alone is a legalistic perversion of God's law. Murder begins in the heart. Jesus sought to look behind the dramatic act of murder to consider everything that can lead up to it. That is why unrighteous anger is condemned by him (Matt. 5:22).

Jesus countered the false ideas of the day that exalted legal rules and ignored love. Erroneous ideas and unrighteous anger often travel together. The result is spiritual and emotional heart failure.

HEART FAILURE: THE BITTER LIFE OF UNRIGHTEOUS ANGER AND TWISTED THINKING

On Saturday night, June 28, 1997, the Fight of the Year turned out to be the Bite of the Century. In one of the most bizarre endings to a world heavyweight boxing championship, Mike Tyson, the ring tyrant, was disqualified after twice digging his choppers into his rival's ears in the third round. The more than 1 million Pay-Per-View audience was stunned. After the fight ended, Evander "The Real Deal" Hollyfield was rushed by ambulance to a hospital where doctors stitched his damaged skin and cartilage. One late-night host would later quip, "Evander became the real meal on pay-per-chew."

Joking aside, the inner rage of Tyson manifested itself in an unusual, wretched manner. Perhaps the sport's one-on-one naked aggression in front of a worldwide audience makes its combatants particularly vulnerable to the cerebral gymnastics that can elevate them to new heights or plunge them into defeat. But Tyson's out-of-control ring tactics reveal something deeper. Behind the ferocious act itself was the pent-up anger that gave rise to it. The fury unleashed that evening was not simply momentary rage but an extension of the red hot anger that had been boiling in his heart for many years.[5]

First, I must emphasize that anger is not always sinful. Righteous anger is a concerned response to injustice, such as the rape of a child or the cold-blooded murder of an innocent human being. God himself experiences righteous anger over sin and injustice. It takes a lot to provoke God's rage, but his anger comes for a holy purpose: to provoke fear ("turn from your evil ways or suffer the dire consequences") and dismantle those who do not heed his warning.[6] Dan Allender and Tremper Longman insightfully say that "God designed and blessed anger in order to energize our passion to destroy sin. Anger can be lovely and redemptive, but it can also be ugly and vindictive."[7]

Unrighteous anger is a negative emotion that causes a person whose own needs are not being met to lash out at others. This dark emotion, with its potential for damaging one's inner stability and outer relations, is extremely volatile. Unrighteous anger seeks to rampage, violate, and gain independence from God and others.[8] Unchecked and not dealt with, this anger draws our deepest sinful desires to the surface and provokes us to say and do things that are hurtful and destructive.

Verbal abuse, name calling, slander, manipulation, pugnacious attitudes, striking someone, and so on—all are manifestations of anger and violate the heart of the Sixth Commandment. Some people live by the revengeful motto, "Don't get angry—get even." This twisted philosophy ignores God's truth, disrespects God's love, and often results in madness. Like the Spanish general who confessed: "I have no need to forgive my enemies. I have had them all shot." Unrighteous anger is the chief cause of spiritual and emotional heart failure. It generates a shrinking heart.

In his book *Wishful Thinking*, Fredrick Buechner explains:

> Of the seven deadly sins, anger is possibly the most fun. To lick your wounds, to smack your lips over grievances long past, to roll over your tongue the prospect of bitter confrontations still to come, to savor to the last toothsome morsel both the pain you are given and the pain you are giving back—in many ways it is a feast fit for a king. The chief drawback is that what you are wolfing down is yourself. The skeleton at the feast is you.[9]

Christians who nurse murderous hearts desperately need the corrective light of God's Word to illuminate their twisted thinking. A believer who holds on to anger always loses. Refusing to deal with it means reaping corruption in life. And that corruption begins in one relationship and works its way into many others. It takes a growing love for God founded on his truth to quell the fires of burning egos and to make an impact on an angry culture. Jesus rooted righteousness in God's love for us and in our love for God. The antidote for the poison of anger is the cultivation of love that flows from the ultimate source of love (1 John 4:7–17). In an age lacking in certainty and filled with angry souls and desperate lives, we must infuse the world with truth and love, restoring to it a portion of its lost heart. Christians who truly live out the covenant love of the Sixth Commandment will become a soothing aroma to an angry culture.

THE REASON WHY MURDER IS FORBIDDEN

The Sixth Commandment prohibits all unlawful killing out of reverence for God, who declares that human life is sacred. For centuries Western culture has held the view of the sanctity of human life. Only recently in our society is this truth degenerating into a quality-of-life standard.

Christians believe that human life is sacred because God made men and women in his own image (Gen. 1:27; 5:1–2). In other words, human beings are like God in ways that other creatures are not. We dimly reflect his glory. "God is a person; we are persons. He desires; we desire. He thinks; we think. He feels, wills, and acts; we feel, will, and act."[10] Human life must be weighed on the scale of God's absolute standard of human value and worth, not on the arbitrary scale of the world's so-called quality of life. Clearly, human beings are distinct from the animal kingdom because we are divine image bearers.[11] The author of human life heralds the inherent goodness of his creative handiwork (Gen. 1:31) and declares that murder is a terrible evil that should reap drastic consequences (Gen. 9:6).

WHAT THE SIXTH COMMANDMENT FORBIDS

The Sixth Commandment in Hebrew gives the divine imperative, "No unlawful killing." That is, killing that violates justice. The word *murder* should also be included. The Sixth Commandment forbids taking an innocent person's life—what the law identifies as unlawful killing and murder.[12]

God's law condemns the shedding of innocent blood (Deut. 19:10). There are numerous ways that the Sixth Commandment is violated. Listed below are the most prominent.

Premeditated murder. This means that the killer intended to take the life of the victim, devising a calculated plan to snuff out the life of someone.

Voluntary manslaughter. This is where a person kills intentionally but without premeditation. The killing is done with intention but under the impulse of burning anger.

Involuntary manslaughter. This refers to the unlawful killing of a human being without express or implied malice. A doctor who carelessly misdiagnoses an illness and administers the wrong medicine, causing the death of the patient, would be in this category. We would not call this professional a murderer since there was no intent to kill, let alone any premeditation of the act. But this would still be a violation of the Sixth Commandment.

Negligent homicide. This is where a person fails to exercise care and somehow causes the death of another. In biblical times, if someone was trying to reduce building costs by not installing a railing around the perimeter of the roof terrace, the home owner could be held liable for the death of anyone who fell from the roof (Deut. 22:8).

Many areas of everyday life fall under the Sixth Commandment. For example, driving a vehicle aggressively, at high speeds, or recklessly has resulted in injuries, deaths, and the heartache of millions. Road rage is another example of negligence and continues to be a dangerous epidemic, resulting in verbal abuse, physical violence, and even murder.

Other examples are pollution caused by nuclear plants and the disposal of nuclear waste or nuclear accidents, such as the one at Chernobyl. All of this goes to show how the life and health of millions of people depend on enforcing proper safety measures.[13]

The life and health of myriads of people are undermined by those who become addicted to tobacco, alcohol, or drugs. Negligence in these areas means that God's law is being violated and his love ignored.

Euthanasia. This term means "good death" (*eu* = good, *thanasia* = death). It is the deliberate act of intending or choosing a painless death for the humane purpose of ending the pain of someone who suffers from incurable disease or injury.[14] The proliferation of life-prolonging technology in recent years has made the controversy over the "right to die" and physician-assisted suicide one of the most explosive medical issues of our day. Dr. Jack Kevorkian's "suicide machine" has commanded front-page coverage for several years, and in 1994 Oregon passed a measure allowing the terminally ill to obtain lethal prescriptions for suicide. Other states have placed similar proposals on their ballots.

Euthanasia can be divided into many different categories (voluntary, involuntary, active/passive, direct/indirect). My objective here is not to offer a full-blown analysis and critique. The traditional view of Western culture which asserts that the basic duties of physicians is to help their patients and to refrain from harming them implies that intending to kill is never right. The doctor is duty-bound to revere human life and to strive to bring healing and a cure. This makes doctor-assisted suicide antithetical to the physician's responsibilities to respect life and restore health.

Euthanasia in general violates the Sixth Commandment, but there are some cases, such as "brain death" or when a person is dying and nothing can be done to reverse the process, which make the withdrawal of artificial life-support permissible. There is no moral obligation to prolong the process of dying through the use of artificial means if it only prolongs the suffering. The moral duty is to prolong life, not to use artificial means to prolong the process of death. In short, it is morally wrong for *anyone* (doctor, family member, or friend) to take an innocent life, whether the individual suffering grants permission or not.[15] It is not morally wrong to allow that person to die. The Christian's overall attitude and intention should be to turn the individual over to God's providence, leaving life and death in God's hands.

Let's consider two more issues related to the Sixth Commandment: suicide and abortion.

SUICIDE

Suicide is the act of taking one's own life. It is distinct from euthanasia, which refers to the actions or omissions of another person that result in the death of the individual who is seriously ill.

The Bible refers to six people who took their own lives: Samson (Judg. 16:23–31), Saul and his armor-bearer (1 Sam. 31:3–5), Ahithophel who had sided with Absalom in his rebellion against David (2 Sam. 17:23), the Israelite king Zimri (1 Kings 16:18–19), and the betrayer Judas Iscariot (Matt. 27:3–5).[16] Suicide is an ancient practice that dates back to classical Greece and Rome. There are numerous extra-biblical accounts of suicide. Perhaps the most familiar is the mass suicide of those at Masada after holding out for several years against the Romans who sought to bring them under their control.

Suicide is a grievous action that is an emotional response to a perceived problem. Suicide is often the violent manifestation of internal anger and rage.[17] Eventually this repressed rage is turned against the self in suicide.

Biblically speaking, human life is sacred. It is sacred because men and women are divine image bearers and because God gives life and sustains it. Since it is his precious gift, we must treat it with care and not reject it. Christians must remember that their lives belong to God. Paul says, "You are not your own; you were bought at a price. Therefore honor God with your body" (1 Cor. 6:19–20 NIV). Suicide is murder because it discards the image of God in man and destroys the sacred vessel given by the author of life to bring glory to his name.

Our culture's love affair with individual autonomy doesn't help. The Scriptures teach that we exist always in relation to God, the author of our entire person who has authority over us. We also exist in relation to each other, the body of Christ, a community that profoundly affects one another. "And if one member suffers, all the members suffer with it" (1 Cor. 12:26). A believer who commits suicide doesn't just take his own life; he takes part of ours, too! We have no authority to take our own lives or the life of an innocent human being. For the Christian, both life-giving and life-taking are divine prerogatives. That is the fundamental reason why suicide or assisted suicide is morally wrong and a form of murder.

In the last several years, suicide has surpassed traffic accidents as the chief cause of death among teenagers and the twenty-something crowd. The Christian church has the unique challenge to reach this young postmodern generation. As a community of faith, hope, and love, we can reach them and others and can become instruments of healing in their lives. When the community of Christ labors together in love and works toward a common purpose of bringing glory to God, hope is infused and life is worth living.

When English cities came under savage air attack in World War II, both alcoholism and suicide declined significantly. Personal problems have a way of fading when a community must rally together to fight off disaster.[18] On any level, when people bind together in community, a renewed drive to move forward is imparted. But when God enters the equation and is at the center of the community, then "new life" is imparted. Love sifts out anger. Truth dispels spurious ideas. And hope fills hungry hearts as they commune in one accord.

When I think of what our response to the hope of the Gospel should be, I am reminded of the story that Larry King, the TV/radio interviewer, told about a visit to Miami's Joe Robbie Stadium before a spring training game. King said manager Tommy Lasorda was introducing him to players and having a good time. They walked past Eddie Murray at first base and Lasorda said, "Hey, Eddie, how you doing?" Murray replied simply, "Okay." At that, Lasorda went wild. "Okay? Okay? Two million dollars a year. It's March. There ain't a cloud in the sky. You're standing there wearing a major-league uniform. You're thirty-three years old, you're going to the Hall of Fame, and you're saying okay? You say, 'Great, Tommy!'" Murray, looking at Lasorda like he was a maniac, seemed at a loss for words. Lasorda tried again, "You say it: I feel great!" So Eddie started saying, "I feel great!"[19]

The Christian has better reasons than any professional athlete to say "I feel great!" The hope of the Gospel is that in Christ all of our sins have been forgiven (Col. 2:13). That is amazing when you think about it carefully. In Christ, we can live a more abundant life in the present with the confidence that a magnificent inheritance awaits us in the future (John 14:1–4; Eph. 1:11–12). When we exit this earth our eternal destination is the unfathomable presence of God, a place of inexpressible beauty (2 Cor. 12:4).

Suicide spurns the authority of the author of life and involves the erosion of community. "Suicide is the final sign of abandonment both by the individual and the society. The individual refuses any longer to fulfill his duties to society and expresses his feeling of being abandoned by it."[20] We as a church community are called to offer faith, hope, and love through the riches of the Gospel. Becoming a Christian means being transferred from one community into another, a new community of hope (see Col. 1:13). Encouraging "one another" with God's promises inspires hope. Gospel hope is the most powerful life-enhancing element in human existence. This is the jewel the Christian community can offer to an insecure postmodern generation.

ABORTION

Back in 1994 the featured speaker at the National Prayer Breakfast in Washington, D.C., was a small, fragile woman with no political credentials. Yet she stood confidently at the podium, surrounded by President Bill Clinton and Mrs. Clinton and various other government officials.

With a steady voice of certainty, Mother Teresa declared: "I feel that the greatest destroyer of peace today is abortion. It is direct war against the child, a direct killing of an innocent child. . . . Any country that accepts abortion is not teaching its people to love but to use any violence to get what they want. . . . By abortion the mother does not learn to love, but kills even her own child to solve her problems. And by abortion the father is told that he does not have to take any responsibility at all for the child he has brought into the world. That father is likely to put other women into the same trouble. So abortion just leads to more abortion."[21]

This Nobel Prize–winning nun put her finger on a central problem—abortion does not model love, but teaches a culture to employ violence to get what it desires. Parents who abort their children do not learn to love, but to use barbaric methods to free them from their responsibilities. Every time an innocent baby is executed, life is devalued and human responsibility is scorned. I share Mother Teresa's concern that our society is more committed to self-interest than love and is becoming a breeding ground for abortion ("abortion just leads to more abortion"). The result is a growing moral paralysis where everyone's personal interests are enshrined. God's law is relegated to obscurity. Abortion has become to many a kind of status symbol of "liberation," where human rights are hallowed as the chief value. The unborn are the only ones who have no rights in a postmodern society.

The number of legal abortions performed in the United States each year is almost two million. Author John Powell calls this tragedy "the silent holocaust." To highlight the deaths of millions of innocent children, Powell constructs a chart of "war casualties," on which each cross represents 50,000 American combatants killed. The Korean and Vietnam wars have only one cross each. World War I has two and a half, and World War II has eleven. But "the War on the Unborn" has no fewer than 240 crosses, representing the 12 million legal American abortions performed up to the beginning of 1981.[22] That number has grown to more than 35 million through 1997.

Any society that can tolerate such ruthless killing, let alone legislate these acts, has ceased to be civilized. The societal barbarism is intensified in light of the horrendous procedure known as partial-birth abortion. On every level it is a mark of an angry, violent culture striving to play god.

Abortion, child sacrifice, and other forms of infanticide were both legal and acceptable in pagan societies from the earliest times. One of the major signs of depravity in ancient Rome was that its unwanted babies were abandoned outside the city walls to die from exposure to the elements or from the attacks of wild foraging beasts.[23] The primitive Canaanites threw their children onto great flaming pyres as a sacrifice to their god Molech. Is our contemporary society any less depraved because it delivers many of its unwanted babies to the hospital incinerator instead of the local garbage dump? Abortion today is even more vicious than the decadent practices of the Romans and the Canaanites since it has been commercialized and is "big business" for certain doctors and clinics. Our society has lost its fear of God. God has been banished from the affairs of men and women, and the sanctity of human life has been exiled with him. Sovereignty has been abducted by foolish finite leaders championing "man's law." By allowing a woman's right to choose to take precedence over a baby's right to live, we may be writing our national epitaph.

Virtually all scientists today concur that zygotes (fertilized eggs), embryos, and fetuses are individuals of the same human species with a unique genetic code (with forty-six chromosomes), which is neither the mother's nor the father's. One's genetic makeup is established at conception determining his/her unique characteristics—gender, eye color, bone structure, hair color, skin color, susceptibility to certain diseases, etc. Leading French geneticist Jerome L. LeJeune, who specializes in mental retardation and diseases of children, while testifying before a Senate subcommittee, asserted: "To accept the fact that after fertilization has taken place a new human has come into being is no longer a matter of taste or opinion. The human nature of the human being from conception to old age is not a metaphysical contention, it is plain experimental evidence."[24]

Dr. Bernard Nathanson was the director of the world's largest abortion clinic and the nation's most prominent abortionist in the 1970s, presiding over 60,000 abortions. Once known as the "abortion king," he performed his last abortion in 1979. The invention of the ultrasound which showed clear moving pictures of the fetus convinced him that he had not been removing mounds of tissue but persons (with all their genetic coding and features being indisputably human). He could no longer wage war against the most defenseless of human beings. He writes:

> After my exposure to ultrasound, I began to rethink the prenatal phase of life. Gradually, I began to understand that two hundred or three hundred years ago, childhood had not been understood as a special time in our lives and that in the seventeenth century, children as young as five years old were made to work in factories. There was no recognition of the phenomenon of childhood or of their needs until the last hundred or so years. Adolescence, adulthood, and senescence—they are all bands in the continuing spectrum of life. When I began to study fetology, it dawned on me, finally, that the prenatal nine months are just another band in the spectrum of life. Ironically, these nine months may be the most important nine months in our lives. That's when our organs are forming, our brain is forming, and we experience our first sensory impressions. In the womb, we can distinguish one kind of music from another. I have put Mozart in a tape player and held it against a womb at, say, seven months, and the baby moved a little, but when I put Van Halen on, the baby was jumping all over the place. The first nine months are a learning time, a time when we are organizing ourselves. To disrupt or abort a life at this point is intolerable—it is a crime. I don't make any bones about using that word: Abortion is a crime."[25]

Today, much of the controversy has moved from the question of when life begins to "a woman's right to choose" and the "quality of life" for the child. Some claim that women have the right to control their own bodies. Therefore, having an abortion is a woman's constitutional right to do with her body as she deems best. For a society as much in love with individual autonomy as ours, this view may appear reasonable to some at first glance, but it is neither reasonable nor lawful. First, laws against suicide and prostitution still exist for the personal and collective well-being of our society. People cannot necessarily do anything they please with their bodies. Second, the unborn fetus carried within the mother's body is not a part of it. The child's genotype is distinct from the mother's, having its own unique and individual gender, blood-type, bone structure, and genetic code.[26] To say that the unborn fetus is part of its mother is to claim that the mother possesses four legs, two heads, two noses, and—with the case of a male conceptus—a penis and two testicles.[27] Certainly a woman has the right to govern her own body, but the unborn entity, although for a time it is attached inside her body, is not part of her body. Therefore, abortion is not justified, since no individual's personal autonomy is so vigorous that it permits the arbitrary execution of a human being.[28]

Moreover, the quality-of-life arguments hurled by pro-choice advocates are disturbing to say the least. Fallible mortals do not have the authority or the discernment to know for sure when the life of a deformed newborn or handicapped child becomes disposable or is to be judged worthless. To move in this direction is to degenerate back to Hitler's abominable Third Reich. "Maurice Baring used to tell the story of one doctor who asked another: 'About the termination of a pregnancy, I want your opinion. The father was syphilitic, the mother tuberculous. Of the four children born, the first was blind, the second dead, the third was deaf and dumb, and the fourth also tuberculous. What would you have done?' 'I would have ended the pregnancy.' 'Then you would have murdered Beethoven.'"[29]

ABORTION AND THE LAW OF GOD

The biblical record confirms that God regards the unborn as human beings and is intimately involved with them. They are considered his handiwork, not lumps of human tissue.

For Thou didst form my inward parts; Thou didst weave me in my mother's womb. I will give thanks to Thee, for I am fearfully and wonderfully made; Wonderful are Thy works, and my soul knows it very well. My frame was not hidden from Thee, when I was made in secret, and skillfully wrought in the depths of the earth. Thine eyes have seen my unformed substance; and in Thy book they were all written, the days that were ordained for me, when as yet there was not one of them. (Ps. 139:13–16)

In Psalm 51 David refers to his spiritual condition at birth; "Behold, I was brought forth in iniquity, and in sin my mother conceived me" (v. 5). From the time of his conception (his personhood), David had been a sinner by nature.

Both Old and New Testaments reveal that God deals with people as human beings made in his image while they are in the womb (Jer. 1; Isa. 49; Gal. 1:15; Luke 1:41–45). At every corner God's Word states or implies that the unborn are just as valuable in his sight as other human beings. Therefore, those who would argue that personhood is an individual with a developed capacity for reasoning, willing, desiring, and relating to others are not carefully considering the scientific/medical and biblical evidence. Philosopher Robert Joyce correctly states that "a person is an individual with a natural capacity for these activities and relationships, whether this natural capacity is ever developed or not—i.e., whether he or she ever attains the functional capacity or not."[30] In other words, a human person is what he is by endowment, not by achievement.[31]

One passage in the Old Testament law bearing directly on the subject of abortion must be considered.

And if men strive together, and hurt a woman with child, so that her fruit depart, and yet no harm follow; he shall . . . pay as the judges determine. But if any harm follow, then thou shalt give life for life, eye for eye, tooth for tooth (Ex. 21:22–24 ASV).

A prevalent interpretation of this passage considers it to refer to an accidental miscarriage of a fetus and the fine imposed as an indemnification to the father because the fetus was lost. If the mother should also die in the accident, then the *lex talionis* is applied (the principle of an eye for an eye and a life for a life from Leviticus 24:17–20).

This unfortunate interpretation of the Exodus passage makes a distinction between fully human life and the life of the fetus. No matter how far the gestation has progressed, the fetus is not considered to be a soul or a fully human person and therefore has less inherent value than a fully born individual. This line of reasoning is often taken one step further to justify the practice of induced abortion.[32]

First, to say that this text allows for or does not forbid abortion, if that is even what it is referring to, is to make a giant leap not supported by the text. Second, the text more than likely does not refer to an accidental miscarriage. The clause rendered in both the KJV and the ASV "so that her fruit depart" literally reads, "and her children come out" (as the marginal reading of the NASB indicates).[33] The verb translated "depart" or "come out" (*yatsa*) usually refers in the Old Testament to a live birth (see Gen. 28:28–30; Ex. 1:5; Deut. 28:57; 2 Sam. 16:11; Job 3:11; Eccl. 5:15; Jer. 20:18). In no case is the word used to indicate a miscarriage. (Its use in Numbers 12:12 refers to the birth of a stillborn child.) The verb for miscarriage (*shakol*) is found in Exodus 23:26 and Hosea 9:14. Thus the Hebrew word used in Exodus 21:22 indicates a premature birth, not a miscarriage, and makes no distinction between mother and child. Therefore, this text actually indicates that God values viable fetuses as highly as he does adults, since the *lex talionis* applies if the child is born dead. This conclusion doesn't settle the abortion issue, but it does refute those who would try to use Exodus 21 as a proof text for liberalizing abortion laws or justifying induced abortion.

Today, pro-choice advocates are playing a language game. The term "abortion" is avoided, and euphemisms like "reproductive health procedure" or "termination of pregnancy" are substituted. The same language game was played by pro-slavery advocates in the 1800s. During the Lincoln-Douglas debates, many of Douglas's statements had a pro-choice quality to them as he relativized the slavery issue (e.g., religious arguments have no place in political debate) in the same manner that pro-choice supporters relativize the argument about abortion. In Andrew Jackson's long farewell address, he spoke about slavery and abolitionism a number of times without once ever using the words "slavery" or "abolitionist."[34]

We find a similar parallel today with pro-choice wordsmiths manipulating language, whereas others say things like "I personally believe abortion is wrong, but I can't allow that to influence the legal or political issues." Hypocritically, morality is reduced to personal taste and everyone's tastes are different.

This is where Lincoln backed the pro-choice Douglas into a corner. Lincoln did affirm that choice was important when dealing with areas of moral indifference (e.g., the state of Virginia should have the right to make laws protecting the oyster business due to an abundance of oysters in Chesapeake Bay, and the federal government has no business interfering). But when dealing with an issue not of personal taste or morality, but interpersonal morality, like slavery, Lincoln argued that these matters could not be left up to individual choice, since that would be sanctioning an immoral, offensive, and destructive practice. Choice is appropriate under amoral circumstances, but when dealing in matters where a third party is affected and does not have a choice, such as a slave, it is no longer an amoral matter. Lincoln went on to say that "unless you want to consider the slave to be basically a farm animal, and if you do that, then of course it should be up to the individual states, but do you really think a slave is the same as a farm animal?"[35] Here, Douglas was pinned in the corner and said that a slave was basically the same as a farm animal—a little bit above a crocodile but below that of a human being. Likewise, many modern abortion advocates preach that the fetus is less than human or they employ language that fools others into thinking so.

Tristam Bylberd declared, "Whoever controls the language controls the culture."[36] What is our responsibility as Christians in the midst of a "culture of death" where the Sixth Commandment is violated every day? How should we respond?

LOVING OUR NEIGHBORS/PROCLAIMING THE TRUTH

God has given us a standard for truth out of his covenant love. It is a universally applicable guide for righteous living and for establishing a peaceful, ordered society. That standard is the law of God embodied in the Ten Commandments. These ten absolutes are as eternal and unchanging as God himself because they are a manifestation of his nature (Mal. 3:6; Heb. 13:8; James 1:17). Jesus said that the entire law and prophets hung on two commandments: "Love the Lord your God with all your heart, and with all your soul, and with all your mind," and "Love your neighbor as yourself" (Matt. 22:37–40). Jesus' reference to "all the Law and the Prophets" means that the entire Old Testament expresses this dual love command. Jesus grounded these love commands in God's law (Lev. 19:18, 34; Deut. 6:5). The law is a transcript of divine character. To transgress God's law violates his character.

Jesus told the classic story of the Good Samaritan to teach us that we must love people (Luke 10:25–37). The point of the parable is that we are to be a loving neighbor to whomever we can, to do good wherever possible, to bind up the wounds of whomever we find injured, to turn sinners from the error of their ways and, above all else, to be people who pursue peace with others (see Matt. 5:9; Rom. 12:18). Scripture associates murder with failure to love one's neighbor (James 2:8–11; 1 John 3:15). When I fail to love people in my path I undermine the Sixth Commandment.

Notably, Jesus linked the command to love others with the command to love God. Theology and ethics cannot be separated. The content of theology has a significant impact on ethical decisions.

In order to respond to the evils in our culture, we must first be committed to the positive aspects of the Sixth Commandment, which require us to seek the health and welfare of others. If we enter the public square with a Rambo abrasiveness, we contribute to the angry cultural ills and become terminators rather than transforming agents of grace. Delinquency in love will invalidate our Christian witness.

In more than sixty countries worldwide, Christians are harassed, abused, arrested, tortured, or executed specifically because of their Christian faith.[37] Richard Wurmbrand, who spent fourteen years suffering in a Communist prison, reminds all believers with less than ideal circumstances that "if the heart is cleansed by the love of Jesus Christ, and if the heart loves Him, you can resist all tortures." He says, "God will judge us not according to how much we endured, but how much we could love."[38] The love of God demonstrated in the lives of his people is potent. Wurmbrand gives an example:

A Christian was sentenced to death. Before being executed, he was allowed to see his wife. His last words to his wife were, "You must know that I die loving those who kill me. They don't know what they do and my last request of you is to love them, too. Don't have bitterness in your heart because they kill your beloved one. We will meet in heaven." These words impressed the officer of the secret police who attended the discussion between the two. Afterward he told me the story in prison, where he had been put for becoming a Christian.[39]

The apostle Paul said, "Do not be overcome by evil, but overcome evil with good" (Rom. 12:21). Even under the most desperate conditions, the light of Christian love must never be turned off.

On the other hand, love is not the only crucial ingredient. Any movement built on the sole principle of love is destined for heresy. God's love gave us the law, and his law is his truth revealed. Truth radiates liberating power, restores the soul, and enlightens the eyes (Ps. 19:7–8). Without it we are like empty bubbles floating on an ocean of subjectivity and despair.

It has been well stated that "truth without love is brutality, but love without truth is hypocrisy."[40] We don't want to be guilty of either. Parenthetically, with the Sixth Commandment in view, I must add that in special cases of self-defense, war, and capital punishment, the Sixth Commandment is not necessarily being violated. What is being prohibited in this command is unjust violence, unlawful killing, and murder. Reverence for God, the author of life, is the highest value. He established the principles for maintaining or forfeiting life. If one person unjustly kills another, then he forfeits his right to life: "Whoever sheds the blood of man, by man shall his blood be shed; for in the image of God has God made man" (Gen. 9:6 NIV). This text bases the capital penalty for murder on the truth that all human beings are made in God's image. Humans are still made in God's image and, therefore, the application of this penalty is still valid today.[41] The taking of human life is also sometimes morally justifiable in maintaining law and order,[42] in self-defense,[43] and in the so-called "just war."[44] Lawful killing should never bring anybody joy, but by enforcing retributive justice (the rightful punishment of vicious lawbreakers) we maintain law and order and highlight God's concern for justice.

God is both loving and just. Love provides the motivation to effect justice. Christians must work hard to bring God's love and justice into the fabric and structure of society. This means demonstrating the reality of God's love concretely. Jesus taught that those who feed the hungry, clothe the naked, take care of the sick, and visit the prisoners express love's tangibility for him and to him (Matt. 25:31–46).

Kindness, concern, and striving to care for others is inherent in the concept of love. Justice is based on rights, such as the right to life (Gen. 9:5–6). Justice is concerned with defending and advancing the rights of all people, including innocent babies who can't speak for themselves.

Our challenge as Christians is not simply to focus on efforts to change the law. We must develop a multifaceted strategy of prevention, including the founding of adoption agencies, crisis pregnancy centers, Christian youth groups, inner-city and rural ministries, and job-training programs stressing human responsibility. Christian journalists must not shrink from exposing abortionists and writing cogently about the sanctity of human life. This is love in action. Biblical love provides the impetus to effect justice. We are called to resist the culture of death by standing up for life.

Conversely, love is not demonstrated nor is justice executed through intimidation, name calling, or hate-driven social and political engineering. This inflames an already angry culture and paints society in conspiratorial "us" versus "them" colors. Culture wars are the result. Christianity, however, is not supposed to be a culture, nor are we called to be at war with the culture. Christianity is socially irrelevant and politically bombastic when it becomes its own elitist subculture within the greater cultural framework. The first casualty of culture war is love.[45] Our battle is not against flesh and blood but against the spiritual forces of wickedness in the unseen realm (Eph. 6:12). Our calling is to love our neighbor in concrete, spiritual, and material ways. This includes making Christian disciples, showing kindness and concern, and seeking the welfare of others.

Reaching a postmodern society does not happen with angry rhetoric, but with love-embodied reality. It doesn't happen with vengeful dogmas, but with truth-incarnate living. The Sixth Commandment beckons us to this kind of authentic walk. When we genuinely love our neighbor, we honor God's truth and fulfill his law (Rom. 13:10).

SMALL GROUP DISCUSSION QUESTIONS

1. The Sixth Commandment forbids "unlawful killing" and "murder." Jesus reminded us that murder and violence are matters of the heart. How is this true? What is meant by "hidden murder"? Discuss some of your personal thoughts and actions that may be in violation of this commandment. What is the solution?

2. Why is murder forbidden? Why is suicide contrary to God's law? How would you discourage a person who is contemplating suicide? How could you encourage that person during this period of depression?

3. Why is abortion legal? How would you explain to the average person subjected to the spirit of the "politically correct" culture that abortion is murder?

4. The Sixth Commandment's positive thrust is to "love our neighbor." Who is our neighbor? How do we love him or her (see Luke 10:25–37 and Matthew 25:31–6)?

5. In Matthew 5:44 Jesus commands us to love our enemies and to pray for those who persecute us. How do we do that? How does this embodied love relate to the Sixth Commandment?

FEARING GOD
IN A PERMISSIVE WORLD

"You shall not commit adultery."

Exodus 20:14

When political consultant Dick Morris fell in August 1996 after a tabloid story detailed his year-long affair with $200-an-hour call girl Sherry Rowlands, the crash shook the capital's notion of what constitutes a proper sex scandal and shed new light on America's fickle attitudes toward adultery in the naughty '90s.[1] A 1996 *Newsweek* poll found that of the five hypothetical shortcomings one could imagine a politician being guilty of (including taking drugs and cheating on income taxes), an extramarital affair was the least likely to cause people to vote against the offender; only 35 percent considered it a reason to choose someone else.[2] A myriad of scandals and three decades of increasingly lurid revelations about the antics of those in high places has apparently persuaded people to look elsewhere for role models. Morris, however, did something worse than shack up with a harlot, according to many women—he carried on a long-term relationship with another woman that went beyond sex into the realm of intimacy.[3]

The word "intimacy" is not meant to imply candlelight, a table for two in a fantasy café, a violinist playing rhythmic melodies as the absorbed couple engages in intensely romantic conversation. Intimacy is deeper and more personal. It is a person's ability to share openly about who he or she really is and to talk about what he or she desires and needs and to be heard by a comforting, caring partner.

For a married man to share intimate partnership with a prostitute is a cold stab in the heart to his wife. The closeness that she hungers for is given to someone else. Even worse, he and all involved pay a heavy, heavy price for his sensuality. Commitment is meaningless. Vows are a sham. Now her own self-worth fades and rejection haunts her unmercifully.

Adultery not only violates covenants, but it is a form of dispassionate communication. It is the way of acting out a message, in the language of behavior, and that message is: "For me, this marriage no longer satisfies me. I would rather bond with someone else."

When the vows of emotional and sexual exclusivity are broken, the reactions on the part of the betrayed mate are shock, hurt, anger, panic, and consternation.[4] Even though the sexual mores of our culture have become more permissive, most spouses continue to feel intensely wounded and distressed by a partner's violation of the sacred boundaries around the marital relationship. A firestorm of fierce emotionality—accusations and anger on the part of the faithful partner; guilt and defensiveness on the part of the extramaritally involved person—rages throughout the entire relationship.

Faithfulness in the covenant of marriage is a prominent theme in Scripture. Keeping promises and staying true to one's vows is a mark of integrity. Our culture, however, has lost sight of its spiritual roots. The bond between biblical fidelity and the American people has deteriorated. America has gradually lost its moral anchor. In his book *Ideas Have Consequences*, Richard Weaver's remarks have never been more applicable: "Every man has been not only his own priest but his own professor of ethics, and the consequence is an anarchy which threatens even that minimum of consensus of value necessary to the political state."[5]

The breaking of vows is the result of our breaking God's law. The Ten Commandments are "Ten Suggestions" in a postmodern society. We live in a permissive world that has lost its reverence for a holy God. The biblical idea of fearing God is a fading doctrine buried under the postmodern, therapeutic masks of self-fulfillment. While "fear" abounds in people's hearts, as attested to by many popular self-help books, because we have lost our Godward roots, it now manifests itself in "free-floating anxiety," low self-esteem, and a host of other ᴄ temporary maladies.[6] Negative emotions bubble to the surface when ever God is reduced to a cosmic hermit. God is too small to be revered.

ADULTERY IN ANCIENT TIMES

God's injunction against adultery, properly fixed in the corpus of Scripture, prohibits sexual relations between a husband and someone else's wife, or of a wife with the husband of another.[7] When a man, for example, has an extramarital affair with a married woman, he violates the marriage covenant of his neighbor. He takes into his possession the woman who has pledged herself to another man. Even if this woman is not officially married, but merely engaged to be married, the same verdict applies: the adulterer has desecrated his neighbor's wife (Deut. 22:24).[8] The man who violates his neighbor's wife violates that neighbor's honor.[9]

The uniqueness of the Seventh Commandment is like a sparkling jewel shining its light on the special covenant relationship that God intended for himself with his own people. This relationship is compared to a marriage of mutual love and faithfulness. It highlights the idea of the permanence of the relationship undergirded by the dual concepts of love and covenant. God's intention was that his people be like a "virgin bride who gives herself willingly, and exclusively to her husband (Jer. 2:2) and thereby becomes his delight" (Isa. 62:5).[10]

Yahweh is pictured as the caring, jealous protector, a God who fights against other gods when his people exhibit the behavior of an unfaithful spouse, forsaking the one and only true God for worthless idols. Like a loving, jealous husband, Yahweh does not tolerate his people whoring after other gods, for in doing so they are committing adultery just like a woman who is being unfaithful to her husband (Jer. 3:6–9; Hos. 2–3).

The marital bond as the pristine focus of man and woman connected in the most dynamic of all human relationships is symbolized by the covenant bond between God and humankind. Adultery is the violation of the unique marriage relationship just as spiritual adultery (idolatry) is a violation of the covenant of love and fidelity that Yahweh has with his people. In the Hebrew Bible the frequency of the prohibition of adultery dolatry. Adultery was considered to be a deplorable sin, the people involved, but against God as well. David's pressing tearful repentance over his act of adultery bear Thee, Thee only, I have sinned" (Ps. 51:4).

JESUS, LUST, AND THE HEART OF THE SEVENTH COMMANDMENT

In the Sermon on the Mount, Jesus gets to the heart of the Seventh Commandment by concluding: "You have heard that it was said, 'You shall not commit adultery'; but I say to you, that everyone who looks on a woman to lust for her has committed adultery with her already in his heart" (Matt. 5:27–28). According to Jesus, the seeds of adultery germinate in the heart. This might sound archaic for those who ride the sensual waves of a permissive society, but from the divine viewpoint it is a vital truth.

In Tom Wolfe's popular novel *The Bonfire of the Vanities*, lead character Sherman McCoy says to himself as he strolls down Fifth Avenue:

> It was in the air! It was a wave! Everywhere! Inescapable...! Sex...! There for the taking...! It walked down the street, as bold as you please...! It was splashed all over the shops! If you are young and halfway alive, what chance did you have...? Who could remain monogamous with this, this, this tidal wave of concupiscence rolling across the world...? You can't dodge snowflakes, and this was a blizzard! He had merely been caught at it, that was all, or halfway caught at it. It meant nothing. It had no moral dimension. It was nothing more than getting soaking wet.[11]

Sexual expression is one of the dominant characteristics of contemporary postmodern culture. We are constantly being inundated by the media's romanticizing of the necessity of sex for self-fulfillment and by the exploitation of sensuality by the gurus of advertising. As the old norms are banished to more primitive eras, sex has become a hedonistic activity engaged in solely for the purpose of pleasure. The words of Jesus are scoffed at by hedonists out to have a "good time."

But the Christian must take his words seriously. Jesus calls his people to purity of heart. He warns that lust is born in the heart and

mind. "Lust is a dehumanizing, depersonalizing drive to in_
sexual appetite."[12] Author Paul Micky says: "Lust is any excessive
desire, any uncontrollable urge for immediate gratification. . . . Lust
may involve a craving for food, alcohol, sports, new fashions, success,
sex. . . . Lust of any type is dangerous because it is self-centered, mech-
anistic, inflexible, and insensitive to the needs of others. . . . Lust is selfish, insensitive self-gratification. Lust is a powerful force that is rooted
deeply in our selfish, rebellious nature."[13]

The Bible does make a distinction between sexual desire and sexual
lust. Sexual desire is healthy and satisfying (Song of Songs 4:1–16).
Sexual lust is unhealthy and sinful (1 Peter 4:1–3). Sexual intimacy was
meant to be encouraged and protected in the personal, public covenant
of marriage.[14] Lust is ultimately using another person to satisfy one's
own sensual hunger. "Lust divorces love, spurns care, denies communion, and disregards commitment."[15] Lust can lead to self-destruction.

Radio personality Paul Harvey tells the story of how an Eskimo kills
a wolf. The account is grisly, yet it offers fresh insight into the consuming, self-destructive nature of sinful lusts:

> First the Eskimo coats his knife blade with animal blood and
> allows it to freeze. Then he adds another layer of blood, and
> another, until the blade is completely concealed by frozen blood.
> Next, the hunter fixes his knife in the ground with the blade up.
> When a wolf follows his sensitive nose to the source of the scent
> and discovers the bait, he licks it, tasting the fresh frozen blood.
> He begins to lick faster, more and more vigorously, lapping the
> blade until the keen edge is bare. Feverishly now, harder and
> harder the wolf licks the blade in the arctic night. So great
> becomes his craving for blood that the wolf does not notice the
> razor-sharp sting of the naked blade on his own tongue, nor does
> he recognize the instant at which his insatiable thirst is being sat-
> isfied by his "own" warm blood. His carnivorous appetite just
> craves more—until the dawn finds him dead in the snow![16]

It is a fearful thing that people, too, can be consumed by their own
lust. These excessive cravings for immediate gratification often lead to
adultery. This heinous sin not only defiles the marriage covenant but

also provides the ground for divorce, the corruption of another's body, the potential for abortion, and the vehicle for the groundswell of sexually transmitted diseases. Lust always competes as a rival god. As it conquers the human heart, it not only has the power to shatter the life and reputation of the lust addict but also leaves broken lives, damaged emotions, and a trail of scarred memories in its wake.

In fact, sexual sin (specifically adultery) leads to the breakdown of numerous relationships. It involves sin against God, against the partner in the affair, against the spouse of each person in the affair, and even against the very bodies of the people engaging in immorality. Paul said that "the immoral man sins against his own body" (1 Cor. 6:18). This is not to mention the children, friends, and relatives who end up sharing in the pain and division caused by sexual sin. Adultery violates God's covenant of love, it demolishes the marriage covenant, and it devastates relationships ordained by God for our joy, fulfillment, and gratitude.

While the Seventh Commandment mentions only one sin, when set in the context of the Holiness Code of Leviticus 18–20 and Christian reality, "Thou shall not commit adultery" has a broader meaning, a deeper significance. The commandment against adultery includes a wide range of other sins. Other impermissible forms of sexual intercourse are mentioned alongside adultery, such as incest, homosexuality, sex with an animal, and prostitution (Lev. 18:6–20, 22–23; 19:29; Deut. 23:17–18). This command also forbids fornication—sexual immorality committed by singles (Deut. 22:22). In fact, the loss of virginity outside of marriage was in itself a shameful thing in Israel (Deut. 22:13–21).[17] The New Testament repeats this commandment many times over in various ways. We are told to flee sexual immorality (1 Cor. 6:13–14). The body is not for immorality, but for the Lord. It is the temple of the Holy Spirit. Therefore, glorify God with your body! (vv. 19–20).

Today, the majority of Americans believe there is nothing morally wrong with having a sexual relationship outside of marriage. The rationalization is that everybody else is doing it too.[18] Our culture celebrates the macho man—an Ernest Hemingway whose life of sensual indulgence is exalted as an "art." For him there is a right way to drink a Margarita, to steal, to kill, and to commit adultery. People who live their lives without moral restraint and fulfill their lusts with artistic style are deemed "authentic." Hemingway, however, said this about his life: "I live in a vacuum that is as lonely as a radio tube when the batteries are dead, and there is no current to plug into."[19] On a sunny Sunday morning in Idaho, he put a shotgun to his head and took his own life. The plain truth is, people rationalize their behavior not wanting to turn from their carnal desires. When one is in the grip of lust, God is never more distant and life is never more hollow. Sexual sin is a cancer that tears away at one's moral fiber, divides human relationships, and leaves personal lives shattered and empty.

We must guard our hearts and minds in Christ Jesus (Phil. 4:7). Only by dwelling on the "higher things" and practicing the truth (vv. 8–9) will the power of sin be broken, halting the inevitable train of sensuality and immorality. Job made a covenant with his eyes so that he would not gaze lustfully at a young woman (Job 31:1). But on a deeper level, we must be enraptured with our God. The passionate gravity of the soul is meant for God. Earthly passion between husband and wife serve as an illustration of this spiritual reality. When the true God comes, the false gods must go. To conquer lust, we turn from it, pursue righteousness, and love God.[20] Loving God will cover a multitude of sins.

THE POSITIVE SIDE OF THE SEVENTH COMMANDMENT: THE MARRIAGE COVENANT

As I have stated already, the Bible assumes positive principles are implicit in their negative form in regard to each commandment. As with murder, we are commanded not only to refrain from killing, violence, and unrighteous anger, but also to love our neighbors and to seek the welfare of others. The Seventh Commandment teaches us not only to abstain from sexual immorality, but calls us to mutual love and marital fidelity. When biblical love shapes a marriage, it leads the husband and wife to care more about the needs of each other than about their own needs. Love does not seek its own (1 Cor. 13:5).

Marriage is God's grand "creation ordinance," his gift of love to all humankind. It is not a human *invention* but a divine *creation*. Marriage was originally intended to be a mirror of the divine-human relationship. Marriage was designed "to represent God: His perfect relationship with Himself—Father, Son, and Holy Spirit—as well as His relationship with His people."[21] A godly marriage provides a lens into the nature of God's relationship with his people.[22] God's plan is for our marriages to reflect his character. "A Christian marriage should be the framework for a bold movement to bring God's beauty and salvation to a dark world of chaos."[23]

Unhappily, God's intention for marriage to be a permanent love relationship that reflects his glory now lies in ruins. The ever-increasing travesty of marital breakdown frustrates his purposes. In our society one in every two marriages ends in divorce. The reasons for this vary, but undoubtedly the decline of commitment to a biblical understanding of the sanctity and permanence of marriage, and the growing attack on traditional concepts of sex, marriage, and family values, top the charts. All too many Christians have been influenced by the spirit of the times. The biblical view of marriage is being traded in for the relational "fool's gold" of a therapeutic culture.

Several years ago, in my first pastorate, I was informed that a woman in the church left her husband so that she could "find herself." This old secular credo finds a warm reception in a postmodern culture. "After all," they rationalize, "people grow apart." Leaving your mate is all part of the normal process of change and personal growth.

The biblical view of marriage as set forth in Scripture declares that the "marriage union is exclusive ('a man... his wife...'), is publicly acknowledged ('leaves his parents'), is permanent ('cleaves to his wife'), and is consummated by sexual intercourse ('become one flesh')."[24] The "one flesh" metaphor does not only signify the sex act but the uniting of the two as a married couple. The sexual union outwardly and physically elucidates the bond that has been formed.

Sex is God's gift to married couples. It is his wedding gift to heterosexual partners, intended for mutual pleasure and the deepening of their union. Sexual intercourse is symbolic of the whole-life sharing that God purposed for soul mates. It seals the souls of the two people who intimately unite.

Sexual intercourse is not merely a physical act but a spiritual union of married love. Thomas F. Jones insightfully describes what happens in the seal of this special union. He says,

In intercourse one person, the man, literally enters the body of the other, the woman. There is in that entrance a symbol of what ought to be happening in his spirit at the same time. He ought to be saying to her, "I am willing to enter into your life, into your whole life. I want to come into who and what you are. I want to discover you in every way. As I discover you, I will love you and accept you. I will not reject what I find that you are. I will care for you, understand you, and always honor you. I will dwell lovingly within your life."

On the other side of the illustration, think of the symbolism of the woman's act of intercourse. She actually opens her body to the man's entrance. She ought to be saying, "You may come into my whole life. I will keep no secrets from you. What I truly am I will permit you to know, to touch. I will trust you wholly with my inner self. You are welcome here inside my life."[25]

Sexual intercourse is deeper than two lovers uniting for personal pleasure. It illuminates the sacred relationship God has given for the purpose of sealing the marriage covenant and "as an outward, bodily symbol of the pledged love of the marriage union."[26] Marriage is the exclusive heterosexual covenant between one man and one woman, sanctioned by God, preceded by a public leaving of parents, consummated in sexual union, issuing in a permanent mutually loving partnership.[27] Sadly, many marriages have departed from the divine ideal, ending in divorce. Even though divorce is permitted under certain circumstances, it is still a breaking of covenant, a treacherous act against one's soul mate, which God says he "hates" (Mal. 2:15–16).

In Deuteronomy 24 we have the only Old Testament passage which refers to guidelines for divorce.

When a man takes a wife and marries her, and it happens that she finds no favor in his eyes because he has found some indecency in her, and he writes her a certificate of divorce and puts it in her hand and sends her out from his house, and she leaves his house and goes and becomes another man's wife, and if the latter husband turns against her and writes her a certificate of divorce and puts it in her hand and sends her out of his house, or if the latter husband dies who took her to be his wife, then her former husband who sent her away is not allowed to take her again to be his wife, since she has been defiled; for that is an abomination before the Lord, and you shall not bring sin on the land which the Lord your God gives you as an inheritance (Deut. 24:1–4).

First, the thrust of this legislation in no way recommends or requires divorce. Yet the presence of divorce required that the religious leaders deal with the problem. Allowance for divorce came about as a concession to the sinful, foreboding times, not as a sanction of God's intent. Rather than giving sanction to or legislating divorce, the Mosaic concession was an attempt to regulate a practice already in operation within the Israelite community. The initial purpose was to protect the rights and health of a divorced woman by explaining why she was being expelled from the household. A cruel husband could lie about her situation and claim that she committed adultery—a capital offense in Hebrew society. A certificate of divorce protected her status and spelled out the real reasons for the dissolution.[28]

Second, even though the law did not encourage divorce, it was a reality among the Hebrews. The general practice already present in the ancient society saw disgruntled husbands divorcing their wives on the grounds that they "found some indecency in her" (Deut. 24:1). According to the Pharisaic parties led by Rabbi Shammai (i.e., 50 B.C.–A.D. 30) the "indecency" was interpreted to be a major sexual offense, such as adultery. Divorce was excluded in all cases except for adultery.[29] Rabbi Hillel, the first-century Palestinian sage, by contrast, was the liberal. He broadened the possibilities of divorce to include anything a husband found disagreeable about his wife (e.g., burning a meal, not able to bear children, being quarrelsome, or simply losing interest in her).

Tragically, Rabbi Hillel's perversion of God's law has leaped many centuries and found a home in the selfish loins of some twentieth-century Christians. Even certain Christian leaders have separated from or divorced a spouse (in some cases remarrying) and continue in positions of Christian leadership. Even worse, some go on a campaign of self-justification and arrogantly chirp: "I believe this is God's will." This banal presumption and crass disobedience is a stench in the nostrils of a holy God.

A few years ago a Christian leader told me that he left his wife on the basis of Proverbs 21:9. "It is better to live in a corner of a roof, than in a house shared with a contentious woman." I wonder if it ever occurred to him that the Proverbs are not principles of conduct, but are sagacious sayings that gather the most instances of good behavior without taking all the exceptions or qualifications.[30] Therefore, generally speaking, a small room in the corner of a house is to be preferred to a large house with a contentious wife. True, but that does not mean that, given a contentious wife, a man can take up a room in another house with another woman or separate from his soul mate that, before God, the man covenanted to stick by until death parted them. Either way, it is a breach of covenant and God hates it!

It is a disgrace when unguarded Christian leaders become dominated by the Enlightenment values that rule American culture: pursuit of happiness, unrestricted freedom of choice, self-authenticating authority. These values thrive in a postmodern culture when everything is understood in relation to our feelings. Pride flourishes in the cesspool of personal exaltation. Pride is the ultimate religious devotion to self-interest. From this extravagant "love of self" spring the moral evils of apathy, indifference, injustice, hate toward one's neighbor, and cruelty to one's spouse.

The liberal Hillel tradition was the most prevalent when Jesus came on the scene. Rather than siding with either of the two options advocated by his contemporaries, Jesus avoided sanctioning divorce under any circumstances. He elevated God's ideal of marriage being a permanent lifetime relationship.

However, I do believe Jesus permitted divorce and remarriage in certain circumstances. To extrapolate on it here would take the focus from the matter at hand—the Seventh Commandment. The intent of Jesus, however, is to exalt God's ideal for marriage and to stress that divorce always constitutes a departure from that ideal. With this in mind, Jesus passionately declared: "Because of your hardness of heart, Moses permitted you to divorce your wives; but from the beginning it has not been this way. And I say to you, whoever divorces his wife, except for immorality, and marries another woman commits adultery" (Matt. 19:8–9).

God hates sexual sin not only because it violates his law but also because it breaks peace and destroys relationships.[31] Adultery is a betrayal of the partner to whom one is joined by a sacred bond. Sexual infidelity is the principal harbinger that causes the rupture of the bond between husband and wife, spawning the eruption of many other relationships affected by the sin. The consequences are enormous.

Before closing this section, it is important that I mention the power of God's healing and forgiveness. No sin is so shockingly evil that it blocks God's forgiveness nor so trivial that it neglects the need for his mercy. Even if a wayward child of God blows it with a heart-tearing divorce and subsequent remarriage—these sins are not "unforgivable." But God's will is that we admit our shortcomings and confess our sins (James 5:16). Unrighteous conduct usually results in negative consequences rather quickly. But true repentance brings restoration and the healing of relationships. Believers who have fallen into sexual sin must present themselves humbly before almighty God in openness and acknowledge responsibility. The love of God is the profound answer to any human struggle when we align our lives with the Word of God. The path of obedience is the road to freedom.

SEX, INTIMACY, AND CHRISTIAN MARRIAGE

The fling from hell in the movie *Fatal Attraction* is now more than ten years old, but it still burns in the minds of moviegoers. Whether you've seen it or not, *Fatal Attraction* is a cultural touchstone ingrained in the public consciousness. This expression is used repeatedly in news articles and magazines. Oftentimes when a jilted lover resorts to harassment or stalking tactics, it's called a fatal attraction. In 1992 a real-life "fatal attraction" brought the eerie fictional account to life when Carolyn Warmus was convicted of brutally murdering her lover's wife.

The movie was in a sense a morality tale for the decadent '80s when sex, drugs, and sexually transmitted diseases were rife. This startling Grimms' fairy tale for adults sent a message: there are terrible consequences to sexual infidelity.

The stimulation of raw sex is usually not the motivation for adulterous encounters. Sexual deviance is oftentimes the outward manifestation signaling an inner need to express one's sexuality and longings for intimacy. Sometimes these potent desires become compulsive, resulting in twisted psychological obsessions, which was the case of Mary Kay LeTourneau, the former grade-school teacher in Seattle who was sentenced to six months in jail for the rape of a teen—one of her pupils. LeTourneau became pregnant and gave birth to a baby girl, now being raised by the boy's mother. After her release, she was caught with the boy (then fourteen) and arrested again after prosecutors learned the relationship with the boy was continuing. Found guilty of the new charges, she was sentenced to 7½ years in prison. Soon after her return to prison, it was confirmed that she was pregnant again. Experts agreed that there was much more than sex involved in the aberrant behavior of LeTourneau. Tragically, she left a husband and four children for a fantasy fling with her fourteen-year-old student.

Extreme cases aside, people enter into extramarital relationships for a variety of reasons. Sometimes they are motivated by the excitement of a new romance. Some are motivated by a desire to "prove" to themselves that they are desirable to the opposite sex. Other reasons might be sexual frustration, curiosity, revenge, boredom, and the need for acceptance and recognition. Although the reasons offered for adulterous affairs are bewildering in their multiplicity and variety, most seem to reveal that the lack of intimacy to some degree has created a vacuum that seeks to be filled. Sexual infidelity is the outworking of the deep longing to give expression to the sexual dimension of one's being. That does not make infidelity right, but it accentuates the human need for intimacy. In the beginning, "Adam's solitude arose from a void that could not be filled by his companionship with animals nor, interestingly enough, even by the presence of the solitary Adam before God"[32] The remedy for this situation was the glorious creation of not merely another human being, but a female counterpart. The void in Adam's existence was sexually and relationally based. God's antidote was to give him Eve—a suitable bonding partner in all aspects of his existence (Gen. 2:18–25).

The introduction of sin into the human race sent everything into a tailspin. Sin is folly. It breeds corruption and destroys peace. Cornelius Plantinga, Jr., says that "sin distorts our character, a central feature of our very humanity. Sin corrupts powerful human capacities—thought, emotions, speech, and act—so that they become centers of attack on others or of defection or neglect."[33]

Sexuality embodies all the elements of a human being that are connected to life as a male or female. Sexuality is a very powerful, deep, and mysterious aspect of our being.[34] When we choose to go outside God's moral parameters to express our sexuality, we establish harmful patterns for our lives and forge an unholy bond with a stranger, wounding the deepest aspect of the human personality—the soul. As Lewis Smedes says, "We cannot take our bodies to bed with someone and park our souls outside in the car to wait."[35] Many try to do so, but the loneliness, guilt, and shame eventually come to the surface in one way or another.

Marriage, and marriage alone, provides the only stable foundation and framework for the full expression of human sexuality. God's intention is for our spouses to be our intimate friends, lovers, and confidants as we live together in a world of good and evil, light and darkness. God calls husbands and wives to be intimate soul mates for life. Growth in marital intimacy involves a commitment to prayer, an openness to think, a willingness to touch, and the tenacity to build an atmosphere of trust. Such a climate will give two image bearers the freedom to search and discover, to feel safe and secure together, and the nutrients to blossom as one.

In a postmodern culture where God's law has been dismantled by the ethics of desire, wants become needs, "the self replaces the soul and human life degenerates into the clamor of competing autobiographies. People get fascinated with how they feel."[36] In such a culture where the self exists to be indulged and explored, Christian couples must be sold on the application of God's truth and radically committed to building strong, godly marriages. To claim that we love God and then to be indifferent and disconnected from our marriage partner is to live a lie. Truth acted upon brings more truth. Failure to obey God's truth will result in a loss of truth (see Matt. 25:28–29). The loss of truth in one's life has devastating consequences and frustrates God's goal of revealing his glory through unadulterated marriages.

No relationship carries more importance to the church or the culture than marriage. Growth in Christian marriages always bears incredible fruit, including a deeper pursuit of God, greater fervor to reach out to lost souls, and a godly application of the Gospel in a permissive world. Most of all, we reveal God to a godless postmodern culture by the covenant love we have for our spouses.

"The fear of the Lord is the beginning of wisdom," declares the psalmist; "a good understanding have all those who do His commandments" (Ps. 111:10). To fear God is to revel in awe of his sovereignty and absolute power over life and death (see Luke 12:4–5). Fearing God is a positive experience for those who love God. To fear him is to know that life without him brings despair, and rebellion against his moral law places us in great danger. Solomon could identify with that and toward the end of his complicated life recorded a crucial decree of wisdom: "Fear God and keep His commandments" (Eccl. 12:13).

The Seventh Commandment calls us to sexual purity and passionate obedience to our God. The moral law is a divine document of covenant love that keeps God-fearing people free. To make an impact on the postmodern culture, we must walk in awesome reverence for God and live in submission to his law. The psalmist agrees wholeheartedly: "My flesh trembles in fear of you; I stand in awe of your laws" (Ps. 119:120 NIV).

SMALL GROUP DISCUSSION QUESTIONS

1. Why are the Ten Commandments oftentimes simply "Ten Suggestions," at best, to the committed postmodernist? Why is it important that believers maintain and proclaim that they are commandments, not suggestions?

2. Why did Jesus point out that adultery is a matter of the heart? What does it mean to lust, and how does it differ from sexual desire? What happens to a person or society consumed by lust?

3. Explain how the Seventh Commandment calls us to mutual love and marital fidelity. What was marriage originally intended by God to be? What is God's plan for our marriages?

4. Discuss the many consequences of adultery. Can healing occur after lives have been torn apart by an adulterous relationship? Explain.

5. What is sexual intimacy? Why is marriage the only stable foundation and framework for the full expression of human sexuality?

APPLYING THE GOLDEN RULE IN A LAW-BREAKING SOCIETY

"You shall not steal."
Exodus 20:15

The Eighth Commandment requires honesty and uprightness in our dealings with others. Jesus built upon that practical principle in the Sermon on the Mount—a virtue that we know today as the Golden Rule.[1] The rule was not first spoken by Jesus, but he phrased the rule positively.

> Therefore, however you want people to treat you, so treat them, for this is the Law and the Prophets (Matt. 7:12).

From the biblical point of view, this verse is not to be understood as a utilitarian formula like "Honesty pays good dividends." The emphasis lies in our responsibilities toward others. We are to treat others the way we would have them treat us, not merely because we expect the same kind of treatment in return but because such conduct honors God and fulfills the loving goal of his law.

We are required to deal with people in a sincere, forthright manner. Jesus' dual-love command is exceedingly comprehensive. He declared that love for God and love for people cannot be separated. As we approach the Lord in passionate obedience, the fountains of divine grace will pour through our hearts, empowering us to apply the Golden Rule to all affairs.

Just as the Sixth Commandment (you shall not murder or kill unlawfully) safeguards the value of human life, and the Seventh Commandment (you shall not commit adultery) defends biblical love, marriage, and the family, the Eighth Commandment (you shall not steal) forbids stealing in general and demands that we respect our neighbors' right to private property.[2]

CRIME

Bob Jackson spent fifteen years in prison. Upon his release, two young reform-minded lawyers, Dan and Linda Smith, provided legal help and attempted to place Bob in a local halfway house program. Jackson was reluctant to trust any authority or supervision after spending a decade and a half in a violent penitentiary. He was determined to make it on his own. The Smiths helped him to find a job, and Jackson began working regularly. Dan and Linda Smith stayed in close contact with Jackson, offering whatever help they could.

Jackson got in the habit of spending time at a local bar every day after work. Several weeks after his release, Dan received a call one evening from the bartender. Jackson was drunk, becoming very disruptive, and the bartender asked Dan to come over and remove him before he got into further trouble. With his wife gone to a meeting and his daughter, Tracy, sleeping, Dan asked a neighbor to watch the house till he got back.

Jackson was indeed drunk and belligerent, but Dan was able to convince him that it was time to go home. They drove to Dan's house, where they watched a football game on TV. Dan fell asleep. Hours later, Dan was abruptly awakened by Jackson holding a butcher knife.

Jackson made it clear that he would kill Dan if he did not cooperate. Disoriented and confused, Jackson was determined to run away and he tied Dan to a chair. Dan silently prayed that Jackson's actions would not awaken his daughter and create further violence.

Linda soon arrived home to the ugly scene. Jackson's hostility soared and he grabbed Linda, taking her as a hostage and sped away in the Smiths's car. They headed for a nearby state. Jackson stopped several times on the way. Linda was raped. He was ready to murder her since he thought he would get the death penalty anyway if caught.

He backed off only after Linda convinced him that the death penalty did not apply to rape. In the midst of the trauma and pain of having been kidnapped and severely violated, Linda tried to figure out a way to get out of the vehicle.

Finally, as they were leaving the highway on an exit ramp she sighted a police car. She quickly opened her door, jumped out, and ran toward the police officer. Jackson was immediately apprehended.[3]

Kidnapping was a capital offense in ancient Israel (Ex. 21:16; Deut. 24:7). Taking someone hostage, holding a person in captivity, or stealing children from their parents are all forms of slavery. God freed Israel from slavery and expressed his desire to keep his people from any future bondage. Slavery is a violation of the Eighth Commandment.[4]

Linda Smith was a tragic victim of one of the Eighth Commandment's worst violators. Her freedom was temporarily stolen, her body robbed of its dignity, and her life wounded by a cruel thief. Here we see God's law being pillaged in brutal fashion.

Many thousands of individuals are victimized by crime each year in the United States. On a nationwide basis, a serious crime (murder, rape, assault, robbery, burglary, larceny, or auto theft) occurs every two seconds, according to the Federal Bureau of Investigation.[5] According to authors James Patterson and Peter Kim of *The Day America Told the Truth*, America's official statistics on crime are somewhat misleading. Their research shows that crime is underestimated by about 600 percent. Thirty-nine percent of the people in America have some kind of criminal offense in their past and more than half of all Americans (60 percent) have been the victims of crime at least once in their lives. It came as no surprise that only a minority of Americans (32 percent) said they feel safe in their neighborhoods. The rest confessed that "we live with continual fear."[6] God's law has fallen on deaf ears in our great land.

The nonviolent, everyday kind of crimes committed by ordinary people are almost as alarming. It's as if smaller thefts, or nonfelonies, are not that bad. Patterson and Kim report some true confessions from the privacy of their interviews:

- A bank teller from Metropolis: "Lots of petty theft when I was a teenager. Now I work in a bank, right."

- A Rust Belt lawyer: "Drugs and theft right up to the present time. I sometimes steal at our office."
- A Southern cop: "I've stolen many items. Little here, little there."
- A receptionist from a rural area in the Northeast: "When I was younger, I stole from department stores. I occasionally hit the malls now."
- A high-school coach from the East: "I stole a leather jacket last year. Every couple of years, I steal something big."
- A young woman from New England who is a fitness instructor: "Attempted larceny. Also, stealing gasoline from cars in the neighborhood."
- A meat cutter from the Midwest: "Dope stealing from work."
- A Midwestern woman who owns a manicuring business: "Stealing in stores and buying drugs."
- A Midwestern woman who now is president of a small company: "Stole paper goods, pens, small machines from a former employer."
- A broker for the federal government: "As a teen, working in a camera shop, I stole a lot of equipment."
- An Old Dixie factory foreman: "I steal packs of cigarettes off our lunch wagon."
- A realtor from the West Coast: "Smoked marijuana and committed petty theft in convenience stores."
- A mother of two from the Rust Belt: "Stole cosmetics at a Mary Kay show."[7]

The authors conclude that "the so-called Protestant ethic is long gone from today's American workplace. Workers around America frankly admit that they spend more than 20 percent of their time (seven hours a week) at work goofing off. That amounts to a four-day work week across the nation. Almost half of Americans admit to chronic malingering, calling in sick when not sick, and doing it regularly. One in six Americans regularly drinks or uses drugs on the job. Only one in four gives work their best effort; only one in four works to realize their human potential rather than merely to keep the wolf from the door."[8] The top five office crimes in America, according to Patterson and Kim, are:

1. Taking office supplies and equipment
2. Lying to a boss or coworker
3. Stealing company funds
4. Affair with a boss or coworker
5. Taking credit for work not done[9]

Employee theft has many faces. The looting of office supplies, stealing company time, or pilfering company funds are all violations of God's eighth absolute: "You shall not steal."

Not wanting to belabor the issues, I have briefly listed some other common ways that the Eighth Commandment is being violated today. If we truly want to honor God and his law, we must carefully consider our own transgressions as we probe the depth of this important command.

Greed: excessive desire for personal gain, self-promotion, and avarice. Jesus, for example, spoke out harshly against the leaders of the people who acted pious while in their greed they devoured the houses of widows (Matt. 23:14). All forms of social injustice are condemned by the Eighth Commandment.

Robbery and extortion: stealing someone else's possessions whether by force (mugging, burglary) or by petty theft.

Fraud: rigging contracts, lying about business-related issues, bribing officials, or being dishonest and unfaithful in general.

Embezzlement: fraudulently taking money or property for one's own use.

Bribery: money or a favor given or promised to a person in a position of trust to influence that person's judgment or conduct.

Tax Evasion: failing to pay the government the amount owed or finding loopholes that violate the spirit of the tax laws.

Credit-Card Debt: Charging items which one cannot pay for or does not expect to pay for. This includes defaulting on loans.

Unjust Prices: charging exorbitant fees for products; not selling at a fair price.

Cheating: deliberately violating the rules dishonestly in order to get something desired (e.g., cheating on a test to get a high grade or engaging in insider trading on Wall Street to get more money).

The list could go on. Stealing in general is a major epidemic on American soil and is all too common even among regular church attenders.

Outright theft is far more common among professing Christians than many care to admit. The great Golden Rule principle ought to govern our attitudes and shape our conduct in our dealings with others. This marvelous truth is not in any way a tenet of salvation, but it must be applied in every believer's life. The apostle Paul reminded the Ephesian Christians, "He who has been stealing must steal no longer" (Eph. 4:28 NIV). Those who practice the Golden Rule refuse to say or do anything that would injure or harm others.

STEALING THE HEART

The writer of Proverbs offers wise counsel: "Watch over your heart with all diligence, for from it flows the springs of life" (4:23). The heart is the core of a person's life. The heart is symbolically described in Scripture as the "real self" holding the body, intellect, emotions, and will in balance. All are united in the heart.

The Bible contains an expression that has to do with being manipulated, a way in which someone can steal the heart of another person (see Gen. 31:20, 26). By promising all kinds of nice things during his popularity campaign, "Absalom stole away the hearts of the men of Israel" (2 Sam. 15:6). In doing so, he laid the groundwork for his enterprise to dethrone King David.[10] Each year on Valentine's Day huge red hearts on cards are reminders to us that the heart is the symbol of love. People are charmed and wooed this time of year. The vapid sentimentality and emotion-tugging often reach a zenith on February 14. Being taken in by another in this manner can be dreamy, poetic, and romantic. But people can be taken in by a deceiver. We can be suckered, fooled, or manipulated.

One of the most high-profile cases of "heart stealing" in this century involved the sinister Charles Manson and his pack of deluded followers, creating shock waves around the world.

An ex-convict and full-fledged sociopath, Manson dominated his disciples with a mishmash of corrupted biblical philosophy and spurious interpretations of the lyrics of Beatles' songs.[11] This, combined with his magnetic sexual attraction for the female members of his so-called "Family," ensured Manson's complete physical, psychological, and spiritual control of the group.

The first publicized murders took place in the summer of 1969, at which time the Family were occupying an abandoned movie-set ranch owned by George Spahn. While at the ranch, Manson organized a fleet of armored dune buggies that would protect the homestead during what he called "Helter Skelter." It was characteristic of Manson's deranged feeblemindedness that for him Helter Skelter was a twisted misinterpretation of the words of a song written by the Beatles—he had no idea that the reference was to a fairground ride. Manson had already decided that the popular rock group's earlier song "Blackbird" represented a call to the blacks of America to rise up against the whites. His crazed irrationality now led him to the conclusion that it was time to get the holocaust started, which would lead to mutual annihilation of the races and ultimately leave the Family in control.

On August 9, 1969, four of Manson's disciples entered the Beverly Hills mansion of actress Sharon Tate and her husband, director Roman Polanski. In a savage killing spree, Manson's crazed followers butchered everyone in the home—Tate and four others. Polanski was away on business.

Two days later, Manson led a group of six devotees on a second murder spree. After inducing and arousing themselves with drugs, the Family invaded the Silver Lake home of businessman Leno LaBianca and his wife, Rosemary; the choice was reportedly random. After stabbing and slashing the LaBiancas to death, Manson and his disciples inscribed the mottos "Death to the Pigs," "Rise," and "Helter Skelter" in blood on the walls.

The Manson killings were inspired by a kind of deranged, hypnotic mysticism of death and violence—a mysticism that had its roots in abused and stolen hearts. Manson, the heart stealer, was himself the victim of psychological battering and abuse. Born illegitimately to a young prostitute and lawbreaker (she was imprisoned for armed robbery when Manson was a child), he felt like an outcast as he was moved from place to place, living with various relatives. He was taken in by an obsessively religious grandmother who drilled him with principles encouraging Christian humility. From there he was dumped on an aunt and uncle determined to turn him away from Christian meekness and to make him a "man." To change him, they sent the young

Manson to school dressed as a little girl where the constant teasing by his classmates threw him into fits of rage that drew out his violent, pugnacious side.

After being moved back and forth among relatives and finally sent to a very strict Catholic boys' institution, Manson escaped to a life of crime and punishment. While not yet a teenager, he was sent to the Indiana School for Boys after a conviction for car theft. There Manson was beaten unmercifully by the guards and his fellow inmates and subjected to frequent sexual abuse. A life of crime, drugs, abuse, and punishment continued into adulthood. In March 1967, Charles Manson was released from Terminal Island reformatory in California, having spent all but a few months of the previous twenty years locked up. He was thirty-two years old.

It is not my purpose here to perform a psychological autopsy on Manson or to provide explanations for his bizarre background. Heart stealing is the issue before us. The words of prophet Jeremiah are sobering: "The heart is more deceitful than all else and is desperately sick; who can understand it" (Jer. 17:9).

For those who respond to God's call he promises a new heart (Ezek. 36:26). For those who reject God's commandments, their fragile hearts will continue to atrophy ("which is being corrupted by its deceitful desires" Eph. 4:22 NIV).

Some say Manson is heartless, like a modern-day Dracula cruelly sucking the life out of his followers, who become his slaves. From a biblical standpoint, apart from God and his law, an abused heart will likely go on to abuse and steal other hearts. The consequences of heart stealing can be devastating.

The world is filled with manipulators and with people open and ready to be dominated by them. Many people, who are naive and searching for acceptance, *allow their hearts to be stolen*. Unfortunately, the rude awakening almost always comes after the damage has been done.

On a less sensational scale, this insidious heart stealing goes on every day in human relationships. We see it in adults who abuse children, spouses who seek to control their partners, and friends who manipulate one another to gain the favor and leverage they seek for self-actualization.

I witnessed more than a fair share of heart stealing in my first full-time pastorate working with single adults. Sometimes even among Christians, self-gratification and longings for intimacy with a person of the opposite sex result in people taking advantage of one another, getting too close too soon, and then being hurt. Dating degenerates into "what can this person do for me?" The fact that the Bible provides life-changing principles for healthy relationships with the opposite sex is of little interest to singles out to benefit only themselves. It is a shame that some Christian singles will manipulate others for their own enjoyment rather than applying biblical truth assuring that God will be glorified and members of the opposite sex will be treated with respect.

Heart stealing of any type is destructive. It injures people, offends God, and is condemned by the Eighth Commandment. The guidelines for knowing how to treat others is to ask ourselves how we would like to be treated if the circumstances were reversed. The Golden Rule is the outworking of the second great command: to love others as we love ourselves. Self-love demands that we think of our own concerns, how we can provide for ourselves. As Christians, we are to treat others the same way. The requirements of God's law are fulfilled by following this profound principle.

GAMBLING: THE LUCK BUSINESS

In 1996, the *Chicago Tribune* ran a story on Buddy Post, a lottery winner who is "living proof that money can't buy happiness." In 1988, he won $16.2 million in the Pennsylvania Lottery. Since then, he has been convicted "of assault, his sixth wife left him, his brother was convicted of trying to kill him, and his landlady successfully sued him for one-third of the jackpot."

"Money didn't change me," insists Post, a 58-year-old former carnival worker and cook. "It changed people around me that I knew, that I thought cared a little bit about me. But they only cared about the money."

Post is trying to auction off seventeen future payments, valued at nearly $5 million, in order to pay off taxes, legal fees, and a number of failed business ventures.

He plans to spend his life as an ex-winner pursuing lawsuits he has filed against police, judges, and lawyers who he says conspired to take his money. "I'm just going to stay at home and mind my p's and q's," he said. "Money draws flies."[12]

Legal gambling, once little more than a tourist attraction in New Jersey and Nevada, spread throughout the United States in the early 1990s and today generates more than $35 billion each year. State lotteries began in 1964 in New Hampshire, but now under the sponsorship of state and local governments, gambling enterprises—lotteries, riverboats, and casinos—have been mushrooming at an explosive rate, with casino revenues alone almost doubling in the last seven years.[13]

Proponents of gambling see the gaming industry as the magic-bullet cure for economic woes. Stories like Buddy Post's are dispassionately chalked up to personal incompetence and irresponsibility, while lobbyists and legislators promote gambling as a means to fiscal salvation. Once an industry created by gangsters like "Bugsy" Seigel, financed through laundered drug monies and other ill-gotten funds, "gaming" and "casino entertainment" are now being operated by business school graduates, financed by conglomerates, and are listed on the New York Stock Exchange.[14]

The merchants of chance declare that just as the government has no business in our bedrooms, it has "no business telling us how to spend our leisure time or our money as long as we are doing so without coercion or harm to others."[15] But that is precisely the point. Gambling does harm. The rise in human tragedies that have followed in the wake of government promotion of gambling is astounding. While proponents exaggerate the benefits of the gambling expansion, they downplay and often refuse to acknowledge its hidden costs—damaged lives, broken relationships, increased criminal activity, and the draining of local economies, resulting in net losses running into the hundreds of millions of dollars in a single state.[16] Many economists and cultural surveyors are asking, "Rather than resort to a desperate political scramble to find a quick fix for deep-seated economic problems, wouldn't it be more prudent to honestly rethink the relationship between cities and publicly sanctioned sin?"[17]

Obviously, the issues are complex and a whole book could be devoted to the subject. I am addressing the issue of gambling somewhat at length because the Christian church in general has largely ignored it, is not aware of the sin inherent in it, and has chosen to remain silent. Too often our silence is construed as approval. We cannot let that happen because gambling, at its bare essence, is a form of stealing. It is not only trying to get something for nothing but trying to gain riches at the expense of other people (the winnings of the few are financed by the losses of the many). The Bible says that "ill-gotten gains do not profit, but righteousness delivers from death" (Prov. 10:2). The Eighth Commandment is broken by gamblers because gambling violates the sacredness of property and the principle of stewardship. Ultimately, any money won through gambling comes at the expense of many other people. While monetary success may be achieved by some, the gods of luck ultimately chip away at our stewardship responsibilities. Here are six reasons why Christians should not be involved in the gambling industry.

1. The sovereignty of God

The biblical doctrine of God's sovereignty stresses that he is the owner of all things in heaven and earth. God is the master of the universe who is always in control even though he is displeased by sin. He is the absolute authority who has the right to influence his creation according to his purposes. "Belief in luck and belief in a sovereign God are mutually exclusive, for if an omniscient, omnipotent Creator God exists then luck makes no sense."[18]

Jesus acknowledged God's sovereign control over all of life (John 19:10–11). God does not exercise his sovereignty in a capricious manner. The Lord's unfailing love surrounds those who put their trust in him (Ps. 32:10). When we fail to trust God, we deny his sovereignty and question his goodness. Worshiping the gods of luck casts aspersions on God's majesty and character. Trusting in luck rather than in God is an idolatrous distraction away from a sovereign, loving God who desires that we trust him along the path of his will for our lives.

2. The corruption of the heart

The Bible says that "the love of money is a root of all kinds of evil. Some people, eager for money, have wandered from the faith and pierced themselves with many griefs" (1 Tim. 6:10 NIV). Money itself, of course, is not evil. Money can do much good by providing for human needs, feeding the hungry, clothing the poor, and furthering God's purposes in the world. But money can be as addictive as cocaine. When the "green god" controls people, it can plunge them into spiritual bankruptcy. Those who fall into a love affair with money may find it easy to love their wealth more than they love God.

Gambling nurtures a covetous spirit. It feeds the "love of money" seduction. It masquerades as an attractive, fun activity where you can win lots of money, but it sucks the generosity and integrity out of those who embrace it.

The gambler violates the Tenth Commandment, "You shall not covet," as well as the Eighth. The covetous person craves someone else's possessions or prestige so strongly that he's tempted to "steal" it. The coveter wants to fill his empty pockets with someone else's riches.

Gambling feeds the seeds of corruption sown in the heart. "Corruption is spiritual AIDS—the mysterious, systemic, infectious, and progressive attack on our spiritual immune system that eventually breaks it down and opens the way for hordes of opportunistic sins."[19]

Gambling's moral corruption is seen in the burgeoning number of people who get hooked by the "luck business" and become overwhelmed by addictive behavior. Arnold Wexler, a former director of the Council on Compulsive Gambling of New Jersey, and his wife, Sheila Wexler, a gambling counselor, create a vivid picture of the drastic consequences to gamblers and others:

> Compulsive gamblers will bet until nothing is left: savings, family assets, personal belongings—anything of value that may be pawned, sold, or borrowed against. They will borrow from co-workers, credit unions, family, and friends, but will rarely admit that it is for gambling. They may take personal loans, write bad checks, and ultimately reach and pass the point of bankruptcy....

In desperation, compulsive gamblers may panic and often will turn to illegal activities to support their addiction.[20]

Compulsive gamblers are not born with this problem. They all started out as casual, recreational gamblers. But gambling feeds covetousness and corruption. Problem gamblers are expensive to their families and themselves. They are costly to their employers, since they tend to be inattentive and unproductive at work, worrying about their debts or contemplating the next scam to borrow money.[21]

Gambling addicts engage in other socially destructive and costly behavior. "They tend to have a higher number of auto accidents, but they often don't have insurance to cover the cost of damages. This not only results in economic losses and physical problems to themselves, but to others involved in the accidents."[22] These accidents occur most often on the way home after a long day of gambling at the casino. Often these accidents are not accidents, but are deliberate suicide attempts.[23] According to one major study, problem gamblers were shown to have a suicide rate five to ten times higher than the rest of the population.[24]

In short, God's Word is clear that Christians are not to be dominated by any person, thing, or activity. The apostle Paul said that he would not be mastered by anything (1 Cor. 6:12). Christ's followers must not be led by the "chiefs of chance" or filled with gluttonous appetites for quick and easy cash. Christians are to be led by and filled with the Spirit of God (Gal. 5:18, 25; Eph. 5:18). God's Word instructs us to develop an eternal perspective. We are exhorted to "lay up for yourselves treasures in heaven, where neither moth nor rust destroys, and where thieves do not break in or steal; for where your treasure is, there will your heart be also" (Matt. 6:20–21).

3. The links to crime

Increased gambling opportunities not only create more gamblers generally but they also lead to a marked increase in crime. Atlantic City, which began casino operations in the late 1970s, is a prime example. In the three years following the opening of its first casino, Atlantic City went from fiftieth to first in the nation in per-capita crime.[25] In the decade following casino gambling, total crimes more than doubled in and around Atlantic City.[26]

Problem gamblers who go into debt to pay for their compulsive behavior frequently do not pay off these debts, nor do they tend to pay their taxes, utility bills, and other debts they owe. Those who do pay what they owe sometimes get the payoff money through criminal activities such as writing bad checks, embezzling money from their employers, not paying taxes, dealing drugs, stealing, and engaging in fraud.[27] Henry Lesieur and K. Puig reported in 1987 that pathological gamblers were responsible for an estimated $1.3 billion worth of insurance-related fraud each year.[28]

In case after case, the introduction of casinos has negatively impacted the lives of ordinary people, resulting in increased numbers of child abuse and neglect cases—from children being left in cars all night while parents gambled to families who were without utilities or groceries because adults had gambled away their paychecks. The rise in human tragedies, social traumas, and criminal behavior is intensified by the gambling industry.[29]

4. The negative impact on youth

Gambling is becoming an enticing "postmodern pastime" for America's youth. The latchkey, broken home Generation Xers are themselves especially susceptible to the enchanting gambling scene. Today's young people are the only ones who have experienced gambling that is both state sponsored and culturally approved. In 1992 Howard J. Shaffer, director of the Harvard Medical School Center for Addiction Studies, predicted, "We will face in the next decade or so more problems with youth gambling than we'll face with drug use."[30] In another study Shaffer found that two-thirds of a random sample of more than three hundred students at an Atlantic City high school had gambled illegally at the local casinos. The gambling attraction is so powerful in Atlantic City that nearly 30,000 underage people are either stopped from entering or ejected from the city's casinos every month.[31]

Teenagers not only are victimized by other family members' problem gambling but oftentimes emulate that behavior. While compulsive adult gamblers tend toward white-collar crimes such as writing bad checks, gambling teenagers tend to steal from their parents. Tragically, our youth are being taught by the disciplers of gambling that the easiest way to get rich is not to study and work hard but to try and hit the jackpot at a promising casino.

The Spirit of God reminds us of our personal and civic responsibility: "For even when we were with you, we used to give you this order: if anyone will not work, neither let him eat. For we hear that some among you are leading an undisciplined life, doing no work at all, but acting like busybodies. Now such persons we command and exhort in the Lord Jesus Christ to work in quiet fashion and eat their own bread" (2 Thess. 3:10–12).

5. The subversion of the Golden Rule

The Phillips translation of the Golden Rule says, "Treat other people exactly as you would like to be treated by them—this is the essence of all true religion." Gambling, however, "creates a condition in which one person's gain is necessarily many other persons' loss."[32] Gambling uses other people as a means to a financial end. It discards the principle of servanthood and love. The Bible says, "Owe nothing to anyone except to love one another; for he who loves his neighbor has fulfilled the law" (Rom. 13:8). Gambling tramples under foot God's most cherished truths: love, justice, and mercy (see Mic. 6:8).

The Golden Rule is the outworking of Christ's command to "love thy neighbor." Love does no harm to its neighbor. Love is not self-seeking (1 Cor. 13:5). Love leads us to seek the good, the welfare, and interest of others.

6. The undermining of the work ethic

Perhaps the most far-reaching, though somewhat intangible, effect of gambling is that it teaches people, especially the youth, to believe in an ethic of chance instead of an ethic of hard work and investment. The luck business undermines the work ethic. It legitimizes debased speculation and nullifies "the importance of stern virtues such as industriousness, thrift, deferral of gratification, diligence, studiousness."[33]

The work ethic is eroding in America, and gambling is contributing to its demise. God is no longer the sacred object of man's labors;

instead labor itself is the enshrined means to an end. The aim is not producing goods for others or for benefiting the common welfare of society but for acquiring "things" for one's personal pleasure. Those laboring for the expansion of gambling enterprises are trading long-term economic growth and prosperity for short-term gain. Even worse, the gambling industry exploits human weakness while people are used and abused as a means for financial gain. We must not ignore the biblical warnings: "A faithful man will abound with blessings, but he who makes haste to be rich will not go unpunished" (Prov. 28:20).

The apostle Paul said, "Let him who steals steal no longer; but rather let him labor, performing with his own hands what is good, in order that he may have something to share with him who has need" (Eph. 4:28). Gambling is a form of theft and is driven by greed. Its corrosive impact on the work ethic is an extension of its greedy promotion of pleasure and profit at the expense of others' pain and loss. This is antithetical to biblical love and truth.

Work is a stewardship to God (Gen. 2:15). It has a spiritual value, for it is rooted in creativity. Work gives expression to our creative gifts and thus fulfills our need for meaning and purpose.[34] Work has a functional value. As citizens in a community, we have a responsibility to our fellow citizens and to God to steward our gifts. Biblical Christianity stresses our duty to be productive members of society. The apostle Paul said, "Make it your ambition to lead a quiet life and attend to your own business and work with your hands" (1 Thess. 4:11). Jesus taught the importance of hard work and financial investment (Matt. 25:27). The application of biblical principles of stewardship and management will bring about spiritual and financial growth. Gambling, however, circumvents the spiritual principles to be learned from biblical financial management. Prudent investment and self-sacrifice are evaded by the luck business. Work has a dignity value, for it is rooted in the divine command to exercise stewardship over the earth, finding significance by participating in the work of creation in a way that honors the Lord. Working helps us to understand our sanctified potential as human beings. The empty promises of gambling militate against the work ethic and violate the principle of stewardship. The counsel of God's Word is, "Do not weary yourself to gain wealth, cease from your consideration of it" (Prov. 23:4).

Rex Rogers, president of Cornerstone College in Grand Rapids, Michigan, sums it up well:

> For many Americans gambling has become a surrogate religion; a pathological hope; a concession to life based on life; an admission that there is nothing to life but determinism, fatalism, nihilism. But gambling is rabbit's foot religion. It's postmodern paganism. Gambling asks people to play the odds, and always, in the long run, gambling wins.[35]

STEALING FROM GOD

The Bible describes another kind of stealing that is more subtle but just as sinful. This is the believer's sin of failing to carry out proper stewardship responsibilities. It is failing to give from what God has given us for his glory. *Leadership Magazine*, known for its colorful cartoons, printed one picturing a conventional-looking church with a large billboard in the foreground advertising its ministry. The sign read:

> The Lite Church
> 24% FEWER COMMITMENTS
> HOME OF THE 7.5% TITHE
> 15-MINUTE SERMONS
> 45-MINUTE WORSHIP SERVICES
> WE HAVE ONLY 8 COMMANDMENTS—YOUR
>   CHOICE
> WE USE JUST 3 SPIRITUAL LAWS
> EVERYTHING YOU'VE WANTED IN A CHURCH ...
>   AND LESS![36]

That is the stewardship-scandal of so many in the contemporary church today—stealing *time* from God due to self-commitment, withholding *talents* and gifts from Christ's service, and hoarding *treasures* instead of giving God what is rightly his. Malachi 3:8 asks: "Will a man rob God? Yet you are robbing Me! But you say, 'How have we robbed Thee?' In tithes and offerings." Stealing means not only taking what is not yours but keeping for yourself what belongs to someone else. Squandering our time, burying our talents, or depositing all of our treasures in worldly affairs rather than investing in kingdom-work is tantamount to theft (see Eph. 5:15–16; Matt. 25:14–30; 1 Cor. 9; 16:1–3). Failing to give back to God is an abuse of his generosity.

FAITH THAT WORKS IN A POSTMODERN AGE

A faith that works is a faith that influences. Bogus faith falls flat. It produces zero results. Charles Swindoll makes the point of this spiritual truth in his book *Improving Your Serve* with the following illustration:

> Let's pretend that you work for me. In fact, you are my executive assistant in a company that is growing rapidly. I'm the owner and I'm interested in expanding overseas. To pull this off, I make plans to travel abroad and stay there until the new branch office gets established. I make all the arrangements to take my family in the move to Europe for six to eight months, and I leave you in charge of the busy stateside organization. I tell you that I will write you regularly and give you direction and instructions.
>
> I leave and you stay. Months pass. A flow of letters are mailed from Europe and received by you at the national headquarters. I spell out all my expectations. Finally, I return. Soon after my arrival I drive down to the office. I am stunned! Grass and weeds have grown up high. A few windows along the street are broken. I walk into the receptionist's room and she is doing her nails, chewing gum, and listening to her favorite disco station. I look around and notice the waste baskets are overflowing, the carpet hasn't been vacuumed for weeks, and nobody seems concerned that the owner has returned. I ask about your whereabouts and someone in the crowded lounge area points down the hall and yells, "I think he's down there." Disturbed, I move in that direction and bump into you as you are finishing a chess game with our sales manager. I ask you to step into my office (which has been temporarily turned into a television room for watching afternoon soap operas).
>
> "What in the world is going on, man?"
>
> "What do ya' mean?"

"Well, look at this place! Didn't you get any of my letters?"

"Letters? Oh, yeah—sure, got every one of them. As a matter of fact, we have had *letter study* every Friday night since you left. We have even divided all the personnel into small groups and discussed many of the things you wrote. Some of those things were really interesting. You'll be pleased to know that a few of us have actually committed to memory some of your sentences and paragraphs. One or two memorized an entire letter or two! Great stuff in those letters!"

"Okay, okay—you got my letters, you studied them and meditated on them, discussed and even memorized them. BUT WHAT DID YOU DO ABOUT THEM?"

"Do? Uh—we didn't *do* anything about them."[37]

Obviously, this kind of behavior is professional buffoonery. In fact, it will put a company out of business in no time. But how much less ludicrous are believers who know the truth but refuse to obey it? A lack of concern about spiritual growth and obedience leads to mediocrity. Mediocre Christians are in a self-absorbed spiritual slumber so consumed with their own little world that violating God's law becomes routine. Their faith is irrelevant to the world around them.

Real religion, said William Penn, does not take men out of the world but puts them into it, in the hope of bettering it.[38] The great sin of omission is to remain quietly uninvolved in our plummeting law-breaking culture. Biblical Christianity lived out in loving action acts as a crucial motivating force inspiring moral conduct.

The literary genius Fyodor Dostoyevsky said that without God, everything is permitted.[39] A society that cuts itself off from the spiritual roots of its Judeo-Christian/moral heritage is doomed to moral deterioration. The proclamation of God's law and the good news of the Gospel are our only hope for a moral uplift. It is the hope of salvation for a downward spiraling postmodern generation.

In the movie *Superman* there is a scene where Clark Kent is angry and frustrated after a football game in which he was restricted to being an assistant manager. He possesses supernatural powers but must hide them from peers who don't accept him because he is not a star, only a team helper confined to the sidelines. Kent's father puts his arm around the soon-to-be "Superman" and says, "Son, you are here for a special reason. I don't know what that reason is—but I know one thing—it's not to score touchdowns."[40]

Like the fictional character Superman, we too are here for a special reason. But *we* are equipped with the power of God (Eph. 3:20). Our responsibility is to apply the Golden Rule in a society riddled with crime and theft. Our mission is to radiate the love of Christ and to proclaim the truth of Christ to a hurting, postmodern culture. We are called to steward our gifts and maximize our lives for the extension of his spiritual kingdom. To shrink back from our calling is to steal from God by withholding the gifts he has given to us for his sovereign purposes. Authentic Christian witnesses will light a candle in the dark and will help replenish the moral capital of our law-breaking society.

SMALL GROUP DISCUSSION QUESTIONS

1. What is the Golden Rule and where is it found in Scripture? Does it regularly or occasionally cross your mind to apply this rule to all areas of your life? Why or why not?

2. What are some of the common ways the Eighth Commandment is violated? How have you seen it violated at your place of work? Do you ever break this command? Discuss.

3. What does the author mean by heart stealing? Have you allowed your heart to be stolen? How can we prevent this from happening to us or avoid doing it to others?

4. After reading the author's critique of gambling, do you believe it violates the Eighth and Tenth Commandments? Why or why not? Explain the reasons why Christians should not be involved in the gambling industry.

5. How do believers steal from God? Does the Eighth Commandment speak to those who withhold their time, talents, and treasures?

6. Discuss the impact authentic Christian witnesses who live out their faith with integrity can have on the postmodern culture.

TELLING THE TRUTH IN AN AGE OF DISHONESTY

"You shall not bear false witness against your neighbor."
Exodus 20:16

We live in an age of dishonesty. This is due in part to the entitlement mentality that has blossomed across our legal landscape in the last few decades. The unrestrained growth of "new rights" has spawned a litigation explosion in America. Taking one another to court is one of our country's most popular indoor legal sports.

Judith Haime claimed to have psychic powers. Several years ago, she sought treatment for a physical problem. The hospital administered a CAT scan and Judith was injected with a dye, which she alleges caused her to lose her psychic abilities. She sued the doctor and the hospital and won nearly $1 million in damages.[1] One can't help but wonder why her psychic powers did not enable her to envision that CAT scans are not "psychic friendly." More than likely, the lust for money was the real power driving her sensibilities.

One day a man named Dan White sneaked into San Francisco's City Hall and savagely gunned down the mayor and city supervisor. Hauled into court, White pleaded temporary insanity. He dogmatically claimed that a steady diet of junk food had raised his blood sugar and corrupted and confused his brain. It became known as the infamous "Twinkie Defense."[2]

A man in California was livid because he found the noise from his neighbor's private basketball court disruptive. He sued; the neighbor countersued. Both sought more than $100,000 in punitive damages.[3]

...rica has become what *Time* magazine called a nation of cry-babies. People just want someone to blame when life doesn't go their way, when things don't turn out just right. It is a hedonistic assumption so widely shared that *Time* calls it an "American faith"—with lawyers as its priesthood.[4]

In biblical times, the Ninth Commandment was primarily concerned with the practice of courtroom justice. Its original focus was on the prevention of perjury by a witness in a judicial trial. In the ancient world, courtroom justice was rather simple. There were no shrewd lawyers like F. Lee Bailey, no fingerprints, no DNA blood tests to be used as evidence. Nor were there any "dream teams" formed on behalf of wealthy clients to strategize a miracle legal defense. Everything in those ancient courtrooms depended on the testimony of *witnesses*. The Old Testament tells us about Naboth who was killed because two scheming witnesses testified against him, saying that he cursed God and the king (1 Kings 21:13). Witnesses could hold decisive sway over life and death.[5] Based on the unanimous testimony of two or three witnesses, the accused could receive the death penalty (Deut. 17:6; 19:15). False witnesses subvert justice, tearing away at the reputation and even the life of their neighbor. Honest witnesses help safeguard the execution of justice.

Like a club and a sword and a sharp arrow is a man who bears false witness against his neighbor. (Prov. 25:18)

The Third Commandment was given to protect God's name and reputation. The Ninth is concerned with protecting the name and reputation of our neighbors. In ancient Israel, a good name was essential for one's preservation. Solomon said, "A good name is to be more desired than great riches, favor is better than silver and gold" (Prov. 22:1). Oftentimes, a good name was necessary not only for human progress but also for survival.

Doctor Sam Sheppard was convicted in 1954 of murdering his wife after a trial that became the basis for the TV series *The Fugitive* and was as sensational as the O. J. Simpson trial. Sheppard served ten years in prison, then was acquitted in a 1966 retrial. Still, many people thought he got away with murder. Hounded out of medicine, he drank himself to death, dying in 1970 at the age of forty-six.[6] A tarnished name can prove fatal.

The justice system exists for the welfare of human beings. This gets messy when justice is not administered impartially or where lying witnesses spout fabrications to protect themselves or to bring others down for a lucrative money deal. The Ninth Commandment was given to safeguard human honor, life, marriage, and property[7] and to encourage "truth-telling." "The Lord detests lying lips, but he delights in men who are truthful" (Prov. 12:22 NIV).

There are many ways this commandment is violated. Here are six for consideration.

THE SIN OF LYING

Clearly recalling the Ten Commandments, Hosea 4:2 mentions five different sins: "cursing, lying and murder, stealing and adultery" NIV. Aimed at preserving the good name of an individual, the Ninth Commandment condemns lying. A lie is a voluntary speaking of an untruth with an intent to deceive or harm.

Parables, figurative speeches, and rhetorical hyperboles are not lies. These are all used as either encounter mechanisms, illumination devices, or merely to make a point. For example, Jesus told parables not with the intent to deceive but to instruct the hearers.[8]

The Ten Commandments are not stuffy principles designed to stifle our joy or cramp our lives. They are liberating absolutes designed to regulate just relationships. "When truth is replaced by deceit in any relationship, that relationship loses its value."[9] Sticks and stones can break our bones, but lies can crack our hearts, ruin reputations, vandalize marriages, and start riots. Martin Luther said, "A lie is like a snowball. The longer it is rolled on the ground the larger it becomes."[10]

Patterson and Kim conclude from their research that "Just about everyone lies—91 percent of us lie regularly." They say that the majority of us find it hard to get through a week without lying. One in five can't make it through a single day—and we're talking about conscious, premeditated lies. In fact, the way some people talk about trying to do without lies, you'd think that they were smokers trying to get through a day without a cigarette.

When we refrain from lying, it's less often because we think it's wrong than for a variety of other reasons, among them the fear of being caught.

We lie to just about everyone, and the better we know someone, the likelier we are to have told them a serious lie.[11]

The Ninth Commandment condemns lying because it leads to the general breakdown of communities. Trust erodes and communication collapses. For societies to advance, there must be at least a minimal degree of trust in communication. Lying often accompanies every other kind of sin, from murder and adultery to tax fraud and stealing. The more lies the liar tells, the more the liar's psychological barriers against lying wear down; lies seem more necessary, less deceitful; the ability to make moral distinctions eventually is lost.

Lying has become a trait of the American character. People lie and don't even think about it.[12] Sadly, many believers are not far behind.

The sin of lying has been a problem throughout history—even in the church. Dr. G. Campbell Morgan called transgressions such as lying "the sins in good standing."[13] Christians can grow so accustomed to lying that it no longer brings conviction.

Bishop Warren A. Candler was preaching about the lies of Ananias and Sapphira (Acts 5:1–11) and asked the congregation, "If God still struck people dead for lying, where would I be?" The congregation snickered a bit, but the smiles disappeared when the Bishop shouted, "I'd be right here—*preaching to an empty church!*"[14]

We live in a postmodern culture of liars. This is the outcome when only one in ten Americans believes in all of the Ten Commandments. Forty percent believe in five or fewer commandments.[15] As our culture moves further away from God's law, more people break their marriage vows, more criminals stalk our streets, and more people lie to and deceive each other.

The problem of lying continues to rage on in the church. As God's law takes a nosedive and the culture presses in on the church, the seeds of lying find fertile soil. The only remedy is to love the truth enough to tell it. Christians must be truth-tellers. Telling the truth builds respect and establishes trust. That is one way we will earn the respect of a falling postmodern culture.

DECEPTION

Deception is a close relative to lying. Deception is a cultural trait embedded in our national character. To deceive is to obliterate one's human dignity. A proper self-evaluation is contorted by a frayed moral conscience. The self-deceived can become like Samson, who "did not know that the Lord had departed from him" (Judg. 16:20).[16]

Deceiving involves masking part of the truth or twisting the details enough to lead others astray. As the poet Sir Walter Scott said, "Oh, what a tangled web we weave when first we practice to deceive."[17]

In the PBS special *The Truth About Lying*, Bill Moyers reported that "the seven astronauts who died in the *Challenger* space shuttle disaster were never told of the dangers of launching in cold temperatures. A behind-the-scenes debate raged between the engineers of Morton Thiokol on one side and that company's managers and National Aeronautics and Space Administration (NASA) officials on the other. To bolster NASA's public image, information about the dangers of the launch was suppressed. When Morton Thiokol's engineers refused to give the go-ahead, they were removed from the decision-making process. In spite of their serious objections, *Challenger* was launched and millions witnessed the disastrous consequences. Once the private debate became public, the world learned of NASA's deception and cover-up.[18]

The Pentagon has a saying, "The truth is so precious it needs to be protected by a bodyguard of lies."[19] But when fallen human beings start applying controversial maxims to everyday affairs, there will be trouble. People are generally more concerned about their own advancement, protection, and preservation than they are about the primacy of reality and truth. "People whose primary agenda is centered on self-will quickly prevaricate when something threatens that self-centered agenda."[20] Deception can lead to innocent people losing their lives.

Libel is one form of deception that can destroy a person's reputation. Libel is deliberately, even maliciously, spreading false information about another person that gives an unfavorable impression. A politician, for example, in the battle to get votes will distort an opponent's ideas so that it looks like the opponent communicated something different from what was actually said. Self-deception quickly follows when the guilty politician tries to justify *to himself* the twisting of his opponents' words (i.e., "The country needs me and my ideas—a few white lies will make my deserved status and credibility overshadow that of my unworthy opponents").

God's law leaves no room for self-justifying deception: "Do not steal. Do not lie. Do not deceive one another" (Lev. 19:11 NIV).

Of course, twisting someone's words is not limited to the politician. We can all plummet to the libel level. Human beings are incredibly self-protective. All forms of lying and deceit are ways to make ourselves look better before other people. They are ways to hide our shame. Eventually, truth is emptied of meaning. Lies and believing lies become the easy road.

GOSSIP

Gossipers are people who chatter idly about others. Gossip is "sharing damaging information about someone or something with another person who is not part of the solution."[21] While the one spreading gossip may not be lying, he or she is still being untruthful, sharing negative information about someone with no intent to preserve that person's good name.

Gossip systematically violates the Golden Rule and is a sign of an unloving heart. Gossipers would not appreciate others talking about their mistakes, faults, or shortcomings in minute detail, but are more concerned with getting a hearing for their own self-promotion and ego-gratification than they are about loving their neighbors. They thrive on nit-picking at half-truths, prattling stories about others to massage their own insecure little hearts. They stir up strife and cause discord whenever they can.

A perverse man stirs up dissension, and gossip separates close friends (Prov. 16:28 NIV).

Those who spread gossip often feel justified in passing on the information, regardless of how much it might hurt another person, because they believe the information is true. They are standing for the truth. But all too often the gossiper is telling only part of the story, a story out of context. Seldom does the gossiper consider that passing along negative truths more often than not plants impressions that are biased and unfair.

The gossiper always finds a ready audience. The information is just too interesting to be ignored, and so the listener passes it on, continuing the chain of gossip. "The words of a whisperer are like dainty morsels, and they go down into the innermost parts of the body" (Prov. 18:8).

Jewish rabbinic tradition forbids speaking negative truths about others unless the person to whom you are speaking needs the information.[22] Two centuries ago, the Swiss theologian Jonathan K. Lavater offered a prudent guideline concerning the spreading of negative information: "Never tell evil of a man if you do not know it for a certainty, and if you know it for a certainty, then ask yourself, 'Why should I tell it?'"[23]

Unfortunately, most gossipers are so fixated with their own needs and struggles that they rarely acknowledge their problem of spreading gossip. Exchanging critical news about others spices up their day. Gossip is the malevolent seasoning people need to invigorate their otherwise boring lives. If they could somehow look past their tongues to examine their hearts in regard to gossip, it may suddenly reveal that the Golden Rule, "Do unto others as you would have others do unto you" is being trampled. Even though most of us want embarrassing information about ourselves kept quiet, most of us refuse to be equally discreet concerning others' shortcomings.[24]

SLANDER

Slander is the spreading of malicious information with the intent to bring harm. While gossip and slander are close cousins, slander always has the intention of hurting someone and, most of the time, the negative information shared is false. Slander is a form of murder. It attacks someone's name and reputation. Some refer to it as "character assassination." Slander violates the Ninth Commandment not only because it violently bears false witness against one's neighbor but also because it reflects a vengeful heart. God's law instructs that we must "not take vengeance, nor bear any grudge against the sons of your people, but you shall love your neighbor as yourself" (Lev. 19:18). Furthermore, the Scriptures tell us that we are never to "pay back evil for evil to anyone," but are exhorted to strive for peace with all men (Rom. 12:17–18).

Words are incredibly powerful. They can bring encouragement and healing ("Pleasant words are a honeycomb, sweet to the soul and healing to the bones" Prov. 16:24), but they can also lead to hatred, pain, and even death ("Death and life are in the power of the tongue" Prov. 18:21).

A Jewish folktale, set in nineteenth-century Eastern Europe, tells of a man who went through a small community slandering the rabbi. One day, feeling suddenly remorseful, he begged the rabbi for forgiveness and offered to undergo any form of penance to make amends. The rabbi told him to take a feather pillow from his home, cut it open, and scatter the feathers to the wind. The man did as he was told and returned to the rabbi. "Am I now forgiven?"

"Almost," was the response. "You just have to perform one last task: Go and gather all the feathers."

"But that's impossible," the man protested, "for the wind has already scattered them."

"Precisely," the rabbi answered.[25]

The rabbi in this story understands that the damage done by slander often cannot be undone. The flames of slander are forever burned into the psyches of the hearers, particularly the busybody types who revel in pernicious stories.

Shakespeare's riveting play *Othello* speaks volumes here. The play is about a jealous husband who listens to and believes slanderous rumors that his wife is having an affair. In his rage he murders his wife, learning almost immediately afterward that the rumors were all lies. For Othello, "Hell," as an old aphorism teaches, "is truth seen too late."[26]

FLATTERY

Flattery is bestowing insincere, excessive praise with self-serving motives. Men who shower women with exaggerated compliments with the goal of taking advantage of them later or getting something in return are stooping to flattery. Women who pamper men with praise out of their own motives of self-interest also are engaging in flattery. Kings, rulers, business executives, leaders, and lovers who flatter others for personal gratification or to boost their position of power break the Ninth Commandment. God's Word speaks to this issue as well:

> Help, Lord, for the godly man ceases to be, for the faithful disappear from among the sons of men. They speak falsehood to one another; With flattering lips and with a double heart they speak. May the Lord cut off all flattering lips, the tongue that speaks great things (Ps. 12:1–3).

Self-flattery, a pleasing self-deception, is also a violation of God's law.[27] To be puffed up with vain conceit, to applaud and commend ourselves in our own minds, and to think that we excel all others in what we have is a clandestine trap of self-flattery. The Bible warns, "I say to every man among you not to think more highly of himself than he ought to think; but to think so as to have sound judgment" (Rom. 12:3).

In postmodern society, the ethic of self-denial is exchanged for the ethic of self-actualization. The postmodernist seeks not to foist his own certainties on others but to find psychological fulfillment in life. Looking out for No. 1 demands self-absorption, self-centeredness, and a constant search for ways to satisfy a state of restless, perpetually unsatisfied desire. Twenty years ago Christopher Lasch, in his provocative book *The Culture of Narcissism*, warned that America was in danger of bargaining away her future.[28] Christians must wage war against the seductive lure of the egocentric, emotionally shallow, narcissistic trends shaping the American mind. God instructs us to find fulfillment in a relationship with him, not in stroking ourselves (John 15:11). While it is important to find satisfaction in our calling and to strive for excellence, our adequacy is not to be in ourselves, but "our adequacy is from God" (2 Cor. 3:5). Although our culture promotes self-flattery, we must glean from the wisdom of Solomon:

> Let another praise you, and not your own mouth; a stranger and not your own lips (Prov. 27:2).

FALSE PROPHETS

By getting a clearer picture on the destructive potential of lying in all forms, it becomes more evident why the Bible fulminates so vehemently against *false prophets*.[29] Liars deceive and lead people astray. False prophets misrepresent the God of truth. They lead people back into slavery by cleverly indoctrinating them with false teaching (Deut. 13:1–18).

Religious pluralism in American has opened the doors to an array of "New Messiahs" who have used biblical terminology and spiritual principles to their own ends. Self-proclaimed prophets, Eastern gurus and New Age teachers abound. Prophet-leaders, like the late David Koresh, make confusing and inflated promises of fellowship and manipulate through emotion and intimidation tactics in order to build their own kingdoms. Where did this so-called prophet lead his loyal followers? On April 19, 1993, (day fifty-one of the siege), the world watched in horror as the Branch Davidian compound burst into flames. Koresh and somewhere between seventy-five and eighty-five of his disciples died in the city-block-sized inferno. The worst of Koresh's apocalyptic prophecies had come to pass.[30]

The 1997 mass suicide of thirty-nine Heaven's Gate cult members was one of the worst in U.S. history. The group's delusionary leader, just days before the mysterious self-imposed deaths, gave the final call: "Your only chance to survive is to leave with us." Videos were recorded of members making a final statement. Then thirty-nine people put on new sneakers, packed flight bags, and poisoned themselves in the belief that a passing UFO will whisk them off to celestial bliss. Instead, the thirty-nine were found on their beds—dead.

We all have vulnerabilities. When someone is feeling exceedingly anxious, uncertain, hurt, lonely, unloved, confused, or guilty, that person is a prime prospect for those who come in the guise of religion offering a way out.[31]

Preserving the truth is a continual struggle. For those who place great emphasis on spiritual experiences, it is easy to succumb to strange religious fervor or the sensational predictions of prophet figures. Emotions become more powerful than logic. New spiritual revelations become more authoritative than biblical truth. Christians must be very careful not to be swayed by the self-authenticating revelations of a man or woman that are contrary to the apostolic body of biblical truth. The faith was once for all delivered to the saints (Jude 3). The Greek term *hapax* means "once for all," because the foundational truths of the

Christian message were given to the church at the beginning; it did not come in installments. The content of the apostolic gospel is fixed, not to be edited or revised for each new generation (Acts 2:42; Rom. 6:17; Gal. 1:23). The foundation truths of the Christian faith cannot be changed. They are nonnegotiable. After all, we cannot effectively battle the vices of lying and deception if we allow the church's vision of the truth to be obscured.[32] Truth and falsehood cannot exist side by side (2 Cor. 6:14).

IS LYING EVER JUSTIFIED?

Lying, as I've already stated, is a falsehood spoken purposely with the aim of deceiving and/or harming someone. But is there any room for justifiable falsehood? Is it a sin to purposely deceive a murderer who asks where his victim has gone or a mad tyrant bent on mass destruction? Is lying justified under these rare conditions? Philosopher Francis Hutcheson paints this picture:

> May not a singular necessity supersede the common rule of veracity, too? Suppose a Genghis Khan, or any such Eastern monster, resolved on the massacre of a whole city if he finds they have given any protection to his enemy, and asking a citizen in whom he confides about this fact, whether his enemy had ever been sheltered by the citizens; and that by deceiving the monster, he can preserve the lives of hundreds of thousands, and of their innocent babes; whereas telling him the truth shall occasion the most horrible slaughter: could a wise man's heart reproach him justly for breaking through the common law of veracity, and conquering the natural impulse toward it, upon such strong motives of humanity?[33]

Would it be wrong to lie to an enemy who is out to destroy those you love? In World War II, for example, the Allies not only kept information concerning the planned invasion of Normandy a secret; they also staged an elaborate hoax to cause the German troops to believe it would happen at a different time and place.

Thomas Aquinas believed that the Bible provided some examples of lying which made it difficult to object categorically to all lies. He distinguished between three classes of lies: the officious, or helpful, lies; the jocose lies, told in jest; and the mischievous, or malicious, lies told to harm another person. Only the latter did Aquinas constitute a sin.

Following Aquinas, Luther distinguished three kinds of lies as well: the humorous (a joke), the helpful (protecting the innocent), and the harmful (to hurt one's neighbor).

Following in the footsteps of Augustine (A.D. 354–430), the greatest theologian among the Latin fathers, many church leaders and theologians rejected the helpful lie, or what some call the "lie of necessity."[34] Augustine did not advocate betraying someone under dire circumstances, but he left no room for a justifiable falsehood. His solution was to remain silent. Evildoers or potentially dangerous perpetrators have no right to the information.

Those who hold this position deserve our respect. They recognize that lies injure people. Truthfulness is essential to the preservation of any society. Even the devils themselves, as philosopher and Anglican minister Samuel Johnson surmised, do not lie to one another, since the society of hell could not subsist without truth any more than others.[35]

Suspicions of widespread professional duplicity can account for much of the loss of trust in our culture. There has been a major decline in public confidence in lawyers, bankers, businessmen, doctors and, especially, politicians. Honesty is still important to people. But simple honesty is no longer that simple. In a postmodern culture, truth claims are subject to endless reinterpretation and are incapable of any precise, explicit meanings. What is "true" for one person may not be "true" for somebody else.

President Bill Clinton, according to psychologist Robert Jay Lifton, is the nation's first "postmodern president." Not bound by objective standards of truth, Mr. Clinton is able to continually reinvent himself, flexibly adapting his ideology, his behavior, and his very personality to the needs of the moment.[36] Lifton meant this as a compliment—a desirable model of his postmodernist psychological theory of mental health. For postmoderns, truth is culturally conditioned and can continually be slanted to meet the needs of the moment. If truth is not absolute, it can be reshaped and revised repeatedly, without any concern about contradictions. "I did not tell her to lie" (in reference to the Monica Lewinsky scandal) may very well be what a postmodernist would say. If there is no truth, it is impossible to lie.[37]

Oftentimes people lie to save face, to get out of a jam, or to avoid embarrassment or humiliation. But even liars don't like to be lied to. It is convenient for them to slip out of their postmodern worldview and embrace a biblical perspective at these times. Liars share with those they deceive the desire not to be deceived. They reserve for themselves the right to view truth as a "matter of interpretation," but expect others to be straight with them. The committed postmodernist swims around in a cauldron of contradictions.

But the question we return to is, "Can lying ever be justified under any circumstances?" While we reject the postmodernist theories and repudiate lying in general, is it possible to condemn lying in every possible case? From my perspective, the Bible contains some examples that appear to support the *lie of necessity* under extreme or dire consequences.

The Hebrew midwives Shiphrah and Puah did not obey Pharaoh's command to put to death the Israelite baby boys. They let the boys live because they feared God (Ex. 1:17). When the king questioned the midwives about this, they responded, "Because the Hebrew women are not as the Egyptian women; for they are vigorous, and they give birth before the midwife can get to them" (v. 19). Clearly they told a lie. The falsehood was not intended to harm, however, but to protect innocent lives. The Bible gives no indication that the midwives sinned. Quite the contrary. They were blessed by God for their mercy on defenseless little babies. "So God was good to the midwives, and the people multiplied, and became very mighty" (v. 20).

Rahab told a lie when she said to the King of Jericho that she did not know where the spies were from or where they went (Josh. 2:4–6). Actually, she knew where they were from, why they were there, and where they were when the king inquired. She had taken them up to the roof and had hidden them under the stalks of flax (v. 6). She is praised for her towering faith because she had welcomed the spies in peace (Heb. 11:31). She was justified by an active faith "when she gave lodging to the spies and sent them off in a different direction" (James 2:25 NIV). Rahab's justifying works included telling a "life-preserving" falsehood as well as receiving the messengers and helping them to escape by another route. If she had told the truth, she would not have been able to help the spies get away.

To me it seems difficult to argue (as many have) that the midwives and Rahab were blessed for their faith, but not for their life-saving lies. The Bible's final verdict is that their faith was expressed definitively in their works. "It is an abstraction to disconnect the *effect* of their acts from the *path* they took to achieve that effect."[38]

The lie of necessity is only justified in *dire circumstances* (i.e., life and death situations). If a serial killer is hunting down your friend or loved one and demands to know where they are, you are morally justified to mislead or deceive him in order to protect an innocent life. Samuel Johnson stated:

> The General Rule is, that truth should never be violated; there must, however, be some exceptions. If, for instance, a murderer should ask you which way a man has gone.[39]

The lie of necessity does not violate the Ninth Commandment but is consistent with other exemptions that arise with other command-ments. For example, we must be in submission to the government (Fifth Commandment), but if the state demands that we worship the governor, we invoke the First Commandment which calls us to give our worship to the one and only true God. Murder is forbidden (Sixth Commandment), but capital punishment and self-defense do not nec-essarily violate this command even though killing is involved. Steal-ing is also forbidden (Eighth Commandment), but God permitted the Israelites to rob the Egyptians just before the Exodus (Ex. 3:22; 11:2; 12:35–36).[40] However, the lie of necessity must only be used in rare situations where it is clear that innocent lives are at stake.

Finally, I must briefly mention what some refer to as the *polite lie*: showing common courtesy and respect for the feelings of others. *Time* magazine ran a cover story on lying back in 1992. The essay makes an interesting point: Who wants to be told the truth all the time? "Gee, what an ugly tie." "Martha, you didn't actually pay for that haircut, did you?" "Frankly, Ted, I think your lack of creativity and basic intelli-gence is going to render you a penniless slob to be cared for by the state for the rest of your life."[41] Brute honesty is certainly insensitive and boorish. This kind of coldhearted speech poisons our moral atmosphere.

In contrast, the so-called polite lie deals more with social etiquette, such as complimenting someone's tie even though it's not one you would buy for yourself, or finding something pleasant to say about their new haircut even though you favored their old style, or saying thank you to an irate customer who is undeserving of any thanks. Generally speaking, we are dealing with social graces, rules of politeness and customs that nourish a friendly climate. Lies seek to lead a person into deception. Sensitivity to others and following edifying etiquette guidelines are not deception.

JESUS CHRIST: FULL OF GRACE AND TRUTH

In Philip Yancey's searching book *What's So Amazing About Grace?* Yancey tells the story of a British conference on comparative religions back in the 1950s, where scholars from around the world debated what, if any, belief was unique to the Christian faith. They began by eliminating the possibilities. Incarnation? Other religions had different versions of gods appearing in human form. Resurrection? Again, other religions had accounts of return from death. The dialogue continued for a considerable period of time until C. S. Lewis wandered into the room. "What's the rumpus about?" he asked, and heard in reply that his colleagues were discussing Christianity's unique contribution among world religions. Lewis responded, "Oh, that's easy. It's grace."[42]

After some discussion, the conferees had to concur that grace is the Christian faith's great distinctive. "The notion of God's love coming to us free of charge, no strings attached, seems to go against every instinct of humanity. The Buddhist eight-fold path, the Hindu doctrine of *karma*, the Jewish covenant, and the Muslim code of law—each of these offers a way to earn approval. Only Christianity dares to make God's love unconditional."[43]

Although the postmodern world is hostile toward Christian certainty in absolute truth, it still thirsts for grace. But a craving for grace without a transcendant standard of truth leads to license. God's biblical attributes of truth, justice, and wrath are watered down, stripped of their theological intent, or rejected altogether. God is not judgmental, but a tolerant, open-minded supreme being of love. The secret hunger for grace keeps the worldliest of humans struggling to fill the void, while God's truth is ignored.

The God of grace entered this world in the person of Jesus Christ. God the Son entered history. Grace was lavished upon the world in superabundance. The apostle John recorded, "For the law was given through Moses; grace and truth were realized through Jesus Christ" (John 1:17). The law can only be properly understood as it moves toward the majestic goal of pointing believers to the Messiah, Jesus Christ. The law serves as the divine tutor to lead us to Christ (Gal. 3:24). The law of grace and truth was brought to completion when the God-man stepped into the world to fulfill the divine salvation plan.

While God suffused the world with his grace,[44] he does not pour out his grace apart from truth. Jesus came full of grace and truth. Truth is the foundation of grace. Faith is the doorway to grace. Paul said, "For by grace you have been saved through faith" (Eph. 2:8). God's grace must be received and his truth believed. It is impossible to get an accurate picture of God apart from his grace and truth.

Here we see evangelical Christianity and postmodernism in contrast. In Christianity, grace is God's undeserved, unmerited favor given to the world carefully packaged in a Savior. But grace is always wrapped in truth. In postmodernism, grace is cast in secular dress (e.g., to be friendly, accepting, tolerant). Truth is a personal, cultural construction (e.g., whatever works for me).

In Christianity, there is an author. We live in a grand story where God's plan will unfold victoriously. We have hope. In postmodernism, there is no author, no grand story, and no future vision. The postmodernist has no hope.

As I mentioned in chapter 7, *gospel hope* is the most powerfully life-enhancing force in all of human existence. Jesus Christ offers hope to a world gone awry. In an insecure postmodern culture where objective truth is denied and reality is what you (or your culture) make it, Christians have the opportunity to demonstrate that there is a unifying center to reality. That center appeared in Jesus Christ—the focal point of God's grand story and the bearer of truth to the world. He is the one who identifies with a suffering world and is the only one that is worthy to dictate ultimate truth. The playlet *The Long Silence* says it all:

> At the end of time, billions of people were scattered on a great plain before God's throne.
>
> Most shrank back from the brilliant light before them. But some groups near the front talked heatedly—not with cringing shame, but with belligerence.
>
> "Can God judge us? How can he know about suffering?" snapped a pert young brunette. She ripped open a sleeve to reveal a tattooed number from a Nazi concentration camp. "We endured terror ... beatings ... torture ... death!"
>
> In another group [an African-American boy] lowered his collar. "What about this?" he demanded, showing an ugly rope burn. "Lynched ... for no crime but being black!"
>
> In another crowd, a pregnant schoolgirl with sullen eyes. "Why should I suffer?" she murmured. "It wasn't my fault."
>
> Far out across the plain there were hundreds of such groups. Each had a complaint against God for the evil and suffering he permitted in this world. How lucky God was to live in heaven where all is sweetness and light, where there is no weeping or fear, no hunger or hatred. What did God know of all that man had been forced to endure in this world? For God leads a pretty sheltered life, they said.
>
> So each of these groups sent forth a leader, chosen because he had suffered the most. A Jew, a Negro, a person from Hiroshima, a horribly deformed arthritic, a thalidomide child. In the center of the plain they consulted with each other. At last they were ready to present their case. It was rather clever.
>
> Before God could be qualified to be their judge, he must endure what they endured. Their decision was that God should be sentenced to live on earth—as a man!
>
> "Let him be born a Jew. Let the legitimacy of his birth be doubted. Give him a work so difficult that even his family will think him out of his mind when he tries to do it. Let him be

betrayed by his closest friends. Let him face false charges, be tried by a prejudiced jury, and convicted by a cowardly judge. Let him be tortured.

"At the last, let him see what it means to be terribly alone. Then let him die. Let him die so that there can be no doubt that he died. Let there be a great host of witnesses to verify it."

As each leader announced his portion of the sentence, loud murmurs of approval went up from the throng of people assembled.

And when the last had finished pronouncing sentence, there was a long silence. No one uttered another word. No one moved. For suddenly all knew that God had already served his sentence.[45]

Illustrations and stories are powerful ways to communicate the Gospel to postmoderns. The grand salvation story of God instructs the mind, tutors the imagination, creates a purposeful vision, and inspires hope. In an age filled with lying and deception, the truth must be told. Christians must be truth-tellers, especially when it comes to telling the great story of God's grace and truth.

Reaching a postmodern culture doesn't happen merely with Christian *rhetoric*, but with love-embodied *reality*. It won't happen by simply declaring carefully formulated doctrines, but by thoughtful, authentic lifestyles. Our lives must be consistent with the message that we speak. What we need more than anything else is not more *textbooks* but more *text-people*.[46] Our character speaks louder than our words. The messenger is as important as the message. It is at this point that telling how God's story intersects with our story will have its greatest impact.

As Christians we must stand against the postmodern denial of truth. But we must tell the truth with gentleness and respect (1 Peter 3:15). Even though truth can be offensive (see Mark 14:61–65), we can still both display the love of Christ and articulate the truth of the Gospel. Chuck Swindoll shares a delightful story of how this can be done in his book *Improving Your Serve*:

A number of years ago, Dr. Waltke, another pastor, a graduate student at Brandeis University (also a seminary graduate), and

I toured the mother church of the First Church of Christ Scientist in downtown Boston. The four of us were completely anonymous to the elderly lady who smiled as we entered. She had no idea she was meeting four evangelical ministers—and we chose not to identify ourselves, at least at first.

She showed us several interesting things on the main floor. When we got to the multiple-manual pipe organ, she began to talk about their doctrine and especially their belief about no judgment in the life beyond. Dr. Waltke waited for just the right moment and very casually asked:

"But, Ma'am, doesn't it say somewhere in the Bible, 'It is appointed unto man once to die and after that the judgment?'" He could have quoted Hebrews 9:27 in the Greek! But he was so gracious, so tactful with the little lady. I must confess, I stood back thinking, "Go for it, Bruce. Now we've got her where we want her!"

The lady, without a pause, said simply, "Would you like to see the second floor?"

You know what Dr. Waltke said? "We surely would, thank you."

She smiled, somewhat relieved, and started to lead us up a flight of stairs.

I couldn't believe it! All I could think was, "No, don't let her get away. Make her answer your question!" As I was wrestling within, I pulled on the scholar's arm and said in a low voice, "Hey, why didn't you nail the lady? Why didn't you press the point and not let her get away until she answered?"

Quietly and calmly he put his hand on my shoulder and whispered, "But, Chuck, that wouldn't have been fair. That wouldn't have been very loving, either—now would it?"

Wham! The quiet rebuke left me reeling. I shall *never* forget that moment. And to complete the story, you'll be interested to know that in less than twenty minutes he was sitting with the woman alone, tenderly and carefully speaking with her about the Lord Jesus Christ. She sat in rapt attention. He, the gracious peacemaker, had won a hearing. And I, the scalp-snatcher, had learned an unforgettable lesson.[47]

Speaking the truth with love honors the incarnational nature of Christianity. God wrapped his grace and truth in a person (John 1:14). God still wraps his grace and truth in his people and places them in a corrupt society to reflect his glory. We are called to be bearers of God's grace and truth—the grace that draws people from every nation, tribe, and tongue, and the truth that dispels the darkness of a world sinking more deeply into deception every day.

Telling the truth consistently in an age of dishonesty is a challenge. Existing deceptive practices and competitive stresses can make it difficult not to conform to the cultural mood. We struggle with the array of choices before us in daily life—whether to lie, equivocate, be silent, or tell the truth in any given situation. These can be difficult decisions because duplicity can take so many forms, be present to such different degrees, and have such different purposes and results.[48] Mark Twain's words come to mind: "When in doubt, tell the truth. It will confound your enemies and astound your friends."[49]

As Christians, we honor God and strengthen our cultural witness when we live authentic lives and tell the truth. We must be truth-tellers in every relationship, starting with God, and then "with parents, children, spouses; coworkers, employers, employees; pastors, parishioners; believer, unbeliever; friend and foe."[50]

Moreover, telling our neighbor the truth about God's grand story is a labor of love requiring two cares: "care for the topic, to get it right; and care for the person receiving your message, that she/he hear it right."[51] In a postmodern culture, we find ourselves talking to people who have never heard of Moses, know little about the Ten Commandments, and have adopted outlooks strikingly removed from that of the Bible. Christians must be involved in *worldview transformation*. That means thinking and speaking with theological precision. That means loving with Christ-centered reality. Truth-incarnate living will open the channels for others to experience and enter into God's truth and his covenant love.

SMALL GROUP DISCUSSION QUESTIONS

1. What was the primary purpose of the Ninth Commandment in ancient Israel? How did "truth-telling" safeguard the execution of justice?

2. What are the consequences of lying for the victim of the falsehoods and the liar? Why do people lie or deceive?

3. What is the difference between gossip and slander? Have you been hurt by gossip or slander? Discuss. From a biblical perspective, how should we respond when somebody spreads negative information about us or someone else? Would you respond differently to a believer than to an unbeliever?

4. Discuss how false prophecy violates the Ninth Commandment. Give some contemporary examples.

5. From the author's perspective, lying is justified in extreme or dire circumstances ("lie of necessity"). Do you agree or disagree? If you happened to be a Hebrew midwife back before the Exodus and were ordered by the king to put all infant boys to death, what would you do? What would you say to the king when he angrily asked for an explanation as to why his orders were disobeyed?

6. We are called to be truth-tellers. How can we communicate the Gospel effectively to postmoderns? Discuss the pros and cons of different approaches to witnessing.

SIMPLICITY AND CONTENTMENT IN A GREEDY, TIRED CULTURE

"You shall not covet."
Exodus 20:17

Proponents of the Enlightenment project assumed that meaning and morality could be found simply within the framework of human reason without any reference to God. Postmodern thinkers have challenged not only Enlightenment meaning but *all* meaning. The death of the doctrine of progress has led many people to abandon all meaning in life. Showered by mass consumerism, dwarfed by our giant technological inventions, and gripped by the postmodern undertow, the contemporary individual has come to feel very small, empty, and meaningless.

Materialism and affluence have risen to fill the void. Money, power, and things are connected with meaning. Michael Jordan's fame and his $44 million in 1994 earnings are coveted by people every day. But then Jordan could look with coveting eyes on Microsoft's CEO Bill Gates's net worth at $42 billion.[1] Many Americans remember the crass materialism of Imelda Marcos, living in splendor amid the deprivation of the Philippines. Having thousands and thousands of shoes and spending $4.5 million over one month in New York was common currency for Imelda Marcos.[2] Americans may scowl at her obsessive spending and ostentatious living, but I wonder how many of those same individuals covet a similar lifestyle for themselves?

In the apostle John's first letter, he warns about the "lust of the eyes" and the boastful pride of life (1 John 2:16). Many interpreters understand

John's statement to mean looking lustfully at someone. But it may mean being obsessed with the sheer act of "looking."[3] Perhaps the inspired apostle was concerned about the lust for looking itself, not just for the thing looked at, but a restless, roaming lust to stare at and visually explore anything interesting or compelling to the consumer appetites.

Television, magazines, advertising, and the like often inculcate covetous desires. These dark desires not only feed the self-absorbed consumer gluttony but also blur all boundaries and distinctions. Madonna is a classic example of the postmodern celebrity who can cross all the lines and still be esteemed as an inspirational role model by popular culture. Theologian David Wells points out that Madonna is "the quintessential virgin whore, by turns sophisticated and vulgar, vulnerable and bullet-proof, seductive and demure. She is, in many ways, a perfect personification of the postmodern reality: sensation without substance, motion without purpose, a self-created persona undergoing perpetual change for its own sake. In her world, everything is fluid and open. All boundaries and taboos are gone. Everything is possible."[4]

Meaning is marketed in a postmodern culture by appealing to and nourishing covetous desires. Since there is no transcendent meaning, we must create our own. The mediums of popular culture coax us to find meaning in life through image, style, wealth, and things. God's law is pushed farther into the mothballs as our culture is suspended in a hypnotic state of finding meaning through inner sensation and "having more."

America's greed has sown the seeds of fatigue. We are a tired culture. The quest for a little bit more kindles the flawed conclusion that happiness and contentment come only by material things and external events. Along with the everyday realities of bills, dirty laundry, excruciating deadlines, grocery shopping, job pressures, business trips, illness, unexpected company, relational difficulties—is it any wonder that we are a tired culture?

This anonymous piece capsulizes it very well.

I'm Tired

Yes, I'm tired. For several years I've been blaming it on middle-age, iron poor blood, lack of vitamins, air pollution, water pollution, saccharin, obesity, dieting, underarm odor, yellow wax build-up, and a dozen other maladies that make you wonder if life is really worth living.

But now I find out, tain't that.

I'm tired because I'm overworked.

The population of this country is 200 million. Eighty-four million are retired. That leaves 116 million to do the work. There are 75 million in school, which leaves 41 million to do the work. Of this total, there are 22 million employed by the government.

That leaves 19 million to do the work. Four million are in the armed forces, which leaves 15 million to do the work. Take from that total the 14,800,000 people who work for the state and city governments and that leaves 200,000 to do the work. There are 188,000 in hospitals, so that leaves 12,000 to do the work. Now, there are 11,998 people in prisons. That leaves just 2 people to do the work. You and me. And you're standing there reading this. No wonder I'm tired.[5]

Simplicity is the answer for people tired and weary. Simplicity is marked by a contented lifestyle that rests in God's grace. It is the commitment to clear out, scale down, and realize the essentials of what we truly need to live well. The intimate search for wholeness is not found by accumulating more things, but by entering into God's presence every single day. The joyful seventeenth-century Carmelite friar Brother Lawrence called it *practicing the presence of God*.[6] Spirituality, authenticity, creativity, understanding, and contentment flourish when the means of grace are applied to life.[7]

Simplicity frees us to recognize that the smallest details of our lives are to be savored because they reside under the sovereignty of God.[8] When we don't set boundaries and instead allow our lives to become too complicated, we lose the ability to see God's hand shaping the ordinary events that give expression to who we are. When we fail to resist the greedy passions that lurk within, God's Spirit is quenched and precious moments of contentment are suffocated by anxiety and distress.

The Tenth Commandment is rooted in the liberating quality of contentment. The other commandments, positively stated from first to last, emphasize loving God, worshiping in spirit and truth, sound theology, eternal life, respect for God-given authority, loving our neighbor, purity and faithfulness in marriage, good stewardship, and truth-telling. This Tenth Commandment, positively stated, affirms the value of contentment. The fullness of life is experienced by learning the secret of being content in all circumstances (Phil. 4:11–12). Contentment turns what we have into enough, and more.

Jesus said, "Take heed, and beware of covetousness: for a man's life consisteth not in the abundance of the things which he possesseth" (Luke 12:15 KJV). In Colossians 3:5 Paul says that covetousness amounts to idolatry. The greedy heart substitutes "possessions" for the proper object of humanity's search and worship—God. The Tenth Commandment tells us what warps our inner peace and tears away at the tapestry of contentment in our lives. "You shall not covet your neighbor's house; you shall not covet your neighbor's wife or his male servant or his female servant or his ox or his donkey or anything that belongs to your neighbor" (Ex. 20:17). The final absolute warns us about the covetous tendencies of the human heart.

DESIRES IN CONFLICT

Our desires have enormous influence over our lives. When God is not at the center of our desires, they can imprison us in despair and compel us to live as slaves to our futile appetites. Misplaced desires generate prayers like that of Augustine who cried out, "Give me chastity and continence, but not yet!" He was afraid that God would respond to his prayer and heal him of his addiction to lust sooner than he desired. The intensity of his inner struggles "laid waste" his soul and inflamed the emotional war within.[9]

The Tenth Commandment is aimed at the corrupt desires that germinate in the heart and are nurtured there. It does not condemn human desires, but the nourishing of desires that are contrary to God's law. Covetousness is normal desire gone out of control. Evil desires allowed to take root in the heart can turn into destructive deeds that cause hurt, division, and even death.

This is seen in the high-profile murder of six-year-old dream child JonBenét Ramsey, whose lifeless body was found gagged and strangled in a windowless room in the basement of the Ramseys' million-dollar mansion. The manifestation of unruly desires that led JonBenét's killer to carry out such horrific evil is complex. The prophet Jeremiah lamented, "The heart is more deceitful than all else and is desperately sick; who can understand it?" (Jer. 17:9). When one becomes intoxicated by the "invisible passion-like drug of self-indulgence" and turns aside to revel in selfish desires, there is no telling how far he or she will plunge into the depths of depravity and wickedness. The application of misplaced desires eventually becomes a cycle of addiction where stimulating encounters, relief, and the mad search for new experiences become ingrained in the recesses of the mind. The insatiable appetite to acquire, to own, to indulge, to take pleasure, to consume, is relentless. Rationality and moral self-control are dominated by the rising lust for power, an insidious power that becomes a sacred goal, a wholly consuming interest.[10]

The Tenth Commandment is God's loving call for his people to examine their hearts. Coveting resides somewhere between the nature and the action, the "disposition and the deed." The Tenth Commandment looks behind the deeds to the passionate heart and the steps taken to implement the plans one has forged there.[11] What lives in the heart will eventually surface in one way or another. Jesus said that out of the abundance of the heart the mouth speaks (Luke 6:45).

In order to stay free we must take God's moral law seriously. A postmodern culture casts aspersions on commands. But in an age of moral bankruptcy, the "thou shall nots" of God's law are important reminders of what offends God, defiles human life, and corrupts human thinking. Christians are not immune to the harmful thoughts that shape covetousness. The only way to guard against the development of malevolent appetites is to properly nurture our desires by setting our minds on things above and dwelling on truth, beauty, righteousness, purity, love, excellence, and the goodness God has ordained (see Col. 3:1–2; Phil. 4:8). As we practice being transformed by the renewing of the mind (Rom. 12:2), our inner as well as our outer lives become expanded, deepened, and richly freed, to enjoy goodness, justice, and lovingkindness (Mic. 6:8). Peace fills our hearts because we are no longer compelled by our own attempts to satisfy the depths of our soul and our longings for self-worth. We are freed to be content and to love because we can trust that God himself will satisfy us and gradually our false notions about him dissipate. Well-nurtured desires free us to pursue our true calling in life—to love God with all our heart, to love our neighbor as ourself, and to impact the world before us.

COVET NO ONE'S POSSESSIONS

Coveting is the excessive desire to have what someone else has. Covetousness amounts to idolatry because it puts self-interest and things in the place of God. Whatever I place my ultimate confidence and trust in, I worship.

The advance of consumerism* has resulted in a preoccupation with the immediate gratification of desire for material things. The Bible's warnings about the "love of money" are ignored as our culture sinks in the quicksand of wealth, materialism, and sensation. As far back as 1931, Christopher Dawson warned:

> We have entered on a new phase of culture—we may call it the Age of the Cinema—in which the most amazing perfection of scientific technique is being devoted to purely ephemeral objects, without any consideration of their ultimate justification. It seems as though a new society was arising which will acknowledge no hierarchy of values, no intellectual authority, and no social or religious tradition, but which will live for the moment in a chaos of pure sensation.[12]

Money, materialism, and the "itch for more" have throttled into high gear in our culture. Today's American dream has changed to: life, liberty, and the purchase of happiness.[13] When interviewers from the University of Michigan's Institute for Social Research asked what hampers the search for the good life, the most common answer was "We're short on money."[14] The research data show that a growing number of college students have a three-pronged strategic plan: money, power, and things (including vacation homes, expensive foreign automobiles,

---

*Consumerism denotes the economic theory that consumption expansion is always good for the economy.

yachts, and even airplanes). In surveys conducted at Duke University, the requests to the faculty were often, "Teach me to be a money-making machine."[15] The incubation of a coveting culture illustrates the old saying, "Know the price of everything but the value of nothing."

The French political philosopher Alexis de Tocqueville made a number of penetrating observations about the individualistic quality of American culture and the penchant for selfishness and amusement. He feared that the "pursuit of immediate material pleasures" and the love of money might eventually extinguish our spirit. "The prospect really does frighten me," de Tocqueville lamented, "that they may finally become so engrossed in a cowardly love of immediate pleasures that their interest in their own future and in that of their descendants may vanish, and that they will prefer tamely to follow the course of their destiny rather than make a sudden energetic effort necessary to set things right."[16]

De Tocqueville's fears were on target as we currently see the media moguls and Americans in general exalting wealth and happiness as the golden ticket to the "good life." Hollywood's Robin Leach reminds us that the *Lifestyles of the Rich and Famous* are the only way to really live. And former Texas Ranger outfielder Pete Incaviglia several years ago wanted us to know that not all professional athletes make $3 million to $4 million a year. "They don't realize that most of us only make $500,000."[17] The cultural obsession of money and possessions has choked the spirit of gratitude, leaving the average American indifferent toward the things of God. The search for truth has been replaced by the pursuit of prestige and success. Believers ensnared by the current hedonistic outlook exude nothing more than a "consumer Christianity" and have little to no impact on life in the here and now.

Covetous desires lead to addictive appetites for possessions, sex, and the like. It is the desire to acquire and accumulate. It differs from envy. The covetous person has a desire to have what others have. The envier does not want others to have either. Cornelius Plantinga, Jr., explains the distinction:

> To covet is to want somebody else's good so strongly ("inordinately," as the Christian tradition says) that one is tempted to

steal it. To envy is to resent somebody else's good so much that one is tempted to destroy it. The coveter has empty hands and wants to fill them with somebody else's goods. The envier has empty hands and therefore wants to empty the hands of the envied. Envy, moreover, carries overtones of personal resentment: an envier resents not only somebody else's blessing but also the one who has been blessed. Coveting focuses much more on objects than on persons: even when it focuses on persons, it tends to see them as objects . . . An envier resents; a coveter desires.[18]

The twisted passions of envy and covetousness erupted in the heart of a Texas cheerleader's mother several years ago. She deeply desired to see her daughter win a spot on the high school cheerleading squad. But something snapped as the weight and pressure of the fraternal twin desires went askance. She ended up hiring a hit man to take out her daughter's rival. Coveting a position for her daughter led to an envious "death wish." She resented somebody else's advance so much that she destroyed it.

Coveting is more than fantasizing, it's the formulating of a plan to get what one wants. In the Decalogue, the commandment forbids not only coveting material possessions such as a house, donkey, or ox (in modern terms, a more luxurious house, car, or truck), but also another's spouse. Coveting creates the surreptitious illusion that *having* constitutes *being*, that indulging brings lasting relief.

The promise of sexual pleasure appears to breathe new life into a person, at least for the moment. When covetous plans are forged, seduction and adultery are a few steps away. Coveting another man's wife often leads to adultery. But adultery strips the body of its intrinsic dignity and treats it as a commodity to be used, managed, even disposed of to suit one's devious desires.[19] The man who seduces another man's wife violates her dignity and his own integrity. Adultery is a defilement of God-ordained sexual wholeness. It leads to the dilapidation of the human being.

C. S. Lewis, in his book *The Abolition of Man*, argued that without the aid of trained emotions, the intellect is powerless against deep-seated appetites and impulses. "Such is the tragi-comedy of our situation,"

Lewis says, "we continue to clamor for those very qualities we are rendering impossible.... We make men without chests [i.e., people who no longer believe in virtue or have any persevering devotion to truth] and expect of them virtue and enterprise. We laugh at honour and are shocked to find traitors in our midst. We castrate and bid the geldings be fruitful."[20] Lewis's penetrating analysis sheds light not only on the contemptible lack of moral restraint in society but also on human superficiality and the loss of meaning. This is the result of the politically correct "emancipation" from the Judeo-Christian tradition.

When possessions are viewed as the barometer for success and completeness and the body is treated as a commodity to be used, the human spirit is crushed and dignity is destroyed. America may be the wealthiest nation on earth with an abundance of amusements, luxuries, and sensual delights, but we are not happier or more fulfilled because of it. "Never has a culture experienced such physical comfort combined with such psychological misery. Never have we felt so free or had our prisons so overstuffed. Never have we been so sophisticated above pleasure or so likely to suffer broken relationships."[21]

As Christians, we are called to set our minds on things above (Col. 3:2). We must hold loosely to things below—our possessions. Having material things is not wrong, but we are not to view these temporal items as if they are all that really matter. Moreover, we must exercise moral restraint. Our desires need to be managed and properly shaped by divine truth (Col. 3:5, 10–17). Our emotions must be complemented by reflective thought. The Word of God must get our full attention, for what we set our minds on determines the direction of our Christian lives.

A wonderful, imaginative short story by Nathaniel Hawthorne illustrates the necessity of having the right focus. It is entitled "The Great Stone Face." The tale centers around a man named Ernest who grew up in a village renowned for a natural wonder that rested just outside its boundaries. Nature had majestically carved in the side of a mountain the features of a human countenance so realistic that from a distance the Great Stone Face seemed positively to be alive.

All the features were noble and the expression was grand and sweet. Ernest, like all the children of the nearby village, was told of an ancient prophecy that at some future day a child would be born in the vicinity who was destined to become the greatest personage of his time and whose countenance, in manhood, would bear an exact resemblance to the Great Stone Face. Upon learning that the promised prophet had not yet appeared, the young Ernest clapped his hands above his head and exclaimed, "I do hope that I shall live to see him!"

Ernest, growing older, never forgot that prophecy learned at his mother's knee. It was always on his mind. And as he grew to manhood, Ernest allowed the Great Stone Face to become his teacher—meditating upon the countenance, looking to it for comfort, reading stories about it, speaking of it to those who would hear.

Years passed. Many came into the village claiming to be the promised one. But each time Ernest went out to meet the pretenders, he came away disappointed and sometimes almost despondent. For although these impostors claimed the honor, Ernest knew better. As a result of his devotion to the Face, he had become an expert on it. Surely Ernest, of all people, would know the one when he came. After each disappointment Ernest would return to the Face, peer into it and ask, "How long?" The granite features seemed to reassure him, "Fear not, Ernest, the man will come!"

Ernest was an old man now, his hair gray and the movement of his body slow. The one great sadness of his life was that he had never seen the prophet long foretold. One day a poet famous for his ode celebrating the Stone Face came to visit Ernest. They enjoyed each other's company and yet each spoke sadly—for they longed to see the Face enfleshed.

The two talked long and, as the day drew to a close, it came time for Ernest's daily discourse on the Great Stone Face. Each evening inhabitants of the neighboring village assembled in the open air for his stirring oration. There Ernest stood and spoke to the people, giving them what thoughts were in his heart and mind. Delivered with eloquence, the words were powerful because they accorded with his thoughts, and his thoughts had reality and depth because they harmonized with the devoted life he had always lived.

The poet, as he listened, grew teary-eyed. The being and character of Ernest were a nobler strain of poetry than he had ever written. The face of Ernest assumed a grandeur of expression, so imbued with benevolence, and with the Great Stone Face looming in the background, the poet suddenly realized what should have been obvious all along. For Ernest, he noticed, had a mild, sweet, beautiful countenance that looked like the Stone Face itself!

Moved by an irresistible impulse, the poet threw his arms aloft and began to shout to all who would hear—"Behold, behold! Ernest is himself the likeness of the Great Stone Face!" And with that all the people sitting about looked at Ernest and noticed that what the poet said was true. The prophecy was fulfilled! Ernest had become like his ideal.[22]

Hawthorne's story reverberates a salient truth, "What gets our attention gets us."[23] God declares in the First Commandment that his people are to focus their attention on him. Likewise, in the New Testament the writer to the Hebrews exhorted Christians to fix their eyes on Jesus (God incarnate) the author and perfecter of faith (Heb. 12:2). We either turn toward God or toward ourselves. When it's the latter we tend to make God into our image. But when our focus is on him, we naturally align ourselves with his Word, falling under his sovereign direction.

Like Hawthorne's Ernest, we can cultivate God-like characteristics and radiate a beautiful countenance by fixing our attention on the Savior. This will keep us from the rootless romanticism of postmodernism where individuals are incapable of forming or sustaining virtuous character, because "the self" abdicates moral control and one's foolish desires take over.

When David's attention was on the Lord he saw God's goodness and his heart was strengthened (Ps. 27:13–14). David's cry must be ours, "When Thou didst say, 'Seek My face,' my heart said to Thee, 'Thy face, O Lord, I shall seek.'" (v. 8).

LEARNING CONTENTMENT IN A WORLD OF SENSATION

More than sixty-six years ago, Aldous Huxley's speculative novel *Brave New World* set off a firestorm of controversy. The provocative Huxleyan vision was set in a futuristic and increasingly technical utopian dictatorship in which men and women lived in a seemingly idyllic environment. In this future time, the major world powers have united to avert the threat of war and the docile masses are manipulated through controlled economy and entertainment.

Yet peace has been achieved at a frightening cost. This chilly and aggressively rational new order dictates the course of human life from birth to death. Children are conceived and born in state-of-the-art factories, then reared and indoctrinated in a discipline that encourages blind acceptance of novel universal "truths."

With their classroom philosophies reinforced by subliminal recordings as they sleep, children grow into smiling, passive puppets who happily accept the doctrines of this "brave new world."

Families are outlawed and viewed as archaic. There are no more heroes, since there is no discernible oppression. Marital commitment is dead, romance is outdated, and promiscuity is encouraged. And if any of this causes a citizen a moment's anxiety, he has only to pop a few Soma pills, a drug that alleviates depression and, in reality, puts people on a comatose pleasure trip, keeping them in line with the laws of the techno-dictatorship.

Huxley's frightening vision of a world in which freedom is dead and all concepts of traditional morality are forgotten is the direction that the West, to some extent, is headed. Our freedom might not be controlled by a despotic government requiring its citizens to take mind-control drugs, but many thousands of Americans inebriate themselves on their own. As in Huxley's novel, the "pleasure principle" rules many American hearts. Drugs like heroin ravage the mind, rattle the senses, and twist human desires. Everyday life subjects the average person to a sea of sensuality. It is conceivable that in any given week of cable TV voyeurism, one may observe more sensual sights than his or her grandparents did in their entire lifetime. Through permissiveness, the craving for pleasure, and the zeal for wealth, the West is headed in a Huxleyan-type direction.

The Bible tells us that in the last days people will be "lovers of self, lovers of money, boastful, arrogant, revilers, disobedient to parents, ungrateful, unholy, unloving, irreconcilable, malicious gossips, without self-control, brutal, haters of good, treacherous, reckless, conceited, lovers of pleasure rather than lovers of God" (2 Tim. 3:1–4).

We should not be surprised to see the destructiveness of evil around us. Sin always rears its ugly head consistently in a godless society. God's command is that we do not allow cultural evils to control our way of living. No Christian is free from temptations. The lure of affluence, sensuality, and power are always before us. If we do not guard our hearts continually from the worldly toxins that attempt to seep into and contaminate the very source of who we are, they will affect everything we touch: our relationships, our marriage, our family, our job, our ministry for the Lord, and our witness to the world.

The apostle Paul challenged the world's view by showing the outcome of trying to find contentment through the pursuit of wealth and worldly pleasure. He warned that it caused people to "fall into temptation and a snare and many foolish and harmful desires which plunge men into ruin and destruction" (1 Tim. 6:9).

In fairness, money and pleasure are not in themselves evil. Money can do much good in providing for people, helping the poor, and furthering God's kingdom. Moreover, God is not against pleasure and provides us with everything for our enjoyment (1 Tim. 6:17). But he calls us to a *balanced* Christian life. Our trust is not to be in money nor our security in pleasure. Those who begin to view either as their life or reason for existing are in danger of being seduced by the narcotic effects of such things. As Paul stated clearly, many foolish and harmful desires will follow. Contentment will never come because misplaced desires tell them they need more wealth and earthly delights. By living horizontally, they continue to feed their greed. Soon their worldly quest makes "wanting more" the only value. Wealth is the grand symbol of self-sufficiency.

Contentment is an abiding soul-sufficiency that is rooted in a growing relationship with Jesus Christ and finding an unwavering sufficiency in him. Being intimately connected with the ultimate source of truth brings us an inner abundance that generates peace and power. Appropriating the truth fosters growth and contented living.

Contentment cleanses our vision so that we can experience the fullness of life. It generates a heart of gratitude that turns what we have into "enough." It turns denial into acceptance, chaos to order, confusion to clarity. But it is a learning, transformative process that flows from an intimate trust in God. Learning the value of contentment enabled Paul to be able to say with conviction, "I can do all things through Christ who strengthens me" (Phil. 4:13).

In a world of consumerism, busyness, and the "rat race" to keep up with (and now surpass) the Joneses, *simplicity* is a key ingredient to maintaining an authentic spiritual journey. In a culture of clutter and confusion, simplicity will preserve us from the burden of extravagance and excess. "Simplicity, simplicity, simplicity!" wrote Henry David Thoreau in his classic *Walden*. "I say, let your affairs be as two or three, and not a hundred or a thousand; instead of a million, count half a dozen, and keep your accounts on a thumb-nail ... Simplify, Simplify."[24] From the introspective Thoreau viewpoint, amid the distractions of our industrial America, the image of youth beside Walden Pond crying out only for simplification becomes for thousands the dream of a green isle in the sea, a respite from distraction, imparting energy to those who admit to themselves, in sleepless nights, that they do after all lead lives of "quiet desperation."

Contentedness involves freedom from inner desperation and anxiety. True contentment flows from godliness in heart (1 Tim. 6:6). The contented heart is a gracious heart. Gratitude gives way to simplicity—the desire for God more than things, holiness more than happiness, and a well-ordered life providing us with the inner peace to appreciate the beauty of each God-given day. Learning the value of contentment will help us see that each day is a path of joy and purpose under the loving hand of God. "For we are His workmanship, created in Christ Jesus for good works, which God prepared beforehand, that we should walk in them" (Eph. 2:10).

Certainly there will not be perfect contentment here in this life. Perfect peace and harmony are only at God's right hand (Ps. 16:11). Yet we can begin on earth to tune our instrument before we play the sweet lesson of contentment exactly in heaven.[25] As we progress by God's grace, learning contentment inspires in us quiet courage to build a godly, authentic life for ourselves and to encourage others to travel the same path of discipleship.

THE CHALLENGE

What is the church to do in a culture that treats history as bunk and defines itself only by the present and champions "privatized truth" over divine truth? In order to thrive in a postmodern age that is essentially nihilistic, and to reach a postmodern world that has lost its center and has contributed to the lingering death of meaning, what is our responsibility?

First, we must not cut the cord from our past. Surrounding us is a postmodern world that is cutting loose from history and bringing about many injurious breaks from our cultural past. These displacements are reshaping the moral and spiritual frameworks from a Judeo-Christian worldview into a blatantly pagan worldview. We must never move away from the fact that the meaning of God as conferred in history is fundamental to our faith and existence. God physically entered history "in the fullness of time" to redeem fallen humanity (Gal. 4:6). This is not a subjective cherished conviction, but an objective historical fact connecting our present spiritual wholeness to the literal redemptive action secured in the past.

The eclipse of history leaves one only with the present. If the present is all one has, there is no future hope. Hope is not inspired by the future but is grounded in the past. For the Christian, hope is built on the eternal work of Christ in history (Heb. 6:18–20).

Furthermore, America was built on Judeo-Christian principles that have served to undergird the moral order. Our nation's first president, George Washington, wrote in his farewell address, "Reason and experience both forbid us to expect that national morality can prevail in exclusion of religious principle."[26] Guenter Lewy, professor of political science at the University of Massachusetts, Amherst, reminds us that "there are nonbelievers who engage in morally praiseworthy deeds, but it should be remembered that their conduct is considered praiseworthy because it is the sort of conduct that has been prescribed by the Judeo-Christian norm that by now is an implicit part of our moral tradition."[27]

These historical acts and cultural realities have objective meaning because they are rooted in God's actions in history and shaped by his truth. The God who is sovereign over history inspires hope for the future where evil will be eradicated and divine truth will cover the globe as the waters cover the sea (Isa. 11:9). Death has been swallowed up in Christ's victory. The mortal will be clothed with immortality—we will be resurrected to eternal life (1 Cor. 15:51–57). Without this divine promise, our faith would be futile and meaningless (v. 17). The most miserable persons have nowhere to search beyond themselves. Yet, we do not coddle in despair but ascertain meaning in an omnipotent God who guides the wings of eternity.

Second, our vision for holy living must be enlarged. We need to continually remind ourselves and each other that this world and its vices are passing away (1 Cor. 7:31). Our commitment to a virtuous, radically different lifestyle that is real, pure, and content will serve as a vehicle of grace to inspire other believers to pursue holiness with determination, joy, and a sense of adventurous, God-honoring liberty. We must stand out and shine. Bishop John Ryle, back in 1879, reminded Christians that "evangelical doctrine is useless if it is not accompanied by a holy life. It is worse than useless; it does positive harm. It is despised by keen-sighted and shrewd men of the world, as an unreal and hollow thing, and brings religion into contempt."[28]

Holiness is never outdated. This is important to remember in an age where the ubiquitous consumer mentality has been injected into the heart of mainstream evangelicalism. It is alarming enough that the inherited influence of a Judeo-Christian outlook has largely dissipated in our culture, but trading in biblical holiness for clever marketing techniques will surely evacuate our Christian heritage. The freedom to grow in holiness is largely dependent on a deliberate cultivation of the spiritual disciplines, such as Bible study and Scripture meditation, prayer, worship, and solitude. Nevertheless, as the church we will be culturally relevant only as our inner lives are renewed, lining up with God's Word, and shaped by his grace in loving service to those seized by the covetous culture.

Sheldon Vanauken, in his book *A Severe Mercy*, recalls the thoughts he penned in his journal regarding the impact Christians can have for good or bad. He wrote:

> The best argument for Christianity is Christians; their joy, their certainty, their completeness. But the strongest argument *against* Christianity is also Christians—when they are somber and joyless, when they are self-righteous and smug in complacent consecration, when they are narrow and repressive, then Christianity dies a thousand deaths.[29]

Christians who live joyful, contented, consecrated lives sustain a passionate God-centeredness and Gospel-centeredness. This points the way to the God who is still there (as Francis Schaeffer used to say). It echoes God's cry to the world and pierces through the postmodern culture's armor of callousness.

Third, we must possess an enormous sense of "destiny," knowing that God's sovereign hand is guiding us personally and corporately. The evangelical church is called to be *the church*. Our vision becomes clouded when we're sidetracked by greed, covetousness, and consumerism. We must rise above the stultifying worldly temptations in the midst of our present cultural breakdown and move forward in undiminished confidence in the power of God's Word.

Joseph had a sense of destiny, even in the face of rejection and injustice. He never forgot his God-given dreams and saw God's hand in the good and bad, molding and shaping his manifold destiny: "And as for you, you meant evil against me, but God meant it for good in order to bring about this present result, to preserve many people alive" (Gen. 50:20).

Living with an eternal perspective is a pungent wake-up call to those besieged by the temporal pleasures of the age. Heralding the meaning of life from the revelation of God's purposes in Scripture confronts the growing cultural nihilism that ultimately declares everything meaningless. We are here to learn how to love, to discover truth, and to grow in responsible stewardship on the earth. Each of us is intended to grow and flourish within the power of our natural talents and spiritual gifts in every dimension of our lives. We are participants in God's "great story." We are not called upon to consume with endless passion, but called to simplicity and contentment—living in a state of grace where our lives contribute to creating a better world. We are called upon to care, live, and give in such a way that the core of who we are is freed to love, enjoy, and glorify God forever.

Finally, we must proclaim *law* and *gospel* in a postmodern age. God's law shows the unbeliever how hopelessly he or she falls short of the righteousness God requires. While "the truth of the Christian faith may no longer travel on the wings of logical argument as it has in the past,"[30] the fact that people are sinners in need of a Savior still must be communicated clearly. But our proclamation about sin must not be reduced simply to citations from Scripture. Postmoderns do not start with Scripture, nor do they accept the view that they are sinners. The doctrine of original sin is often dismissed as archaic or simply ignored altogether.

Still, that should not dissuade us from explaining that all sin is understood in relation to God, in contrast to the postmodern view that sin or wrongdoing is understood in relation to ourselves. Sin is offensive to God and a violation of his moral law.

Reminding postmoderns of some of the horrific evils of history may move them to reconsider their denial of sin. Hitler's mass executions of more than six million Jews, turning eastern Europe into a "vast slaughterhouse," is one example.

In 1960, Israeli undercover agents orchestrated the daring kidnapping of one of the worst of the Holocaust masterminds, Adolf Eichmann. After capturing him in his South American hideout, they transported him to Israel to stand trial.

There, prosecutors called a string of former concentration camp prisoners as witnesses. One was a small haggard man named Yehiel Dinur, who had miraculously escaped death in Auschwitz.

On his day to testify, Dinur entered the courtroom and stared at the man in the bulletproof glass booth—the man who had murdered Dinur's friends, personally executed a number of Jews, and presided over the slaughter of millions more. As the eyes of the two men met—victim and murderous tyrant—the courtroom fell silent, filled with the tension of the confrontation. But no one was prepared for what happened next.

Yehiel Dinur began to shout and sob, collapsing to the floor.

Was he overcome by hatred? by the horrifying memories? by the evil incarnate in Eichmann's face?

No. As he later explained in a riveting *60 Minutes* interview, it was because Eichmann was not the demonic personification of evil that Dinur had expected. Rather, he was an ordinary man, just like anyone else. And in that one instant, Dinur came to the stunning realization that sin and evil are the human condition. "I was afraid about myself," Dinur said. "I saw that I am capable to do this ... exactly like he."

Dinur's remarkable statements caused Mike Wallace to turn to the camera and ask the audience the most painful of all questions: "How was it possible for a man to act as Eichmann acted? Was he a monster? A madman? Or was he perhaps something even more terrifying? Was he normal?"

Yehiel Dinur's shocking conclusion? "Eichmann is in all of us."[31]

The same is true when considering serial killers, such as the early-twentieth-century "cannibal killer," Albert Fish, who violently assaulted more than one hundred young girls, murdering twelve of them and engaging in the hideous activities of torture, necrophilia, and cannibalism. Or the grotesque murders of the late Jeffrey Dahmer in the late twentieth century, who butchered, cooked, and ate his victims. When scanning the evils perpetrated in the twentieth century alone, a very bleak picture of sin and human fallenness is painted. Martin Luther's insight on sin's deceptiveness is still relevant. "The ultimate proof of the sinner is that he doesn't know his own sin. Our job is to make him see it."[32]

In a postmodern age where "greed is good" and covetousness is turbulent, believers will be most influential as a God-glorifying community. Christians become better Christians and more effective witnesses as we join together in community, in our churches, in our families, among our peers, in our schools, at our jobs, where there is the meeting of hearts in interaction. We must make sure, however, that the popular notion of church "community" does not simply become another strategy for self-fulfillment. Strengthening one another and feeling more "connected" is good, but if we pursue community just to feel better about ourselves rather than for God's honor and the extension of his kingdom, the community movement will either fade or degenerate into spiritual encounter groups. We must work toward the establishment of God-centered, truth-bearing community. In order for postmodern generations to consider the plausibility of Christianity, they must be convinced of its authenticity and stirred by its community-building characteristics.

SIMPLICITY AND CONTENTMENT REVISITED

Most Americans, including most in our churches, have been so shaped by the popular culture that no thoughtful Christian can afford to ignore the impact.[33] Much in the media titillates our sin of covetousness. This reinforces self-indulgence, instant gratification, self-promotion, greed, and narcissism. Americans are tired and are sprinting through life, looking for relief and meaning, with their eyes on the wrong target.

Simplicity as a conscious choice restores our equilibrium and illuminates our vision to see reality. Our inner resources are cleansed and our spiritual centers flourish when we resolve to live simple, uncomplicated lives. The late pioneer missionary Jim Elliot resolved:

> The wisest life is the simple life.... Be on guard, my soul, of complicating your environment so that you have neither time nor room for growth.[34]

To reach the postmodern world, we must be spiritually healthy. The Tenth Commandment forbids coveting because it offends God and causes spiritual erosion. Living beyond our means or "going for all the gusto we can" are harmful aims. Living godly, contented, unencumbered lives will free us to touch the world in a way that honors the Lord.

SMALL GROUP DISCUSSION QUESTIONS

1. What does it mean to "covet"? Discuss how television, magazines, and advertising often arouse covetous desires.

2. What happens to our desires when God is not at the center of our lives? How do we guard against the development of evil desires?

3. What is the difference between coveting and envy? What happens when covetous plans are forged in the heart? Discuss the importance of having the right focus (see Heb. 12:2; Col. 3:1–5).

4. Define contentment. How do we find contentment? What does "simplicity" have to do with personal growth and contentment? What are the obstacles to contentment?

5. Why is meaning linked to God's actions in history? Why are we here in this world? What is our purpose on the earth?

6. How does obedience to the Tenth Commandment put us in a better position to reach postmoderns with the Gospel?

WHOSE VALUES WILL PREVAIL?

On Day Six of the ill-fated mission of *Apollo 13*, the astronauts needed to make a critical course correction. If they failed, they might never return to Earth.

To conserve power, they shut down the onboard computer that steered the craft. Yet the astronauts needed to conduct a thirty-nine-second burn of the main engines. How to steer?

Astronaut Jim Lovell determined that if they could keep a fixed point in space in view through their tiny window, they could steer the craft manually. That focal point turned out to be their destination—Earth.

As shown in the 1995 hit movie *Apollo 13*, for thirty-nine agonizing seconds, Lovell focused on keeping the Earth in view. By not losing sight of that "fixed reference point," the three astronauts avoided disaster.[1]

God has provided us with an absolute moral framework to keep us on the path of life away from disaster. God's moral law stems from his character and is the "fixed reference point" that engenders prosperity and success. The Lord reminded Joshua at a crucial time in Israel's history:

> Only be strong and very courageous; be careful to do according to all the law which Moses My servant commanded you; do not turn from it to the right or to the left, so that you may have success wherever you go.
>
> This book of the law shall not depart from your mouth, but you shall meditate on it day and night, so that you may be careful to do

according to all that is written in it; for then you will make your way prosperous, and then you will have success (Josh. 1:7–8).

Western culture has for the most part cut itself off from God's immutable standard of right and wrong. People are a law to themselves. Success is purchased by setting aside what is fixed and eternal for the gloss and glitter of popular culture.

From the divine viewpoint, genuine growth and success comes from meditating (e.g., studying, absorbing, memorizing, reflecting, applying) on God's law. Nothing has meaning apart from his truth. Faithful obedience to the law of God paves the path to abundance, inspiring courage and removing the fear (v.9). Ravished by its goodness and power, those who align themselves with it find it to be the perfect guide into the blessed life in God (see Ps. 119). "To be sure, law is not the source of rightness, but it is forever the course of rightness."[2]

The law of God has always been about liberation. True freedom is not giving in to our every impulse. Freedom is doing what we were designed to do. As human beings created by God we were designed to love, to discover and grow in truth, to enjoy and glorify God eternally. By developing into the people God designed us to be we find freedom and "keep it" as long as we do not depart from his law (Josh. 1:8).

A leading philosopher, Dallas Willard, laments at the fading popularity of the Ten Commandments. This is truly lamentable, for as Willard observes, "Even a fairly general practice of them would lead to a solution of almost every problem of meaning and order now facing Western societies. They are God's best information on how to lead a basically decent human existence."[3] Not only do we find little resolute conformity to the Ten Commandments, but there is a remarkable reticence to even acknowledge that these truths were foundational to the Western moral tradition. Reticence has led to ignorance, cultural illiteracy, and deep moral confusion. Increasingly, today's young people know little or nothing about the moral directives of the Judeo-Christian heritage.

This was recently demonstrated by *Tonight Show* host Jay Leno. Leno frequently does "man-on-the-street" interviews, and one night he collared some young people to ask them questions about the Bible.

"Can you name one of the Ten Commandments?" he asked two col-
lege-age women. One replied, "Freedom of speech?" Mr. Leno said
to the other, "Complete this sentence: Let he who is without sin. . ."
Her response was, "have a good time?" Mr. Leno then turned to a
young man and asked, "Who, according to the Bible, was eaten by a
whale?" The confident answer was, "Pinocchio."[4]

Culturally, the average person, especially today's young people, live
in a moral haze. We must not forget that there exists a core of non-
controversial ethical issues rooted in God's law that were settled a long
time ago. We cannot allow future generations to remain morally illiterate. All healthy societies pass along their moral and cultural traditions to their children.[5] Moreover, as Christians we can take a stand
against the divisive unlearning that is corrupting the integrity of our
society by communicating that "The Ten Commandments are not the
Ten Highly Tentative Suggestions."[6] We can dispel some of the moral
confusion by applying the ten absolutes to all areas of life. The divine
decree still stands: "Righteousness exalts a nation, but sin is a disgrace
to any people" (Prov. 14:34). God's law not only liberates individual
devotees, but brings about saner, safer, more dignified, morally
enlightened societies as well.

America has a rich tradition of commitment to the law of God as the
basis for a well-ordered society. The American experiment was built on
the acceptance of divine law from two sources: the law of nature and
the law of Scripture.[7] Both reflect an unabated adherence to God's law.
In spite of the multicultural onslaught, we do have a common culture
in this country, based on shared ideas developed first in the civilizations of antiquity, later matured in western Europe.

Our political traditions come from the common-law tradition,
which English authorities such as Coke and Blackstone saw as based
on Holy Scripture.[8] They are not based on Darwinian, atheistic world-
views. Our aesthetic ideals are derived from many rich sources, such
as Shakespeare, Renaissance painters, and classical music, not neopagan folklore, existential artistry, or New Age chants. Our ethics come
from the Bible, not Eastern religions.

All of life is ethical and requires a moral standard of right and wrong.
In any society, someone's values must prevail. If America isn't governed

by the Judeo-Christian ethic, it will be ruled by the neopagan doctrines of postmodernism. For the consequences of the latter, consider the latest statistics on drug use, the breakdown of schools and the family, the suicide rate, and the astounding amount of precipitous greed in the culture.

Until quite recently the Ten Commandments enjoyed unchallenged prestige. They were basic to the religious training that Western nations gave to their children and youth. Today, posting the Ten Commandments is viewed as an intolerable display of favoritism toward the Judeo-Christian values on which our nation was founded, or unconstitutional because they allegedly advance a religious agenda. It is unfounded, however, to assume that the use of religious materials must have a religious agenda. The Ten Commandments are of important distinction because of their "significant secular impact on the development of the secular legal codes of the Western World."[9] Banishing the Ten Commandments to the private world of religion is obstructing the transmission of the best guidelines of our political and cultural heritage. Our nation's youth are kept from knowing the truth about our Founding Fathers' religious beliefs and how these beliefs influenced the attitudes of the times and the structure of our government, and how these beliefs can positively affect our nation's future.[10]

It is dishonest to pretend that the nation's history was different than it was. The nation's roots were primarily (though not exclusively) Christian, and the Christian faith has been the prominent faith throughout American history. I am not saying that the Founding Fathers' intention was to establish a "Christian nation." It would be unconstitutional as well as wrong to impose the Christian faith upon non-Christians. Civil government defines what is lawful, not what religion one must accept. But the liberal cultural elite have abandoned our historical connection to the residual Judeo-Christian worldview that played a dominant role in the framers' minds.

Stephen Carter, one of the nation's leading experts on constitutional law, says in his popular book *The Culture of Disbelief* that "one need not go that far in order to appreciate the importance of teaching children about the role of religion at crucial junctures in the nation's history, from the openly religious rhetoric of the Founding Generation, through the religious justifications for the abolition of slavery, the

GOD'S TEN COMMANDMENTS	THE NEW TEN COMMANDMENTS
1. Thou shalt have no other gods before Me.	1. Thou shalt worship any god that makes you feel good about yourself.
2. Thou shalt not make for yourself an idol.	2. Thou shalt attempt to create anything which brings you pleasure and success.
3. Thou shalt not take the name of the Lord your God in vain.	3. Thou shalt not object to anybody's god or religion. All religions worship the same God but call him or her by a different name.
4. Remember the Sabbath day, to keep it holy.	4. Remember yourself and don't worry, be happy.
5. Honor your father and your mother that your days may be prolonged in the land which the Lord your God gives you.	5. You are the ultimate authority. You determine your own destiny.
6. Thou shalt not murder.	6. Thou shalt not oppose abortion.
7. Thou shalt not commit adultery.	7. Thou shalt not oppose pornography.
8. Thou shalt not steal.	8. Thou shalt look out for No. 1 ("self").
9. Thou shalt not bear false witness.	9. Thou shalt uphold relativism.
10. Thou shalt not covet.	10. Thou shalt seek to fulfill one's desires even at the expense of others.

"social gospel" movement to reform American society and industry, or even the civil rights movement of the 1950s and 1960s."[11] You cannot have an accurate portrayal of American history or culture and leave out the Judeo-Christian framework which shaped it.

Tragically, that is what is happening. The legal culture that guards the public square views God as a hobby, someone who should be worshiped and discussed in private. Popular culture views God as an inner amoral force, or as the peachy keen cosmic blanket who will accept just about anybody's point of view. The Ten Commandments have undergone significant revision. Our culture is experiencing sharp divisions as God's Ten Commandments are being replaced by man's postmodern commands of tolerance.

THE JUDEO-CHRISTIAN IMPACT ON CULTURE

America has rich traditions and institutions of proven strength and efficacy. Historically, many of these institutions were surrendered to secular control as a large segment of the evangelical church retreated into a religious ghetto. Christians have contributed to our society's spiritual and moral erosion not only by the past cultural withdrawal but also by removing the Ten Commandments from their instruction. Joshua 1:7–8 reminds us that God's people need an objective, fixed, eternal standard for instruction and direction. A church that abandons God's law also abandons the blessings of his presence. A society that abdicates God's law also abdicates the blessings of his presence. Christians must rediscover God's law and reflect the power of his truth and presence through passionate hearts. People see God most clearly through human vessels alive to him.

We cannot afford to be indifferent about our culture.[12] Those who believe that cultural destruction is inevitable should not contribute to its demise by going AWOL. The fact that the culture is in a state of moral and spiritual decline is not a signal to stick our heads in the sand, but to act as responsible stewards of God's creation, taking a stand for righteousness and truth. We are constantly being challenged about how we spend our time, talents, and treasures in light of our greater calling to love God with all of our heart and love our neighbor as ourselves. The problem of evil continues to be exceptionally acute as we see incessant violence, immorality, abortion, greed, and family disintegration. This is the dirty cultural air my children are breathing. They are growing up in an unstable, morally confused postmodern culture. Rather than live in isolation, I want to be a change agent to help alleviate the instability, to lessen the confusion. The church must think about future generations and how they might be influenced. Postmodernism will totally absorb the culture if the church retreats.

"The only thing necessary for the triumph of evil," Edmund Burke wrote in 1795, "is for good men to do nothing."[13]

An intellectually credible, pastorally sensitive Christian response bathed in God's unchanging law is all-important. This is an extension of God's covenant love in faithful operation.

It is the Judeo-Christian heritage which combats the moral nihilism and nourishes and replenishes the moral capital of our society. The church can help renew this legacy if she gets her house in order. The moral law is God's revealed and objective standard, which sets our course for righteous living. It restores our moral center, empowering us to bring change to the disintegration of the ethical fabric of life today.

Most agree that murderers, abusers, swindlers, cheaters, and liars who violate societal norms should be punished. So there still exists a moral texture to life in our culture that demands, albeit rather selectively, the application of the Golden Rule. Still, the majority of Americans have enough "moral sense" to recognize a rapid moral decline. Unfortunately, the American people are unclear on how to bring about renewal.

Education is often proclaimed as the "new Messiah," and changing laws and public policy are another way to influence the culture, but as important as these are, the culture will change only if the people change.

Ultimately, what holds a society together is not law or public policy but moral persuasion. Righteousness exalts a nation. The late Francis Schaeffer said that what works best is a nation that operates out of a moral consensus that is Christian. The Christian faith should not be legislated by the state. Rather "government and laws exist ideally as a kind of spillover of Christian sensibility, reflecting God's values as revealed in the Bible: peace, respect for life; environmental, racial, and economic justice."[14]

But Christians must be godly moral agents who set standards, raise aspirations, develop transforming ideas, stimulate, and inspire. When the church loses its moral bearings, society becomes less honest, more corrupt, and extremely self-indulgent. God's people must be the change agents who inject moral acumen into our declining society by helping to influence new laws that discourage unproductive and harmful behavior. Long-term, meaningful change must be grounded in permanent moral principles. Faithful adherence to the Ten Commandments will give us the wisdom and power we need to help make this world a better place than it otherwise would be.

Although the founders disconnected the functions of church and state, all of them believed in the necessary relationship between religious values and a stable moral framework as well as affirming the role of religion in making a democracy run well. Robert Bellah confirms that there has not been a major issue in the history of the United States on which religious bodies did not speak out, publicly and vociferously.[15] Throughout American history, Christian leaders led the way in moral crusades that politically correct theorists erroneously view as progressive. Christians led the charge in the antislavery movement, and it was Christianity's influence that brought an end to this evil practice. It was also Christianity that inspired the first hospitals, drove the early labor movement, women's suffrage, human-rights campaigns, and civil rights. It was under the leadership of the Reverend Martin Luther King, Jr., that the civil rights movement used methods of nonviolent resistance to force the nation to change its laws.[16] It did this by articulating the biblical and republican strands of our national history, enabling a large number of Americans to recognize the glaring failures of collective national responsibility. Churches, both black and white, provided the buildings, the volunteers, and the theological underpinnings to properly support the movement, ensuring that justice and dignity were extended to people of every race.

Those inclined to doubt the important role played by religion in upholding the moral order may want to confront the question posed by Dennis Prager, a Jewish writer and editor in Los Angeles:

Imagine that you are walking alone at night down a dark alley in a bad neighborhood in Los Angeles, and you see several strapping young men walking toward you. Would you or would you not be relieved to know that they had just attended a Bible class?

It is a sure bet, Prager maintains, that "even if you are a member of Atheists United, if you are a member of Down with God, Inc., you, too, would breathe a major sigh of relief if you were walking in a dark alley and you knew they had just been studying Genesis [or the Ten Commandments]. Because while it is possible they will mug or rape you, deep in your gut you know that the likelihood is that they won't.[17]

Mark it down. If our culture is to survive and flourish, it must stay connected to the religious vision out of which it arose[18] and be nurtured by God-fearing believers who radiate his power and presence, and love his law. "I will keep Thy law continually, forever and ever . . . I love Thy law" (Ps. 119:44, 113).

God is with us and the world is before us. We have the opportunity of retelling the great old story to a brand-new postmodern age. Surely, we must offer a significant degree of creativity, ingenuity, and originality. But we have at our disposal the greatest laws of liberation the world has even known—documented in the ancient writings and autographed on our hearts. To love God's Ten Commandments will refresh our souls and preserve the truth of our moral identity. To love the God who gave us those priceless treasures and to know his covenant love is the supreme "liberating force" and the avenue to blessing, confidence, strength, and character. We have an opportunity to restore a good measure of moral dignity to our culture. But we must be energized by a mutually elevating love relationship with the one true God. That means passionate obedience and affirming a deep respect for our true spiritual and ethical capacity rooted in God's moral law. The Ten Commandment treasures must be excavated, proclaimed, and lived out if we are going to be a powerful voice among the cacophony of lifestyles and ideas that are evolving in today's chaotic postmodern world.

NOTES

Chapter One: God's Law in a Postmodern Society

1. As an aside, prominent social economist Thomas Sowell says that any discussion of overpopulation is *relative*. He suggests three factors that must be evaluated: land, natural resources, and food. Based on the amount of space each person in the world actually has, it is obvious that there is theoretically enough room for many times the number of people presently on the earth (approximately six billion). The entire population of the earth could fit inside the state of Texas, with each person having about 1,700 square feet of space. See Thomas Sowell, *The Economics and Politics of Race: An International Perspective* (New York: William Morrow, 1983), 209.

2. Ted Turner, from a speech printed in *Sermons Illustrated*, 949 (February 1990).

3. George Gallup and James Castelli, *The People's Religion* (New York: Macmillan, 1989), 60.

4. James Patterson and Peter Kim, *The Day America Told the Truth* (New York: Plume, 1992), 25–26.

5. Robert N. Bellah et al., *Habits of the Heart: Individualism and Commitment in American Life* (Los Angeles: University of California Press, 1996 updated edition), 75.

6. Patterson and Kim, *The Day America Told the Truth*, 200–1.

7. Bellah, *Habits of the Heart*, 77.

8. "Deciding Whether to Discuss Religion Prompts Debate," in *Dear Abby* (September 19, 1989).

9. Stanley J. Grenz, *A Primer on Postmodernism* (Grand Rapids: William B. Eerdmans, 1996), 12.

10. Jim Leffel and Dennis McCallum, "Postmodern Impact: Religion," in *The Death of Truth: What's Wrong With Multiculturalism, The Rejection of Reason, and The New Postmodern Diversity*, ed. Dennis McCallum (Minneapolis: Bethany House, 1996), 200.

11. Ibid., 31.

12. Grenz, *A Primer on Postmodernism*, 5.

13. Ibid., 5.

14. Ibid., 9.

15. Ibid., 9.

16. The exception here would be the command to keep the Sabbath, although I argue in chapter 4 that the Sabbath pointed toward the Messiah, Jesus Christ, and was God-centered in orientation. See also Donald Richardson, *Eternity in Their Hearts* (Ventura, Calif.: Regal, 1981). Richardson shows that God's principles, whether adhered to or not, still existed for centuries in hundreds of cultures throughout the world.

17. See J. Budziszewski, *Written on the Heart: The Case for Natural Law* (Downers Grove, Ill.: InterVarsity Press, 1997).

18. Gene Edward Veith, Jr., *Postmodern Times: A Christian Guide to Contemporary Thought and Culture* (Wheaton, Ill.: Crossway, 1994), 198.

19. Some think these are artificial distinctions without biblical warrant. While the Bible does not explicitly classify laws according to the scheme of civil, ceremonial, and moral laws, it does not categorize itself according to most of our topics in systematic theology (e.g., the word "Trinity"). Assigning priority to the moral aspect of the law over both its civil and ceremonial aspects can be observed in a host of passages in the Prophets (1 Sam. 15:22–23; Isa. 1:11–17; Jer. 7:21–23; Mic. 6:8, as well as many Psalms, such as Ps. 51:16–17). The moral law of God took precedence over the civil and ceremonial laws in that it was based on the character of God. The civil and ceremonial laws functioned only as further illustrations of the moral law. See Walter C. Kaiser, Jr., "The Law As God's Guidance for the Promotion of Holiness," Greg L. Bahnsen et al., *The Law, The Gospel, and the Modern Christian: Five Views* (Grand Rapids: Zondervan, 1993), 189–96.

20. Ibid., 303, 306, 400. Kaiser points out a number of places in Scripture that teach that there were priorities and rankings within the one law of God. For example, 1 Samuel 15:22 urges: "to obey is better than sacrifice." See also Psalm 51:16–19, Isaiah 1:11-20, Hosea 6:6, Jeremiah 7:21–24, Micah 6:6–8, among others. Kaiser finds the teaching that the entire law has been abrogated erroneous, which he says is the invention of another "replacement theology." He astutely points out that the view espousing that the law of Christ (or the royal law—James 2:8) is a separate and different law from the law the Father revealed to Moses is also erroneous. To make God's law and Christ's law different or antithetical is a strange replacement theology. He warns that those who hold such a view have adopted "semi-Marcionism."

21. See Kaiser, "The Law as God's Guidance," 195. Kaiser asks, "If the law were such a monolithic unity, how is our Lord himself able to require of us something that our definitions tell us is impossible?"

22. Ibid., 305.

23. Michael S. Horton, *The Law of Perfect Freedom: Relating to God and Others Through the Ten Commandments* (Chicago: Moody Press, 1993), 23.

24. See Kaiser's response to Greg Bahnsen, in "The Theonomic Reformed Approach to Law and Gospel," *The Law, The Gospel, and the Modern Christian*, 153. Kaiser points out that the civil and ceremonial laws carry principles within them that are still normative today. But to take all the civil duties of the theocracy unique to Israel and urge the church to hold present day (non-theocratic) forms of government responsible for carrying all of the "civil provisions" is to slip categories and to confuse Israel with the church and theocracy with every other form of government.

25. Walter C. Kaiser, Jr., *Toward Old Testament Ethics* (Grand Rapids: Zondervan, 1983), 32.

26. George Barna, *The Barna Report: What Americans Believe* (Ventura, Calif.: Regal, 1991), 83–85, 292–94.

27. Veith, *Postmodern Times*, 213.

28. George Barna, *The Frog in the Kettle: What Christians Need to Know About Life in the Year 2000* (Ventura, Calif.: Regal, 1990), 121.

29. Doug Bandow, *Beyond Good Intentions: A Biblical View of Politics* (Wheaton, Ill.: Crossway, 1988), xii.

30. Ibid.

31. Kaiser, "The Law As God's Guidance," 198. Kaiser insightfully states that the Proverbs are a veritable republication of the law of God in proverbial form, as can be seen in the marginal references to Exodus, Numbers, and Deuteronomy.

Chapter Two: The First Commandment, Part 1

1. Grace Palladino, *Teenagers: An American History* (New York: Basic Books, 1996), 127–30.

2. *Christianity Today* (April 25, 1994), 44.

3. Richard Keyes, *True Heroism: In a World of Celebrity Counterfeits* (Colorado Springs: NavPress, 1995), 87.

4. Os Guinness and John Seel, eds., *No God But God: Breaking with the Idols of Our Age* (Chicago: Moody Press, 1992), 32.

5. Ibid., 34.

6. Ibid., 23.

7. Donald W. McCullough, *The Trivialization of God: The Dangerous Illusion of Manageable Deity* (Colorado Springs: NavPress, 1995).

8. Ibid., 32.

9. Ibid., 30.

10. Ibid., 15.

11. Michael S. Horton, *The Law of Perfect Freedom: Relating to God and Others Through the Ten Commandments* (Chicago: Moody Press, 1993), 61.

12. Norman L. Geisler and William D. Watkins, *Worlds Apart: A Handbook on World Views*, 2nd ed. (Grand Rapids: Baker, 1989), 47.

13. See Michael Denton, *Evolution: A Theory in Crisis* (Bethesda, Md.: Adler & Adler, 1997).

14. "New Battle Over Darwinian Theory," *Buffalo News* (December 26, 1982).

15. Ibid.

16. Carl Sagan, *Cosmos* (New York: Ballatine, 1985), 1.

17. Ibid., 241–42.

18. Gary DeMar, *Surviving College Successfully: A Complete Manual for the Rigors of Academic Life* (Brentwood, N.J.: Wolgemuth & Hyatt, 1988), 75.

19. Herbert Schlossberg, *Idols for Destruction: Christian Faith and Its Confrontation with American Society* (Nashville: Thomas Nelson, 1983), 6.

20. Ezekiel Hopkins, *A Short Exposition of the Ten Commandments* (London: Printed by J. Paramore at the Foundry, Moorfield, 1784), 15.

21. Geisler and Watkins, *Worlds Apart*, 147–48.

22. Charles B. Sanford, *The Religious Life of Thomas Jefferson* (Charlottesville, Va.: University Press of Virginia, 1984), 85, 175. Jefferson rejected orthodox Christianity's theology regarding original sin, the divinity of Christ, the doctrine of the atonement, the doctrine of the Trinity, and biblical miracles. He did, however, have an optimistic view of human improvement by education and social reform based upon his religious beliefs and "Christian social action" (pp. 175–77).

23. Geisler and Watkins, *Worlds Apart*, 181.

24. Gary Friesen, with J. Robin Maxson, *Decision Making and the Will of God: A Biblical Alternative to the Traditional View* (Portland, Ore.: Multnomah Press, 1980). I do agree with a large portion of Friesen's perspective. His book provides a wealth of inspiring biblical insight. I do, however, disagree with his basic thesis that God has no personal will for his people. From my perspective, this view spawns functional deism.

25. M. Blaine Smith, *Knowing God's Will: Finding Guidance for Personal Decisions* (Downers Grove, Ill.: InterVarsity Press, 1991), 234.

26. Dallas Willard, *In Search of Guidance: Developing a Conversational Relationship with God* (San Francisco: Harper, 1993), 50. I believe there are special times when God will speak to his people through dreams and visions. Missionary and adjunct seminary

professor Herbert Kane told me that while he was ministering in China, the Communists took control of the government and sent all known Christians to "re-education camps." The Christians were stripped of their Bibles, religious literature and, in some cases, separated from their fellow believers. They received meager portions of food, got very little sleep, and were forced to sit through rigorous deprogramming and indoctrination sessions. During this time God spoke to these persecuted believers through dreams, visions, an inner voice, etc. God's intimate presence preserved them during these fearful, trying times.

27. Ibid., 107.

28. Smith, *Knowing God's Will*, 238.

29. Willard, *In Search of Guidance*, 52.

30. E. Stanley Jones, *A Song of Ascents* (Nashville: Abingdon, 1979), quoted in Willard, *In Search of Guidance*, 52.

31. Willard, *In Search of Guidance*, 223. This may include selecting a mate, various vocations, educational institutions, or places of residence.

32. Ibid., 50.

33. Geisler and Watkins, *Worlds Apart*, 217.

34. Rodney Clapp, "Fighting Mormonism in Utah," *Christianity Today* 26 (July 16, 1982), 30. See also Geisler and Watkins, *Worlds Apart*, 228.

35. Harry L. Ropp, *The Mormon Papers* (Downers Grove, Ill.: InterVarsity Press, 1978), 13–17.

36. Ibid., 15. See also Michael G. Moriarty, *The New Charismatics: A Concerned Voice Responds to Dangerous New Trends* (Grand Rapids: Zondervan, 1992), 322.

37. See Robert M. Bowman, Jr., "Ye Are Gods? Orthodox and Heretical Views on the Deification of Man," *Christian Research Journal* (Winter/Spring 1987), 20.

38. David L. Miller, *The New Polytheism: Rebirth of the Gods and Goddesses* (New York: Harper & Row, 1974).

39. Ibid., 4, 37.

40. Ibid., 37.

41. J. Douma, *The Ten Commandments: Manual for the Christian Life*, trans. Nelson D. Kloosterman (Phillipsburg, N.J.: P & R, 1996), 30–33.

42. Ibid., 17.

43. A. W. Tozer, *The Knowledge of the Holy* (San Francisco: Harper & Row, 1961), 1.

44. Jack Finegan, *Myth & Mystery: An Introduction to the Pagan Religions of the Biblical World* (Grand Rapids: Baker, 1989), 126, 133.

45. This is a paraphrase from the great literary scholar C. S. Lewis.

46. C. S. Lewis, *The Four Loves* (New York: Harcourt, Brace, 1960), 3.

47. Michael J. Wilkins, *In His Image: Reflecting Christ in Everyday Life* (Colorado Springs: NavPress, 1997), 11.

48. This is a familiar paraphrase of the ancient church father Augustine.

Chapter Three: The First Commandment, Part 2

1. Michael Horton, *Made in America: The Shaping of Modern American Evangelicalism* (Grand Rapids: Baker, 1991), 94. It must be noted that Enlightenment thinkers did not totally abandon religion (outside of French skeptics like Voltaire). However, revelation was deprived of its sole authority status and subjected to human reason. Furthermore, if the Enlightenment is to be viewed as the age of reason, reason must be understood as the alternative to dogma or in terms of broad intellectual autonomy.

2. Roger Lundin, *The Culture of Interpretation: Christian Faith and the Postmodern World* (Grand Rapids: William B. Eerdmans, 1993), 53.

3. Ibid., 61.

4. Ibid., 67.

5. Ibid., 71.

6. Ralph Waldo Emerson, "The Divinity School Address," in *Emerson: Essays and Lectures*, ed. Joel Porte (New York: Library of America, 1983), 75–76.

7. Lundin, *Culture of Interpretation*, 75. Lundin explores the complicated developments that led from the epistemological confidence of Romanticism to the interpretive skepticism of postmodernism (72–75).

8. Robert N. Bellah et al., *Habits of the Heart: Individualism and Commitment in American Life* (Los Angeles: University of California Press, 1996 updated edition), 221.

9. Shirley MacLaine, *Out on a Limb* (New York: Bantam Books, 1983), 347, 387.

10. Guenter Lewy, *Why America Needs Religion* (Grand Rapids: William B. Eerdmans, 1996), 28.

11. Alasdair MacIntyre, *Whose Justice? Which Rationality?* (Notre Dame, Ind.: University of Notre Dame Press, 1988), 6, quoted in Lundin, *Culture of Interpretation*, 133.

12. Alexis de Tocqueville, *Democracy in America*, ed. J. P. Mayer, trans. George Lawrence (Garden City, N.Y.: Anchor, 1969), 431–32, 508.

13. Bellah et al., *Habits of the Heart*, 37.

14. George Marsden, *Fundamentalism and American Culture: The Shaping of Twentieth Century Evangelicalism: 1870–1925* (New York: Oxford University Press, 1980). Marsden points out how American evangelicalism has ahistorical individualism at its roots.

15. Dinesh D'Souza, *The End of Racism* (New York: Free Press, 1995), 147. D'Souza points out that Matthew Arnold in the nineteenth century used the term "culture" in contrast to "civilization." The term "civilization" comes from the Latin word *civis*, meaning citizen. Civilization implies a certain level of achievement in human society. The term "culture" comes from the Latin word *cultura*, meaning to grow or cultivate. This term described individuals who were highly educated in morals and taste. English anthropologist Edward Taylor later framed a more inclusive definition for culture that highlights and describes the knowledge, beliefs, customs, and habits of any given society or group of people. This is what most people today think of when hearing or referencing the world "culture."

16. Matt Friedeman, *The Master Plan of Teaching: Understanding and Applying the Teaching Styles of Jesus* (Wheaton, Ill.: Victor, 1990), 90.

17. Ibid.

18. *Wall Street Journal* (July 11, 1980), 1, quoted in Friedeman, *The Master Plan of Teaching*, 90.

19. Ibid.

20. Harold O. J. Brown, *Heresies* (Grand Rapids: Baker, 1984), 364.

21. This does not mean that we must ostracize ourselves from the culture. We must remember that Jesus is Lord over creation. We can enjoy the culture without compromising our biblical standards as long as we are not dominated or influenced by its idols.

22. See Kenneth A. Myers, *All God's Children and Blue Suede Shoes: Christians and Popular Culture* (Wheaton, Ill.: Crossway, 1989), 17–23.

23. From a letter to Mars Hill audio subscribers by Michael Cromartie.

24. Quoted in Cal Thomas, *The Death of Ethics in America* (Dallas: Word, 1988), 110.

25. Michael S. Horton, *Beyond Culture Wars: Is America a Mission Field or a Battle Field?* (Chicago: Moody Press, 1994), 159. Horton adds, "Unless we truly believe that it is the business of the government to force people to become Christians, the first table of the Law is not to be legislated by the state, but is rather to be proclaimed by the church and is to shape the witness of the church as it is properly related to God by the Gospel. It is the duty of every person, but it cannot be and ought not to be the duty of the state to enforce it."

26. From a short essay by Joseph Stowell entitled "The Power of a Life Well-Lived."

27. Harold Kushner, *To Life: A Celebration of Jewish Being and Thinking* (Boston: Little, Brown, 1993), 291.

28. Douglas Groothuis. *The Soul in Cyberspace* (Grand Rapids: Baker, 1997), 120.

29. Robert L. Wilkin, *Remembering the Christian Past* (Grand Rapids: William B. Eerdmans, 1995), 62.

30. Ibid.

Chapter Four: The Second Commandment

1. Richard Keyes, "The Idol Factory," in Os Guinness and John Seel, eds., *No God But God: Breaking With the Idols of Our Age* (Chicago: Moody Press, 1992), 33.

2. Walter C. Kaiser, Jr., "Exodus," *The Expositor's Bible Commentary*, ed. Frank E. Gaebelein (Grand Rapids: Zondervan, 1990), 422–23.

3. Steven Charnock, *The Existence and Attributes of God*, vol. 1 (1853; reprint, Grand Rapids: Baker, 1979), 187–88. Charnock says:

"If God were not a Spirit, he could not be the most perfect being. The more perfect anything is in the rank of creatures, the more spiritual and simple it is, as gold is the more pure and perfect that hath least mixture of other metals. If God were not a Spirit, there would be creatures of a more excellent nature than God, as angels and souls, which the Scripture call spirits, in opposition to bodies. There is more of perfection in the first notion of a spirit than in the notion of a body. God cannot be less perfect than his creatures, and contribute an excellency of being to them which he wants himself. If angels and souls possess such an excellency, and God wants that excellency, he would be less than his creatures, and the excellency of the effect would exceed the excellency of the cause. But every creature, even the highest creature, is infinitely short of the perfection of God; for whatsoever excellency they have is finite and limited; it is but a spark from the sun—a drop from the ocean; but God is unboundedly perfect, in the highest manner, without any limitation; and therefore above spirits, angels, the highest creatures that were made by him: an infinite sublimity, a pure act, to which nothing can be added, from which nothing can be taken. 'In him there is light and no darkness,' spirituality without any matter, perfection without any shadow or taint of imperfection. Light pierceth into all things, preserves its own purity, and admits of no mixture of anything else with it."

4. Neil Postman, *Technopoloy: The Surrender of Culture to Technology* (New York: Vintage, 1992), xii.

5. Neil Postman, *Amusing Ourselves to Death: Public Discourse in the Age of Show Business* (New York: Penguin, 1986), 12.

6. Ibid., 51.

7. Ibid., 7.

8. Ibid., 122–23.

9. Kenneth A. Myers, *All God's Children and Blue Suede Shoes: Christians & Popular Culture* (Wheaton, Ill.: Crossway, 1989), 162.

10. Ibid., 162.

11. Quoted in Charles Colson with Nancy R. Pearcey, *A Dangerous Grace* (Dallas: Word, 1994), 19.

12. Myers, *All God's Children*, 164.

13. Jane M. Healy, *Endangered Minds: Why Children Don't Think and What We Can Do About It* (New York: Simon and Schuster, 1990), 51.

14. Ibid.

15. Ibid.

16. Ibid., 74–82.

17. Arnold Scheibel, "The Rise of the Human Brain," a paper presented at the symposium "The Ever-Changing Brain" in San Rafael, Calif., August 1985, quoted in Healy, *Endangered Minds*, 54.

18. Ibid., 56.

19. George Barna, *The Frog in the Kettle: What Christians Need to Know About Life in the Year 2000* (Ventura, Calif.: Regal, 1990).

20. Coleen Cook, *All That Glitters: A News-Person Explores the World of Television* (Chicago: Moody Press, 1992), 165.

21. Postman, *Amusing Ourselves to Death*, 121.

22. David Augsburger, *A Risk Worth Taking* (Chicago: Moody, 1973), 39.

23. The movie *Network*, quoted in Cook, *All That Glitters*, 138.

24. Philip Elmer-Dewitt, "Cyberpunk!" *Time* (October 15, 1993), quoted in *Virtual Gods: The Seduction of Power and Pleasure in Cyberspace*, ed. Tal Brooke (Eugene, Ore.: Harvest, 1997), 17.

25. Ibid., 8.

26. Arthur Kroker and Michael Weinstein, *Data Trash: The Theory of the Virtual Class* (New York: St. Martin, 1994), 1–2. The authors explain what a technically feasible medium of cyberspace can accomplish in virtual reality.

"Virtual reality is the dream of pure telematic experience.... In virtual reality, flesh vaporizes into virtuality as twentieth-century bodies are repackaged with twenty-first century cybernetic systems for speeding across the electronic frontier.

"The wired body is perfect. Travelling like an electronic nomad through the circulatory flows of the mediascape, it possesses only the virtual form of a multi-layer scanner image. Abandoning the heavy referential history of a central nervous system, the wired body actually grows a telematic nervous system that is freely distributed across the electronic mirror of the Internet. A product of neural tapping and image processing, the wired body is the (technoid) life-form that finally cracks its way out of the dead shell of human culture.

"Technotopia is about disappearances: the vanishing of the body into a relational data base, the nervous system into 'distributive processing,' and the skin into wetware. As technology comes alive as a distinctive species, we finally encounter the end of (human) history and the beginning of virtual history."

27. Alexander Brooks, "The Faustian Bargain—Computers and Human Potential," in *Virtual Gods*, 100.

28. Neil Postman, *The End of Education: Redefining the Value of School* (New York: Alfred A. Knopf, 1995), 38, quoted in Douglas Groothuis, *The Soul in Cyberspace* (Grand Rapids: Baker, 1997), 15.

29. Ibid.

30. Ibid.

31. Douglas Groothuis, *The Soul in Cyberspace* (Grand Rapids: Baker, 1997), 160.

32. Douglas Groothuis, "Losing Our Souls in Cyberspace," *Christianity Today* (September 1, 1997), 55. See Tal Brooke, "Cyberspace: Storming Digital Heaven," in *Virtual Gods*, 27. Brooke says that Irwin Winkler, who produced the movie *The Net*, which is among a new wave of cyberspace intrigue films released in the summer of 1995 (others are *Virtuosity* and *Johnny Mnemonic*), now describes himself as an "Internet widower." He says his wife has been disappearing for long hours on the Net. Once greeted cheerfully with a martini and meal prepared, Winkler is now all but ignored by his wife when he comes through the door. His wife stares transfixed at a computer screen while navigating the World Wide Web, barely acknowledging his presence.
An interesting aside: cyber-addiction now has therapy that ironically comes via the computer. Interaction with a cyber-therapist costs approximately $90 per hour.

33. Douglas Groothuis, "It Takes More Than a Virtual Village," in *Books and Culture* (May/June 1997), 15.

34. David F. Wells, *God in the Wasteland: The Reality of Truth in a World of Fading Dreams* (Grand Rapids: William B. Eerdmans, 1994), 48.

35. Groothuis, "It Takes More Than a Virtual Village," 15.

36. Ibid.

37. Tal Brooke, "Virtual Gods, Designer Universes," in *Virtual Gods*, 126.

38. Richard Keyes, "The Idol Factory," in *No God But God*, 44.

39. Tal Brooke, "Virtual Gods, Designer Universes," in *Virtual Gods*, 126.

40. Groothuis, *Soul in Cyberspace*, 162.

41. Clifford Stoll, *Silicon Snake Oil: Second Thoughts on the Information Superhighway* (New York: Doubleday, 1995), 138, quoted in Groothuis, *Soul in Cyberspace*, 162.

42. Maggie Gallagher, *The Abolition of Marriage: How We Destroy Lasting Love* (Washington, D.C.: Regenery, 1996), 27.

43. Ibid., 123.

44. Charnock, *The Existence and Attributes of God*, 212. Charnock says, "It is, therefore, as much every man's duty to worship God in Spirit, as it is their duty to worship him. Worship is so due to him as God, as that he that denies it disowns his deity; and spiritual worship is so due, that he that waives it denies his spirituality. It is a debt of justice we owe to God, to worship him; and it is as much a debt of justice to worship him according to his nature."

45. William Temple, *Readings in St. John's Gospel*, First Series (London: Macmillan, 1939), 68.

46. Ben Patterson in *Christianity Today*, quoted in Robert Wenz, *Room for God? A Worship Challenge for a Church-Growth and Marketing Era* (Grand Rapids: Baker, 1994), 55.

47. D. A. Carson, *The Gospel According to John* (Grand Rapids: William B. Eerdmans, 1991), 225–26.

48. John Piper, *Desiring God: Meditations of a Christian Hedonist* (Portland, Ore.: Multnomah, 1986), 65.

49. Guinness and Seel, *No God But God*, 28.

Chapter Five: The Third Commandment

1. Sinclair Lewis, *Elmer Gantry* (New York: Signet, 1927; reprint, New York: Penguin, 1980). The book's back cover claims that *Elmer Gantry* is the "record of a period, a reign of grotesque vulgarity, which but for Lewis would have left no record of itself." Lewis studied the preachers and evangelists of the early 1920s for the writing of this

novel. Unfortunately, he focused on the worst of the worst, giving some the impression that most preachers resemble Elmer Gantry. His model for the novel was the Reverend L. M. Birkhead, a Unitarian and an agnostic. Birkhead described himself as "an immoralist" who wouldn't try to reform Lewis and had a wide Protestant experience that could be of real use to the novelist. He told Lewis that after his fundamentalist faith failed him, he enrolled at Union Theological Seminary, became an agnostic even while still preaching Methodism, and at last lapsed over to Unitarianism (p. 421).

2. Ibid., back cover.

3. Ibid., 429.

4. John Piper, *The Pleasures of God: Meditations on God's Delight in Being God* (Portland, Ore.: Multnomah, 1991), 101.

5. J. Douma, *The Ten Commandments: Manual for the Christian Life*, trans. Nelson D. Kloosterman (Phillipsburg, N.J.: P & R, 1996), 75.

6. Ibid.

7. Ibid., 82–83.

8. Ibid., 76.

9. Ibid.

10. Piper, *The Pleasures of God*, 109. Piper demonstrates how a God-centered prophet like Ezekiel handled the terrible setback for the reputation of God. This is God's answer through Ezekiel concerning the captivity of his people which he himself brought about.

"But when they came to the nations [during captivity], wherever they came, they profaned my holy name, in that men said of them, 'These are the people of the Lord, and yet they had to go out of his land.' But *I had concern for my holy name*, which the house of Israel caused to be profaned among the nations to which they came. Therefore say to the house of Israel, 'Thus says the Lord God: "It is not for your sake, O house of Israel, that I am about to act, but *for the sake of my holy name*, which you have profaned among the nations to which you came." And I *will vindicate the holiness of my great name*, which has been profaned among the nations, which you profaned among them; and the nations will know that I am the Lord, says the Lord God, when through you I vindicate my holiness before their eyes'" (Ezek. 36:20–23). Similarly in Ezekiel 39:25 God says, "Now I shall restore the fortunes of Jacob, and have mercy on the whole house of Israel; and *I shall be jealous for My holy name*" (italics added).

11. Gary North, *Chronicles: A Magazine of American Culture* (December 1992), 15.

12. Will Durant, *The Reformation: The Story of Civilization* (New York: Simon and Schuster, 1957), 338–39.

13. Laurence Moore, *Selling God: American Religion in the Marketplace of Culture* (New York: Oxford University Press, 1994), 251–52.

14. Jim Bakker, *I Was Wrong: The Untold Story of the Shocking Journey from PTL to Prison and Beyond* (Nashville: Thomas Nelson, 1996).

15. Ibid., back cover.

16. Richard Pierard, "Radical Resistance," *Christian History* 10, no. 4 (1991), 30, quoted in Erwin W. Lutzer, *Hitler's Cross: The Revealing Story of How the Cross of Christ Was Used As a Symbol of the Nazi Agenda* (Chicago: Moody Press, 1995), 101.

17. Robert R. Reilly, *National Review* (November 25, 1996), 60–61.

18. Michael S. Horton, *The Law of Perfect Freedom: Relating to God and Others Through the Ten Commandments* (Chicago: Moody Press, 1993), 101.

19. Donald W. McCullough, *The Trivialization of God: The Dangerous Illusion of Manageable Deity* (Colorado Springs: NavPress, 1995), 50.

20. Piper, *The Pleasures of God*, 111.

21. Thomas C. Reeves, *The Empty Church: The Suicide of Liberal Christianity* (New York: Free Press, 1996), 2.

22. Alister E. McGrath, *Intellectuals Don't Need God and Other Modern Myths: Building Bridges to Faith through Apologetics* (Grand Rapids: Zondervan, 1993), 151.

23. J. Gresham Machen, *Christianity and Liberalism* (1923; reprint, Grand Rapids: William B. Eerdmans, 1983).

24. H. Richard Niebuhr, *The Kingdom of God in America* (New York: Harper & Row, 1959), 193.

25. Quoted in Reeves, *The Empty Church*, 180. Reeves quotes a prayer used in Minneapolis at a Sunday communal "blessing of milk and honey" which reads in part: "Our maker Sophia, we are women in your image.... With the hot blood of our wombs we give form to new life.... With nectar between our thighs we invite a lover, we birth a child; with our warm body fluids we remind the world of its pleasures and sensations.... We celebrate the sweat that pours from us during our labors. We celebrate the fingertips vibrating upon the skin of a lover."

26. *Milwaukee Journal* (January 29, 1994). Quoted in Reeves, *The Empty Church*, 180.

27. Carl E. Braaten and Robert W. Jenson, eds., *Either/Or: The Gospel or Neopaganism* (Grand Rapids: William B. Eerdmans, 1995), preface, 3–4.

28. Benton Johnson, Dean R. Hoge, and Donald A. Luidens, "Mainline Churches: The Real Reason for Decline," *First Things* 31 (March 1993), 15, quoted in Braaten and Jenson, *Either/Or*, 5.

29. Ibid.

30. C. S. Lewis, *Mere Christianity* (New York: Macmillan, 1952), 56.

31. Quoted in R. Kent Hughes, *Disciplines of Grace* (Wheaton, Ill.: Crossway, 1993), 53.

32. Douma, *The Ten Commandments*, 92.

33. Hughes, *Disciplines of Grace*, 57.

34. Edith Schaeffer, *Ten Things Parents Must Teach Their Children (And Learn for Themselves)* (Grand Rapids: Baker, 1994), 77.

35. Horton, *The Law of Perfect Freedom*, 109.

36. The historic praise hymn *The Doxology* is derived from the Greek word *doxa*. In its earlier history *doxa* referred to a person's reputation. When applied to God in the New Testament, it conveys the idea of enhancing his reputation.

Chapter Six: The Fourth Commandment

1. John N. Drakeford, *Humor in Preaching* (Grand Rapids: Zondervan, 1986), 17–18.

2. I am indebted to the brilliant scholar Kenneth Kantzer for these insightful pieces of information about the thought of Karl Barth.

3. J. Douma, *The Ten Commandments: Manual for the Christian Life*, trans. Nelson D. Kloosterman (Phillipsburg, N.J.: P & R, 1996), 110.

4. Ibid., 142–143.

5. Walter C. Kaiser, Jr., "The Law as God's Guidance for the Promotion of Holiness," in Greg L. Bahnsen et al., *The Law, The Gospel and the Modern Christian: Five Views* (Grand Rapids: Zondervan, 1993), 188.

6. Fred G. Zaspel, "Divine Law: A New Covenant Perspective," *Reformation & Revival: New Covenant* 6, no. 3 (Summer 1997), 157–58.

7. Ibid., 160.

8. Michael S. Horton, *The Law of Perfect Freedom: Relating to God and Others Through the Ten Commandments* (Chicago: Moody Press, 1993), 122.

9. Ibid., 117.

10. William Barclay, *The Ten Commandments for Today* (New York: Harper & Row, 1973), 40.

11. R. Kent Hughes, *Disciplines of Grace* (Wheaton, Ill.: Crossway, 1993), 71.

12. *To the Magnesians 9:1*, see also *Epistle of Barnabas 15:9*, quoted in Ajith Fernando, *The Supremacy of Christ* (Wheaton, Ill.: Crossway, 1995), 255.

13. D.A. Carson, ed., *From Sabbath to Lord's Day: A Biblical, Historical and Theological Investigation* (Grand Rapids: Zondervan, 1982), 378. Carson notes that the post-apostolic church hardly references the Fourth Commandment. He quotes New Testament scholar Andrew Lincoln: "It is almost as if the Sabbath commandment were not a part of the Decalogue."

14. Barclay, *The Ten Commandments*, 32.

15. Douma, *The Ten Commandments*, 111.

16. Kaiser, "The Law as God's Guidance," 190.

17. Sunday has never been a day of rest for everybody. Police officers are on duty and doctors and nurses are at work in hospitals. Even in the Old Testament, the Sabbath was not a day of inactivity. On the Sabbath, Joshua led Israel around Jericho seven times (Josh. 6:15–20). People visited each other on the Sabbath (2 Kings 4:23). Acts of love and service could be performed on the Sabbath (Mark 2:23–28). The Pharisees turned the Sabbath into a legalistic system of deprivation, but Jesus rebuked them saying, "The Sabbath was made for man, and not man for the Sabbath" (v. 27). In other words, it was instituted for the good of the people, not for the sake of the Sabbath. As Lord of the Sabbath, Jesus had the authority to define its proper observances. Ultimately, Christ was their rest, but the Pharisees chose works-righteousness.

18. Horton, *The Barna Report: Law of Perfect Freedom*, 128.

19. Ibid., 126.

20. George Barna, *The Barna Report: What Americans Believe* (Ventura, Calif.: Regal, 1991), 249–250. See also Donald S. Whitney, *Spiritual Disciplines Within the Church: Participating Fully in the Body of Christ* (Chicago: Moody Press, 1996), 17–18.

21. Eugene H. Peterson, "Confessions of a Former Sabbath Breaker," *Christianity Today* (September 2, 1988), 26.

22. Eugene H. Peterson, *Working the Angles: A Trigonometry for Pastoral Work* (Grand Rapids: William B. Eerdmans, 1987), 52, quoted in Hughes, *Disciplines of Grace*, 81.

Chapter Seven: The Fifth Commandment

1. Bob Greene, "I Know I Have at Least One Fan," *Chicago Tribune* (August 15, 1993), sec. 5, p. 1, quoted in Craig Brian Larson, *Illustrations for Preaching & Teaching* (Grand Rapids: Baker, 1993), 168.

2. J. Douma, *The Ten Commandments: Manual for the Christian Life*, trans. Nelson D. Kloosterman (Phillipsburg, N.J.: P & R, 1996), 12.

3. Quoted in R. Kent Hughes, *Disciplines of Grace* (Wheaton, Ill.: Crossway, 1993), 98.

4. Douma, *The Ten Commandments*, 171.

5. Dana Mack, *The Assault on Parenthood: How Our Culture Undermines the Family* (New York: Simon & Schuster, 1997), 35.

6. I believe that obedience to some extent continues throughout all of life if parents have provided righteous instruction and the children have responded lovingly to their parents' godly example from the earliest years.

7. Hughes, *Disciplines of Grace*, 104.

8. John R. W. Stott, *The Message of Ephesians* (Downers Grove, Ill.: InterVarsity Press, 1979), 238–39. Stott says that parental authority and child obedience do not depend on special revelation but are part of the natural law which God has written on all human hearts. It is not confined to Christian ethics; it is the proper standard of behavior in every society.

9. Ibid., 239.

10. Ibid., 241. Stott points out that during the time of the theocracy, when Israel was both a nation and a church over which God ruled, God's covenant blessings were closely tied to the promised land (e.g., prosperity and a long life). The promised land, however, fades from view. God's covenant people are now an international community, and his blessings are largely spiritual in Christ. What is promised is probably not so much a long life to each child who obeys his parents as social stability to any community in which children honor their parents. Personally, I think a long, prosperous individual life still holds, but I do not think we should absolutize this promise.

11. William Kilpatrick, *Why Johnny Can't Tell Right From Wrong: And What We Can Do About It* (New York: Touchstone, Simon & Schuster, 1992), 246.

12. Ibid., 247.

13. Wade F. Horn, "Why There Is No Substitute for Parents," *Imprimis* 26, no. 6 (June 1997), 2.

14. Ibid.

15. Ibid.

16. Sheila Weller, *Saint of Circumstance: The Untold Story Behind the Alex Kelley Rape Case: Growing Up Rich and Out of Control* (New York: Pocket, 1997).

17. Kilpatrick, *Why Johnny Can't Tell Right From Wrong*, 258.

18. Ibid.

19. Dan B. Allender and Tremper Longman III, *Intimate Allies: Rediscovering God's Design for Marriage and Becoming Soul Mates for Life* (Wheaton, Ill.: Tyndale, 1995), 22. These authors say that "the goal of marriage is twofold: to reveal the glory of God and to enhance the glory of one's spouse."

20. J. B. Cheaney, "Selling Our Birthright: The culture shifts but the church does not have to go along," *World* 26 (January 10, 1998).

21. Ibid.

22. Kilpatrick, *Why Johnny Can't Tell Right From Wrong*, 249.

23. Horn, "Why There Is No Substitute for Parents," 2.

24. Mack, *Assault on Parenthood*, 15.

25. Ibid. Mack cites the popular article by Barbara Dafoe Whitehead in the April 1993 *Atlantic Monthly* entitled, "Dan Quayle Was Right."

26. Cited by William Peterson, *Martin Luther Had a Wife* (Wheaton, Ill.: Tyndale, 1983), 75.

27. James Dobson and Gary Bauer, *Children At Risk*, 169–70, quoted in Kilpatrick, *Why Johnny Can't Tell Right From Wrong*, 251.

28. Horn, "Why There Is No Substitute for Parents," 2.

29. Ibid., 3.

30. David A. Seamands, *God's Blueprint for Living: New Perspectives on the Ten Commandments* (Wilmore, Ky.: Bristol, 1988), 84. John Ruskin is credited for this remark.

31. Kevin Graham Ford, *Jesus for a New Generation: Putting the Gospel in the Language of Xers* (Downers Grove, Ill.: InterVarsity Press, 1992), 20.

32. Ibid., 24–25. When I say "this generation" or "this group" I do not intend to convey that all people in this so-called Generation X fit neatly in all categories. James Davidson Hunter suggests that this generation may be more of an "anticulture" than a culture, and he dismisses the notion that there is an identifiable "Baby Buster" or "Gen X" generation with its own outlook and values.

33. Jimmy Long, *Generating Hope: A Strategy for Reaching the Postmodern Generation* (Downers Grove, Ill.: InterVarsity Press, 1997), 188.

34. Deborah Caldwell, "Questions of Faith," *Dallas Morning News* (January 25, 1995), 1G, quoted in Long, *Generating Hope*, 192.

35. David Lipsky and Alexander Abrams, *Late Bloomers* (New York: Random House, 1994), 87, quoted in Long, *Generating Hope*, 43.

36. Leighton Ford, *The Power of Story* (Colorado Springs: NavPress, 1994), 122.

37. Michael S. Horton, *The Law of Perfect Freedom: Relating to God and Others Through the Ten Commandments* (Chicago: Moody Press, 1993), 136.

38. Rodney Clapp, *Families at the Crossroads: Beyond Traditional and Modern Options* (Downers Grove, Ill.: InterVarsity Press, 1993), 35–36.

39. Michael Cromartie, "Up to Our Steeples in Politics," in *No God But God: Breaking With the Idols of Our Age*, eds. Os Guinness and John Seel (Chicago: Moody Press, 1992), 53. Cromartie quotes Randell Terry, leader of Operation Rescue: "Our time of withdrawal is over. We've joined the battle, and are prepared to make serious sacrifices before it's too late. This is a winner-take-all battle for every soul of the country."

40. John Seel, "Nostalgia for the Lost Empire," in *No God But God*, 68.

41. William Lee Miller, *The First Liberty* (New York: Knopf, 1985), 361–63.

42. Patrick J. Buchanan, "Hollywood's War on Christianity," *Washington Times* (July 27, 1988), F3, quoted in Os Guinness, "More Victimized Than Thou," in *No God But God*, 87.

43. Richard John Neuhaus, "The Christian and the Church," *Transforming Our World*, ed. James M. Boice. (Portland, Ore.: Multnomah, 1988), 120.

44. John Seel, "Nostalgia for the Lost Empire," *No God But God*, 73.

Chapter Eight: The Sixth Commandment

1. Ted Peters, *Sin: Radical Evil in Soul and Society* (Grand Rapids: William B. Eerdmans, 1994), 70.

2. Paul Johnson, *Intellectuals* (New York: Harper & Row, 1988), 245–46.

3. Quoted in Michael S. Horton, *The Law of Perfect Freedom: Relating to God and Others Through the Ten Commandments* (Chicago: Moody Press, 1993), 159.

4. Doug Webster, *The Easy Yoke* (Colorado Springs: NavPress, 1995), 106.

5. Theologians often make a distinction between *thumos* (rapid, explosive anger) and *orgé* (lasting, pent-up anger). In either case, however, the anger can result in murderous actions and is a violation of the Sixth Commandment. See also José Torres, *Fire & Fear: The Inside Story of Mike Tyson* (New York: Popular Library, 1989).

6. Dan B. Allender and Tremper Longman III, *Cry of the Soul: How Our Emotions Reveal Our Deepest Questions About God* (Colorado Springs: NavPress, 1994), 71.

7. Ibid., 58.

8. Ibid., 63.

9. Frederick Buechner, *Wishful Thinking* (San Francisco: Harper & Row, 1993), quoted in *Contemporary Illustrations for Preachers and Teachers*, ed. Craig Brian Larson (Grand Rapids: Baker, 1996), 15.

10. Dan B. Allender and Tremper Longman III, *Intimate Allies: Rediscovering God's Design for Marriage and Becoming Soul Mates for Life* (Wheaton, Ill.: Tyndale, 1995), 19.

11. See J. Douma, *The Ten Commandments: Manual for the Christian Life*, trans. Nelson D. Kloosterman (Phillipsburg, N.J.: P & R, 1996), 214. Douma warns that we must not say all life is sacred. He mentions Albert Schweitzer who viewed reverence for life as that we should not so much as pluck a leaf from a tree or pick a flower or kill a fly. Schweitzer advised people of his day (before air-conditioning) that if someone were to work indoors on a summer evening, it would be better to keep the windows closed and breathe stale air than to watch insect after insect fall to its death with wings singed by the candlelight. Douma prudently prefers to speak of reverence for God rather than reverence for life.

12. Ibid. The word *murder* alone is probably too restrictive since the commandment includes far more than what most people usually mean by murder (e.g., involuntary manslaughter). However, unlawful killing proves to be deficient by itself since certain governments sanction killing, such as in cases of abortion, making this inhumane practice lawful. Therefore, both murder and unlawful killing are needed to adequately explain the Sixth Commandment.

13. Ibid., 227.

14. David K. Clark and Robert V. Rakestraw, *Readings in Christian Ethics*, vol. 2, *Issues and Applications* (Grand Rapids; Baker, 1996), 95.

15. An ad hoc committee of the Harvard Medical School defined brain death—irreversible coma—by four criteria: 1) unreceptivity and unresponsivity (no stimuli of any sort evokes any kind of response); 2) no movements or spontaneous breathing for at least an hour; 3) no reflexes, and fixed dilated pupils; 4) flat brain wave (flat EEG) for at least ten minutes, preferably twenty. All four must apply, and they must still be true of the patient twenty-four hours after first tested. Another case where euthanasia may be permissible is where a terminal patient, according to the best medical judgment, will die within hours regardless of what's done. Trying to maintain life at all costs seems tantamount to refusing to accept the fact that it is the person's time to die.

16. Some contend that Saul's case should not be considered suicide since 1 Chronicles 10:4, 14 reports that the Lord killed him. Others point out that Saul willfully fell on his own sword. Both versions together may describe divine capital punishment carried out through the shameful impulses of a disgraced king.

17. Michael Lewis, *Shame: The Exposed Self* (New York: The Free Press, 1992), 11. Lewis distinguishes anger (a response to the blockage of a goal) from rage (a response to an attack on the self). Lewis believes that "shame" is the underlying cause of anger and rage and often leads to murder, suicide, and child abuse. See also H. Norman Wright, *Crisis Counseling: Helping People in Crisis and Stress* (San Bernardino, Calif.: Here's Life, 1985), 99. Wright cites repressed rage as one of the chief causes of suicide.

18. Walter McQuade and Ann Aikman, *Stress: What It Is: What It Can Do to Your Health: How to Fight Back* (New York: Bantam Books, 1974), 36n.

19. Quoted in Matt Friedeman, *Accountability Connection* (Wheaton, Ill.: Victor, 1992), 137.

20. John S. Feinberg and Paul D. Feinberg, *Ethics for a Brave New World* (Wheaton, Ill.; Crossway, 1993), 120.

21. Paper by Joseph M. Stowell, "The Power of a Life Well-Lived." See also John Stott, *Involvement: Social and Sexual Relationships in the Modern World* (Old Tappan, N.J.: Fleming H. Revell, 1984), 188.

22. John S. J. Powell, *Abortion: The Silent Holocaust* (Allen: Argus Communications, 1981), 20–39.

23. See Will Durant, *Caesar and Christ* (New York: Simon & Schuster, 1944). Also see George Grant, *Grand Illusions: The Legacy of Planned Parenthood* (Brentwood, Tenn.: Wolgemuth & Hyatt, 1988), 189.

24. Stephen M. Krason, *Abortion: Politics, Morality and the Constitution* (Lanham, Md.: University Press of America, 1984), 341. In a custody dispute over seven human embryos, Professor Jerome LeJeune testified that each human being has a very unique beginning—the moment of conception. He stated:

"And if I can say so, I would say that life has a very long history, but each of us has a unique beginning, the moment of conception. We know and all the genetics and all the zoology are there to tell us that there is a link between the parents and the children. And this link is made of a long molecule that we can dissect the DNA molecule which is transmitting information from parents to children through generations and generations. As soon as the program is written on the DNA, there are twenty-three different pieces of program carried by the spermatozoa and there are twenty-three different homologous pieces carried by the ovum. As soon as the twenty-three chromosomes carried by the sperm encounter the twenty-three chromosomes carried by the ovum, the whole information necessary and sufficient to spell out all the characteristics of the new being is gathered.... You have to figure out what is a DNA molecule. I would say it's a long thread of one meter of length, cut in twenty-three pieces. Each piece is coiled on itself very tightly to make spiral of spiral of spiral so that finally it looks like a little rod that we can see under the microscope that we call a chromosome. And there are twenty-three of them carried by father, twenty-three of them carried by mother. I said the minuteness of the language is bewildering because if I was bringing here in the Court all the one meter long DNA of the sperms and all the meter long of the ovums which will make every one of the five billions of human beings that will replace ourselves in this planet, this amount of matter would be roughly two aspirin tablets. That tells us that nature, to carry the information from father to children, from mother to children, from generation to generation, has used the smallest possible language. And it is very necessary because life is taking advantage of the movement of the particles, of molecules, to put order inside the chance development of random movement of particles, so that chance is now transformed according to the necessity of the new being."

Testimony of Professor Jerome Lejeune, M.D. (University of Paris): Circuit Court for Blount County, Tennessee, at Maryville, Equity Divisions (Div. I), published by Michael J. Woodruff, director, Center for Law & Religious Freedom, Annandale, Virginia.

25. Bernard N. Nathanson, M.D., *The Hand of God: A Journey From Death to Life by the Abortion Doctor Who Changed His Mind* (Washington, D.C.: Regenery, 1996), 130.

26. Ibid., 125–47.

27. Francis J. Beckwith, "Answering the Arguments for Abortion Rights," "Part Two: Arguments from Pity, Tolerance and Ad Hominem," *Christian Research Journal* (Winter 1991), 31.

28. Ibid.

29. Quoted in John Stott, *Involvement: Social and Sexual Relationships in the Modern World*, II (Old Tappan, N.J.: Fleming H. Revell, 1984), 211.

30. Robert E. Joyce, "When Does a Person Begin?" in David K. Clark and Robert V. Rakestraw, *Readings in Christian Ethics*, vol. 2 (Grand Rapids: Baker, 1996), 47–48.

31. Ibid., 24.

32. See the article by Virginia Ramey Mollenkott, "Reproductive Choice: Basic to Justice for Women" in Clark and Rakestraw, *Readings in Christian Ethics*, 26–31.

33. Jack W. Cottrell, "Abortion and the Mosaic Law" in Clark and Rakestraw, *Readings in Christian Ethics*, 33.

34. George McKenna, "Lincoln and Abortion" (Charlottesville, Va.: Mars Hill), demo tape, side 2.

35. Ibid. See also *The Lincoln-Douglas Debates*, ed. Harold Holzer (New York: Harper Collins, 1993), 151. Douglas states: "I hold that a negro is not and never ought to be a citizen of the United States. . . . I do not believe that the Almighty made the negro capable of self-government."

36. Quoted in Grant, *Grand Illusions*, 118.

37. Paul Marshall with Lela Gilbert, *Their Blood Cries Out: The Worldwide Tragedy of Modern Christians Who Are Dying for Their Faith* (Dallas: Word, 1997), back cover.

38. Richard Wurmbrand, *Tortured for Christ* (Bartlesville, Okla.: Living Sacrifice, 1967), 41.

39. Ibid., 45.

40. Warren W. Wiersbe and David W. Wiersbe, *10 Power Principles for Christian Service: Ministry Dynamics for a New Century* (Grand Rapids: Baker, 1997), 41.

41. It is important to note that Jesus did not repudiate the death penalty. Capital punishment was instituted by God long before Moses received the law. "Whoever sheds the blood of man, by man shall his blood be shed; for in the image of God has God made man" (Gen. 9:6 NIV). Later Mosaic legislation commended the death penalty for premeditated killing. Romans 13:1–7 shows that it is God's design that the judicial system enforce retribution. God practiced retribution in both OT and NT times. In my opinion, capital punishment should be used sparingly only in cases of proven premeditated murder. The proper distribution of justice does not denigrate life, but establishes the value of human life.

42. Human government has the right to use appropriate force in order to prevent murderous tyranny or mass killings. This may involve killing to uphold law and order. Scripture authorizes the state to punish those who violate human life or break laws (Rom. 13:1–7). New Testament lexicographer Marvin Vincent says that the sword Paul refers to in Romans 13:4 "is borne as the symbol of the magistrate's right to inflict capital punishment." See Marvin R. Vincent, *Word Studies in the New Testament* (Wilmington, Del.: Associate Publishers and Authors, 1972), 746.

43. In Exodus 22:2 we have a situation where a thief was caught breaking and entering and received a fatal death blow in the dark. This was not considered murder or unlawful killing. That is not to say that anyone should strive to kill someone in self-defense. But if one kills another while defending his life or the life of someone else, this does not necessarily violate the Sixth Commandment.

44. No rational, sane person likes war. But in a fallen world war is not totally unavoidable. The biblical view maintains the state's responsibility to enforce justice and equity, and permits the state to use force to defend people (Rom. 13:3–4; 1 Peter 2:13–14; cf. Ex. 22:2–3). Furthermore, some of the most godly OT saints engaged in military action. Abraham rescued his nephew by military action (Gen. 14:13–16). Joshua, the judges, and David spent a good deal of their administrations in military conflict, and there is no hint that their actions met with divine disapproval. In fact, the writer of Hebrews says that by *faith* they conquered kingdoms, enforced justice, became mighty in war, and put foreign armies to flight (Heb. 11:33–34). See John S. Feinberg and Paul D. Feinberg, *Ethics for a Brave New World* (Wheaton, Ill.: Crossway, 1993), 364.

War should never be glorified, but in cases where it is unavoidable, it can be conducted in a "just way." The purpose of a just war is to ultimately limit further war and killing. Unfortunately, in a fallen world the evils of war sometimes cannot be avoided. This position is a peace position without pacifism. We are called to be peacemakers. This sometimes means that human values and human lives are worth protecting or fighting for and even dying for. Yet I do believe that we should allow individuals the right of conscientious objection if they cannot in good conscience participate in a war.

45. John Ortberg, "Do They Know Us By Our Love? The first casualty of the culture wars is not truth," *Christianity Today* (May 19, 1997), 25.

Chapter Nine: The Seventh Commandment

1. Jerry Adler, "Adultery: A New Furor Over an Old Sin," *Newsweek* (September 30, 1996), 54.

2. Ibid., 58.

3. Ibid., 56.

4. William H. Masters and Virginia E. Johnson, *Human Sexual Inadequacy* (Boston: Little, Brown, 1970), 51.

5. Richard Weaver, *Ideas Have Consequences* (Chicago: University of Chicago Press, 1984), 2.

6. Edward T. Welch, *When People Are Big and God Is Small: Overcoming Peer Pressure, Codependency and the Fear of Man* (Phillipsburg, N.J.: P & R, 1997), 97.

7. R. Kent Hughes, *Disciplines of Grace* (Wheaton, Ill.: Crossway, 1993), 127.

8. J. Douma, *The Ten Commandments: Manual for the Christian Life*, trans. Nelson D. Kloosterman (Phillipsburg, N.J.: P & R, 1996), 243.

9. Ibid., 244. Some commentators point out that adultery in Israel was a crime against private property. People were forbidden to violate a neighbor's wife (Seventh Commandment) as they were the life or possession of another (the Sixth and Eighth Commandments). However, the Seventh Commandment is much deeper because the man who violates his neighbor's wife violates that neighbor's marriage covenant and his honor.

10. Stanley J. Grenz, *Sexual Ethics: An Evangelical Perspective* (Louisville, Ky.: Westminster John Knox, 1997), 61.

11. Tom Wolfe, *The Bonfire of the Vanities* (New York: Farrar, Straus, Giroux, 1987), 54, quoted in Doug Webster, *The Easy Yoke* (Colorado Springs: NavPress, 1995), 120.

12. Ibid., 122.

13. Paul A. Mickey, "Get Rid of the Lust in Your Life," TSF *Bulletin* (March–April 1986), 11, quoted in Webster, *The Easy Yoke*, 122.

14. Ibid.

15. Ibid.

16. Quoted in *Illustrations for Preaching & Teaching From Leadership Journal*, ed. Craig Brian Larson (Grand Rapids: Baker, 1993), 146.

17. Douma, *Ten Commandments*, 246.

18. James Patterson and Peter Kim, *The Day America Told the Truth* (New York: Plume, 1992), 94–99.

19. Joseph M. Stowell, *Following Christ: Experiencing Life the Way It Was Meant to Be* (Grand Rapids: Zondervan, 1996), 71. See also Paul Johnson, *Intellectuals* (New York: Harper & Row, 1988), 138–73.

20. Peter Kreeft, *Back to Virtue: Traditional Moral Wisdom for Modern Moral Confusion* (San Francisco: Ignatius, 1992), 169. See Webster, *The Easy Yoke*, 126.

21. Dan B. Allender and Tremper Longman III, *Intimate Allies: Rediscovering God's Design for Marriage and Becoming Soul Mates for Life* (Wheaton, Ill.: Tyndale, 1995), xviii.

22. Ibid., 26.

23. Ibid., 124.

24. John Stott, *Involvement: Social and Sexual Relationships in the Modern World*, II (Old Tappan, N.J.: Fleming H. Revell, 1984), 163. Genesis 2:24 ("For this reason a man will leave his father and mother and be united to his wife, and they will become one flesh" NIV) implies that a marriage exists in God's sight when a man leaves his parents with the intent and commitment to cleave to his wife and become one flesh with her.

25. Thomas F. Jones, *Sex & Love When You're Single Again* (Nashville: Oliver Nelson, 1990), 33.

26. Ibid.

27. Stott, *Involvement*, 163. Stott also adds to the marriage definition that it's normally crowned with children based on Genesis 1:28: "Be fruitful and multiply."

28. For a good discussion on Deuteronomy 24:1–4 see John S. Feinberg and Paul D. Feinberg, *Ethics for a Brave New World* (Wheaton, Ill.: Crossway, 1993), 310–16. The Feinbergs also add a second reason for the Mosaic concession: to curtail the possibility of a woman to have multiple divorces and remarriages. While the law was meant to protect the woman and her rights, it did not warrant multiple marriages (p. 311).

29. Some believe that the Shammai school left the sexual offense undefined so that it was not limited to adultery but included homosexuality and bestiality. Others would say that sodomy and sexual intercourse with an animal are adultery. It would include more than a sexual act with a person of the opposite sex.

30. I owe this wise explanation to Walter C. Kaiser, Jr., expressed to me via e-mail on September 8, 1997.

31. The inspired penman of Psalm 51, traditionally ascribed to David after his adultery with Bathsheba, views his sin primarily as a sin against God and his law (Ps. 51:1–4).

32. Grenz, *Sexual Ethics*, 32.

33. Cornelius Plantinga, Jr., *Not the Way It's Supposed to Be: A Breviary of Sin* (Grand Rapids: William B. Eerdmans, 1995), 2.

34. Grenz, *Sexual Ethics*, 21.

35. Quoted in Jones, *Sex & Love*, 32.

36. Plantinga, *Not the Way It's Supposed to Be*, 83.

Chapter Ten: The Eighth Commandment

1. See Bishop Ezekiel Hopkins, *A Short Exposition of the Ten Commandments* (London: Printed by J. Paramore, at the Foundry, Moorfields, 1784), 66.

2. Michael S. Horton, *The Law of Perfect Freedom: Relating to God and Others Through the Ten Commandments* (Chicago: Moody Press, 1993), 198.

3. As told in Mark Umbreit, *Crime and Reconciliation: Creative Options for Victims and Offenders* (Nashville: Abingdon, 1985), 36–37.

4. Slavery did occur with Yahweh's approval in the ancient world, but the slaves were foreigners who were among the spoils of war who had been procured in a foreign country. This was unlike the ravages of Civil War slavery. The Law did contain provisions to make the life of a slave secure and bearable (Ex. 21:16; Deut. 23:15–16). The New Testament condemns kidnapping as well (1 Tim. 1:10, men stealing). However,

slavery was a reality in the Roman world. Undoubtedly, some slaves were mistreated even though Roman legislation did regulate the treatment of slaves. First-century slaves were generally well treated and were not only skilled laborers but often managers and trained members of the various professions (doctors, nurses, teachers, musicians, skilled artisans). They were paid for their services and could eventually purchase their freedom. I say this not to justify slavery but to show that it was quite different than the abominable Civil War slavery.

5. Umbreit, *Crime and Reconciliation*, 39.

6. James Patterson and Peter Kim, *The Day America Told the Truth* (New York: Plume, 1992), 173.

7. Ibid., 174–75.

8. Ibid., 155.

9. Ibid., 157.

10. J. Douma, *The Ten Commandments: Manual for the Christian Life*, trans. Nelson D. Kloosterman (Phillipsburg, N.J.: P & R, 1996), 289. Jacob also "stole" Laban's heart by not telling him he wanted to flee (Gen. 31:26). But when Jacob stole away with both his wives and possessions, Laban felt deceived; he said to Jacob, literally, "What have you done, that you have stolen my heart and carried away my daughters like captives taken with the sword?" (Gen. 31:26 NKJV).

11. Colin Wilson and Damon Wilson, *The Killers Among Us* (New York: Warner, 1995), 103–5.

12. Quoted in *Fresh Illustrations for Preaching and Teaching from Leadership Journal*, ed. Edward K. Rowell (Grand Rapids: Baker, 1997), 221.

13. Robert Goodman, *The Luck Business: The Devastating Consequences and Broken Promises of America's Gambling Explosion* (New York: Free Press, 1995), vii–xiv.

14. Ibid., 5.

15. William N. Thompson, *Legalized Gambling: A Reference Handbook* (Santa Barbara, Calif.: ABC-CLIO, 1994), 13, quoted in Rex M. Rogers, "America's New Love Affair With Gambling," *Christian Research Journal* 20, no. 3 (January–March 1998), 18.

16. Goodman, *The Luck Business*, xi. John Kindt, professor of commerce and legal policy at the University of Illinois, says, "Legalized gambling is inherently parasitic on any economy. . . . [Gambling] always hurts the economy, it always creates large socioeconomic problems. And that intensifies the needs for tax dollars to address the new problems that they are creating by legalizing gambling." See Mitchell Zuckoff and Doug Bailey, "Cities Weigh Quick Cash vs. Social Costs," *Boston Globe* (September 30, 1993), 1.

17. Goodman, *The Luck Business*, 57.

18. Rogers, "America's New Love Affair With Gambling," 21.

19. Cornelius Plantinga, Jr., *Not the Way It's Supposed to Be: A Breviary of Sin* (Grand Rapids: William B. Eerdmans, 1995), 32–33.

20. Arnold Wexler and Sheila Wexler, "Facts on Compulsive Gambling and Addiction," New Jersey Alcohol/Drug Clearing House, Center of Alcohol Studies, Rutgers University, Piscataway, N.J. (1992), quoted in Goodman, *The Luck Business*, 48.

21. Ibid., 50.

22. Ibid., 51.

23. Valerie Lorenz, "Dear God, Just Let Me Win," *Christian Social Action* (July–August 1994), 25–27.

24. Henry Lesieur, "Compulsive Gambling," *Society* (May–June 1992), 44, quoted in Goodman, *The Luck Business*, 51.

25. Robert Goodman, "Legalized Gambling As a Strategy for Economic Development," (March 1994), quoted in report by Ronald A. Reno, "You Bet Your Life: The Dangerous Repercussions of America's Gambling Addiction" (Colorado Springs: Focus on the Family, 1995), 5.

26. Andrew J. Buck, Hakim Simon, and Spiegel Uriel, "Casino, Crime, and Real Estate Values: Do They Relate?" *Journal of Research in Crime and Delinquency* 28, no. 3 (August 1991), 228–303, quoted in Reno, "You Bet Your Life," 5.

27. Goodman, *The Luck Business*, 46–55.

28. Lesieur, "Compulsive Gambling," *Society*, 45, quoted in Goodman, *The Luck Business*, 47.

29. Jeffrey L. Bloomberg, *Testimony at Hearing on the National Impact of Casino Gambling Proliferation*, Committee on Small Business, U.S. House of Representatives (September 21, 1994).

30. William C. Rhoden, "Newest Concern for Colleges: Increase in Sports Gambling," *New York Times* (April 28, 1992), A1.

31. Howard J. Shaffer, "The Emergence of Youthful Addiction: The Prevalence of Underage Lottery Use and the Impact of Gambling," Technical Report No. 011394-100, Massachusetts Council on Compulsive Gambling, Boston (January 13, 1994).

32. Rogers, "America's New Love Affair With Gambling," 22.

33. George Will, "In the Grip of Gambling," *Newsweek* (May 8, 1989), 78, quoted in Reno, *You Bet Your Life*, 15.

34. Chuck Colson and Jack Eckerd, *Why America Doesn't Work* (Dallas: Word, 1991), 178.

35. Rogers, "America's New Love Affair With Gambling," 25.

36. *Leadership* 4, no. 3 (Summer 1983), 81.

37. Quoted in Charles R. Swindoll, *Improving Your Serve* (Waco, Tex.: Word, 1983), 170–71.

38. Quoted in Matt Friedeman, *The Master Plan of Teaching: Understanding and Applying the Teaching Styles of Jesus* (Wheaton, Ill.: Victor, 1990), 85.

39. Fyodor Dostoyevsky, *The Brothers Karamazov*, trans. Constance Garnett (New York: Modern Library, 1937), 629.

40. See Matt Friedeman, *Accountability Connection* (Wheaton, Ill.: Victor, 1992), 60.

Chapter Eleven: The Ninth Commandment

1. Charles Colson with Nancy R. Pearcey, *A Dance With Deception: Revealing the Truth Behind the Headlines* (Dallas: Word, 1993), 70.

2. Ibid., 68.

3. Ibid., 70.

4. Ibid., 70–71.

5. J. Douma, *The Ten Commandments: Manual for the Christian Life*, trans. Nelson D. Kloosterman (Phillipsburg, N.J.: P & R, 1996), 314.

6. Laura Parker, "DNA tests point to Sheppard's innocence," *USA Today* (March 15, 1998), 3A. I do not mean to imply that Sheppard was innocent or guilty, but only that a bad name or marred reputation could be life threatening. In the ancient world, a bad name often ended one's career or trade.

7. Douma, *The Ten Commandments*, 315.

8. Ezekiel Hopkins, *A Short Exposition of the Ten Commandments* (London: Printed by J. Paramore at the Foundry, Moorfields, 1784), 79.

9. Michael S. Horton, *The Law of Perfect Freedom: Relating to God and Others Through the Ten Commandments* (Chicago: Moody, 1993), 228.

10. *Quotes & Idea Starters for Preaching & Teaching*, ed. Edward K. Rowell (Grand Rapids: Baker, 1996), 105.

11. James Patterson and Peter Kim, *The Day America Told the Truth* (New York: Plume, 1992), 45–46.

12. Ibid., 7.

13. Quoted in Warren W. Wiersbe, *Be Complete: How to Become the Whole Person God Intends You to Be* (Wheaton, Ill.: Victor, 1984), 105.

14. Ibid., 107.

15. Patterson and Kim, *The Day America Told the Truth*, 200.

16. R. Kent Hughes, *Disciplines of Grace* (Wheaton, Ill.: Crossway, 1993), 163.

17. Quoted in *Oxford Dictionary of Quotations*, 3rd ed. (Oxford: Oxford University Press, 1980), 417.

18. Cited in Doug Webster, *The Easy Yoke* (Colorado Springs: NavPress, 1995), 138.

19. Ibid., 140.

20. Stowell, *Shepherding the Church into the 21st Century*, 136.

21. Ibid., 134.

22. Rabbi Joseph Telushkin, "Words That Hurt, Words That Heal: How to Choose Words Wisely and Well," *Imprimis* 25, no. 1 (January 1996), 4.

23. Ibid.

24. Ibid.

25. Ibid., 3.

26. Ibid., 4.

27. See Hopkins, *Ten Commandments*, 91.

28. Christopher Lasch, *The Culture of Narcissism: American Life in an Age of Diminishing Expectations* (New York: Warner, 1979).

29. Douma, *Ten Commandments*, 324.

30. See Kenneth Samples et al., *Prophets of the Apocalypse: David Koresh & Other American Messiahs* (Grand Rapids: Baker, 1994), 80–86. These researchers argue that Koresh believed that he, as the Lord, would loose fire upon the faithful, killing off their old nature and transforming them into flaming, glorified individuals. Based on a mishmashing of biblical texts, such as Amos 2:5, Joel 3:14–17, Isaiah 4, and Nahum 2:3–13, Koresh expected to transform the Davidians into living instruments of fiery judgment whose mission was to slaughter the armies of the world.

31. Ibid., 17. A partial quote from sociologist Ronald Enroth.

32. Douma, *Ten Commandments*, 324.

33. Sissela Bok, *Lying: Moral Choice in Public and Private Life* (New York: Vintage, 1978, 1989), 107.

34. Douma, *Ten Commandments*, 326.

35. Bok, *Lying*, 18–19.

36. Gene Edward Veith, "A Postmodern Scandal: If truth is relative, it's impossible to lie," *World* (February 21, 1998), 24.

37. Ibid.

38. Douma, *Ten Commandments*, 327. Douma also lists military deception as justifiable in some cases. He says it is difficult to condemn this kind of deception, since the Lord himself recommended such tactics in Joshua's battle against Ai and in David's fight against the Philistines (Josh. 8:1–26; 2 Sam. 5:22–25).

39. Bok, *Lying*, 40.

40. Douma, *Ten Commandments*, 330.

41. Quoted in Horton, *Law of Perfect Freedom*, 226.

42. Philip Yancey, *What's So Amazing About Grace?* (Grand Rapids: Zondervan, 1997), 45.

43. Ibid.

44. Interestingly enough, Jesus never defined or analyzed grace. Instead he communicated grace through parables and stories. Many define grace something like "God's unmerited favor which we don't deserve." Grace is the power of God's love and favor that penetrates our lives undeservedly and, sometimes, unexpectedly. The power of God's grace saves and continues to empower and restore God's people.

45. John R. W. Stott, *The Cross of Christ* (Downer's Grove, Ill.: InterVarsity Press, 1986), 336–37.

46. Quoted in Matt Friedeman, *The Master Plan of Teaching: Understanding and Applying the Teaching Styles of Jesus* (Wheaton, Ill.: Victor, 1990), 50. Friedeman credits Abraham J. Heschel with this piece of insight.

47. Chuck Swindoll, *Improving Your Serve: The Art of Unselfish Living* (Waco, Tex.: Word, 1981), 119–20.

48. Bok, *Lying*, 88–89.

49. Ibid., 145.

50. Horton, *Law of Perfect Freedom*, 236.

51. Walter Wangerin, *As for Me and My House* (Nashville: Thomas Nelson, 1987), 123.

Chapter Twelve: The Tenth Commandment

1. See David Myers, "Money & Misery," in *The Consuming Passion: Christianity & the Consumer Culture*, ed. Rodney Clapp (Downers Grove, Ill.: InterVarsity Press, 1998), 63.

2. See Ted Koppel and Kyle Gibson, *Nightline: History in the Making and the Making of Television* (New York: Random House, 1996), 270, 295.

3. Ken Myers, "Television & Christian Discipleship," *Mars Hills Lectures* tape, side 1 (Charlottesville, Va.: n.d.).

4. David F. Wells, *God in the Wasteland: The Reality of Truth in a World of Fading Dreams* (Grand Rapids: Eerdmans, 1994), 48.

5. Quoted in Charles R. Swindoll, *Laugh Again* (Dallas: Word, 1992), 58.

6. Brother Lawrence, *The Practice of the Presence of God with Spiritual Maxims* (Grand Rapids: Spire, 1958, 1967 reprint).

7. For an excellent study on the spiritual disciplines, see Dallas Willard, *The Spirit of the Disciplines: Understanding How God Changes Lives* (San Francisco: Harper San Francisco, 1988), especially pages 156–92.

8. The writings of Henry David Thoreau have some excellent insights on simple living. One must dig through the pantheistic philosophies that sometimes surface, yet his views on simplicity, at times, are instructive.

9. Augustine, *Confessions*, bk. 8, trans. John K. Ryan (New York: Doubleday, Image, 1960), 189, 194–95.

10. For an example, see Ted Peters, *Sin: Radical Evil in Soul and Society* (Grand Rapids: William B. Eerdmans, 1994), 137. National Socialist Hermann Goering was so inebriated with power, it became his god. Hitler was the personification of power with which he identified. Goering's adoration of Hitler's power carried him into religious ecstasy. He once said: "We each possess just so much power as the Führer wishes to give. And only with the Führer and standing behind him is one really powerful, only then does one hold the strong powers of the state in one's hands; but against his will,

or even just without his wish, one would instantly become totally powerless. A word from the Führer and anyone whom he wishes to be rid of falls. His prestige, his authority are boundless.... It is not I who live, but the Führer who lives in me."

11. J. Douma, *The Ten Commandments: Manual for the Christian Life*, trans. Nelson D. Kloosterman (Phillipsburg, N.J.: P & R, 1996) 341.

12. Quoted in Craig M. Gay, "Sensualists Without Heart," in *The Consuming Passion*, 19.

13. Ibid., David Myers, "Money & Misery," 52.

14. Ibid.

15. Ibid.

16. Ibid., Gay, "Sensualists Without Heart," 26. See Alexis de Tocqueville, *Democracy in America*, trans. George Lawrence (Garden City, N.Y.: Doubleday, Anchor, 1969), 691–92.

17. Ibid., David Myers, "Money & Misery," 57.

18. Cornelius Plantinga, Jr., *Not The Way It's Supposed to Be: A Breviary of Sin* (Grand Rapids: William B. Eerdmans, 1995) 162–63.

19. Charles Colson and Nancy Pearcey, "Why Fidelity Matters," *Christianity Today* (April 27, 1998), 104.

20. C. S. Lewis, *The Abolition of Man* (New York: Macmillan, 1996 edition), 35–37.

21. David Myers, "Money & Misery," 60.

22. Nathaniel Hawthorne, *Hawthorne: Tales and Sketches* (New York: Penguin, 1982), 1068–86.

23. Quoted in Matt Friedeman, *The Master Plan of Teaching: Understanding and Applying the Teaching Styles of Jesus* (Wheaton, Ill.: Victor, 1990), 25.

24. Henry David Thoreau, *Walden* (New York: Signet, 1980), 66.

25. Thomas Watson, *The Art of Divine Contentment* (Morgan, Penn.: Soli Deo Gloria, 1835 reprint edition), iv.

26. George Washington, *The Farewell Address: The View From the Twentieth Century*, ed. Burton Ira Kaufman (Chicago: Quadrangle, 1969), 24–25, quoted in Guenter Lewy, *Why America Needs Religion: Secular Modernity and Its Discontents* (Grand Rapids: William B. Eerdmans, 1996), 124. When Washington used the word "religion," he was referring to the various Christian persuasions: Puritans in the North, Episcopalians in the South, Quakers in Pennsylvania, Catholics in Maryland, Baptists in Rhode Island, Reformed in New York, and Presbyterians, Methodists, Lutherans, along with unorthodox groups such as Unitarians and Universalists, and also the Jews. Yet Washington understood Christianity to be a historical religion. Religion to Washington meant the transcendent authority of Christianity, broadly speaking, and Judaism. He considered religion and morality to be the pillars of society and, therefore, to be encouraged by the government.

27. Lewy, *Why America Needs Religion*, 137.

28. J. C. Ryle, *Holiness* (England: Evangelical Press, first printed in 1879, eighth edition, 1997), introduction.

29. Sheldon Vanauken, *A Severe Mercy* (New York: Harper Collins, 1977, 1980), 85.

30. Wells, *God in the Wasteland*, 224. Personally, I think it is a mistake to abandon logical argument as some evangelicals seem to advocate. The apostle Paul reasoned like a skilled logician in a pluralistic age and we should follow his example (Acts 17:17–34; 18:4–5, 19, 28; 19:8). Yet, it must be underscored that this is not the only way to reach postmodern pluralists, nor even the primary way.

31. From a transcript of *60 Minutes*, vol. 15, no. 21, broadcast by CBS television network (February 6, 1983), cited in Charles Colson and Ellen Santilli Vaughn, *The Body* (Dallas: Word, 1992), 187–88.

32. Ibid., 191.

33. See D. A. Carson, *The Gagging of God: Christianity Confronts Pluralism* (Grand Rapids: Zondervan, 1996), 46–52.

34. Elizabeth Elliot, *Shadow of the Almighty: The Life & Testament of Jim Elliot* (San Francisco: Harper & Row, 1967), 117.

Chapter Thirteen: Culture Shift

1. Quoted in Edward K. Rowell, *Fresh Illustrations for Preaching & Teaching* (Grand Rapids: Baker, 1997), 73.

2. Dallas Willard, *The Divine Conspiracy: Rediscovering Our Hidden Life in God* (New York: Harper Collins, 1998), 142.

3. Ibid., 56–57.

4. Christina Hoff Summers, "Are We Living in a Moral Stone Age?" *Imprimis* 27, no. 3 (March 1988), 1.

5. Ibid., 4.

6. Ibid.

7. H. Wayne House, ed., *The Christian and American Law: Christianity's Impact on America's Founding Documents and Future Direction* (Grand Rapids: Kregel, 1998), 9.

8. Ibid.

9. Stephen L. Carter, *The Culture of Disbelief: How American Law and Politics Trivialize Religious Devotion* (New York: Anchor, 1993), 208.

10. Ibid.

11. Ibid., 206–7.

12. Kenneth A. Myers, *All God's Children and Blue Suede Shoes: Christians and Popular Culture* (Wheaton, Ill.: Crossway, 1989), 26.

13. Edmund Burke letter to William Smith (January 9, 1775).

14. Philip Yancey, "A State of Ungrace," *Christianity Today* (February 3, 1997), 34.

15. See Robert N. Bellah et al., *Habits of the Heart: Individualism and Commitment in American Life* (Los Angeles: University of California Press, 1996 updated edition), 219–49.

16. See Stephen B. Oates, *Let the Trumpet Sound: A Life of Martin Luther King, Jr.* (New York: Harper & Row, 1982).

17. Quoted in Guenter Lewy, *Why America Needs Religion: Secular Modernity and Its Discontents* (Grand Rapids: William B. Eerdmans, 1996), 133–34.

18. Ibid., 131.

We want to hear from you. Please send your comments about this
book to us in care of the address below. Thank you.

ZondervanPublishingHouse
Grand Rapids, Michigan 49530
http://www.zondervan.com